*Content-Area Reader*

**TEACHER'S GUIDE**

# A World in Transition
## The Fall of Rome to the Early Modern Era

Senior Consultant
**Dr. Judith Irvin**
Florida State University

**HOLT, RINEHART AND WINSTON**

A Harcourt Classroom Education Company

Austin • New York • Orlando • Atlanta • San Francisco • Boston • Dallas • Toronto • London

# Staff Credits

## EDITORIAL

**Manager of Editorial Operations**
Bill Wahlgren

**Executive Editor**
Patricia McCambridge

**Senior Editor and Project Editor**
Eileen Joyce

**Component Editors:** Jane Archer Feinstein, Carolyn Logan, Stephanie Wenger

**Assistant Editor:** Tracy DeMont

**Copyediting:** Michael Neibergall, *Copyediting Manager;* Mary Malone, *Copyediting Supervisor;* Christine Altgelt, Joel Bourgeois, Elizabeth Dickson, Emily Force, Julie A. Hill, Julia Thomas Hu, Jennifer Kirkland, Millicent Ondras, Dennis Scharnberg, *Copyeditors*

**Project Administration:** Marie Price, *Managing Editor;* Lori De La Garza, *Editorial Operations Coordinator;* Heather Cheyne, Mark Holland, Marcus Johnson, Jennifer Renteria, Janet Riley, Kelly Tankersley, *Project Administration;* Ruth Hooker, Casey Kelly, Joie Pickett, Margaret Sanchez, *Word Processing*

**Writers:** Colleen Hobbs, Elizabeth Smith

**Editorial Permissions:** Susan Lowrance, *Permissions Editor*

## ART, DESIGN, AND PHOTO

**Book Design**
Richard Metzger, *Design Director*

**Graphic Services**
Kristen Darby, *Manager*

**Design Implementation**
The Format Group, LLC

**Image Acquisitions**
Joe London, *Director;* Jeannie Taylor, *Photo Research Supervisor;* Rick Benavides, Terri Janecek, *Photo Researchers;* Sarah Hudgens, *Assistant Photo Researcher;* Michelle Rumpf, *Art Buyer Supervisor;* Gillian Brody, Joyce Gonzalez, *Art Buyers*

**Cover Design**
Curtis Riker, *Director*
Sunday Patterson, *Designer*

## PRODUCTION

Belinda Barbosa Lopez, *Senior Production Coordinator*
Beth Prevelige, *Prepress Manager*
Carol Trammel, *Production Supervisor*

## MANUFACTURING/INVENTORY

Shirley Cantrell, *Supervisor of Inventory and Manufacturing*
Wilonda Ieans, *Manufacturing Coordinator*
Mark McDonald, *Inventory Planner*

Cover Photo Credits: (Astrolabe by Gualtiero Arsenio, Museo della Scienza, Florence, Italy), Scala/Art Resource, NY; (Abou Bakr Ibn Iousouf, Astrolabe, 1216 CE, Musee Paul Depuy, Toulouse, France), Giraudon/Art Resource, NY; (Castillos de las Herguijuelas, Caceres, Spain), Scala/Art Resource, NY; (Atlas Coelestis 1660), © Planet Art.

15 16 17 18   1186   17 16 15

4500542905

# Contents

## CHAPTER 5

## Forces of Change: Renaissance, Reformation, and Scientific Revolution

## CHAPTER 6

## Oceans of Exploration: From Europe to the Americas

## *Selection Tests*

## CHAPTER 1

## Empire on the Edge: The Fall of Rome

## CHAPTER 2

## Lasting Legacies: From the Islamic World to Africa

## CHAPTER 3
## Looking to the East: China and Japan

## CHAPTER 4
## The Making of the Middle Ages: Europe and Japan

## CHAPTER 5
## Forces of Change: Renaissance, Reformation, and Scientific Revolution

## CHAPTER 6
## Oceans of Exploration: From Europe to the Americas

# Content-Area Reading Strategies

# Blackline Masters for Graphic Organizers

# Using This Teacher's Guide

## This Teacher's Guide is intended to

- *provide maximum versatility and flexibility*
- *serve as a ready resource for background information on each selection*
- *act as a catalyst for discussion, analysis, interpretation, activities, and further research*
- *provide reproducible blackline masters that can be used for either individual or collaborative work, including discussions and projects*
- *provide multiple options for evaluating students' progress*

The Selection Notes, Selection Tests, reading strategies essay, and blackline masters in this Teacher's Guide have been created to provide support for teaching the selections and features in the *Content-Area Reader* Pupil's Edition. In this Teacher's Guide, you will find instructional background and other resources that will help you to effectively teach content-area reading skills to all of your students.

## Selection Notes

Selection Notes, arranged by chapter and selection, are included for every selection in the Pupil's Edition, providing teachers with the tools they need to help students get the most out of their content-area reading.

- **Before Reading** activities introduce students to important issues in the selection, provide further background for the teacher, offer instruction in both high-utility and content-area vocabulary, and present basic reading skills and reading strategies to implement those skills.
- **During Reading** activities provide extra information about selection features, such as the side-margin features and the art that accompanies the selection. In addition, teaching suggestions for Learners Having

Difficulty, English-Language Learners, and Advanced Learners are offered to help teachers meet the needs of all students.

- **After Reading** activities provide answers to the **Reading Check** questions in the Pupil's Edition so that you can assess students' content comprehension. A **Reteaching** feature for students who had difficulty with the reading skill and strategy helps ensure that all students learn content-area reading skills. **Connecting to Language Arts** activities offer students in the language arts classroom a chance to create a personalized response to the selection, using such approaches as journal entry writing, ad or brochure copy writing, video presentations, and interviews involving role-playing. **Connecting Across the Curriculum** provides activities to extend students' interest by researching materials related to the selection topic and completing a project based on their investigations. **Rubrics for Cross-Curricular Activities** in the Pupil's Edition are provided at the end of each chapter.

## Selection Tests

- A **Selection Test** for each title offers multiple-choice questions about the content and multiple-choice or matching questions to assess vocabulary comprehension. The vocabulary that is tested appears underscored in the selections in the Pupil's Editions.

## Content-Area Reading Strategies for the Language Arts Classroom

In this section of the Teacher's Guide, Senior Consultant Dr. Judith Irvin provides an informative essay on content-area reading skills and offers eleven strategies for approaching content-area reading in the classroom. In order to successfully read expository text, students need to be aware of the basic text structures used in nonfiction literature. Students also need to have access to a variety of tools—strategies—for understanding expository text. Dr. Irvin's reading strategies are cross-referenced throughout the Selection Notes in the first section of the Teacher's Guide, and graphic organizers to support various reading strategies are provided in reproducible blackline masters in the final section of the Teacher's Guide.

## Graphic Organizers

A selection of various graphic organizers in reproducible blackline masters form appears at the back of the Teacher's Guide. These graphic organizers can be used with the various reading strategies presented in the selection Teaching Notes.

## CHAPTER 1

# Empire on the Edge
## The Fall of Rome 753 B.C.–A.D. 476

---

### *from* **The Roads to the Spiceries**

from *Roman Roads*

by VICTOR W. VON HAGEN
*(student text page 3)*

**CONTENT-AREA CONNECTIONS**

HISTORY •⎯⎯
GEOGRAPHY •⎯

---

**Reading Level:** Above Average

### Text Summary

Trajan's use of legions to provide security made it safe to build a system that brought goods into Rome from all over the world. Eager buyers awaited the spices, jewels, ivory, and cloth carried by ship and camel from far away lands to the market in Rome.

---

## BEFORE READING

### Make the Connection

Ask students if they have ever been to a place that they could not reach by a car, bus, or bicycle. Ask students to consider how their lives today would be different if they did not have access to roads and the products conveyed on them. [Students might say that they would not be able to go very far from home and probably would have to walk to school. Their families would depend on what they could grow, make themselves, or buy from close neighbors or markets.]

### Build Background
■ More About the Topic

The Emperor Trajan's roads were just one of his ambitious building projects. Trajan's Bridge, the first one built across the Danube River, was a half-mile long; no one built a longer bridge for a thousand years. Trajan's Forum in Rome was an enormous complex of structures that covered an area the size of nine football fields. One may still see Trajan's Column in the ruins of the forum; the sculpture that covers the tall marble monument still boasts of the emperor's military victories.

### ⌐ *Vocabulary Tip* ⎯⎯⎯⎯⎯⎯

**Using Prefixes** Point out the prefixes *un–* and *in–*, which both mean "not," and have students brainstorm a list of words using these prefixes.

### Vocabulary Development

The following words are underscored and defined in the student text.

**unruly:** difficult to manage; undisciplined.

**hewn:** shaped with a tool such as an ax.

**sheen:** glistening appearance; shininess.

**invulnerable:** unable to be injured; not open to attack.

**cultivated:** grew or tended.

Before assigning the reading, you may want to introduce students to any words that could cause pronunciation or definition problems.

### ⌐ CONTENT-AREA VOCABULARY ¬

Although the following words are important to an understanding of the text selection, some of them may be unfamiliar to students. You may want to introduce the words to students before they begin reading. Put the words on the chalkboard or on an overhead transparency. Pronounce each word and ask students to define the words if they can. Write their definitions and add the ones given below if students have not covered those particular meanings. You may want to ask students to predict what they will read about in a selection using these words.

**caravan\*:** a group of merchants traveling together.
**trade winds:** constant, steady winds.
**imports:** goods that are brought for sale from another country.
**cargo:** goods being transported.

*Although students may be familiar with some meanings of this word, the word as used in the selection has a specific meaning that pertains to the content area.

## Reading Informational Materials

### Reading Skill
Finding the Main Idea
Explain to students that the main idea is the topic that is developed in an article or in a section of an article. Recognizing key words can help students form a statement of the main idea.

▶ **Teaching Tip**
*Text Features* Point out to students that words set off by unusual treatment, such as italics, boldface, boxes, or bullets will have special meaning. Explain also that they will find information about the topic in the head note and the "You Need to Know" feature. Previewing the vocabulary will familiarize students with unusual words and meanings that are particular to this topic.

### Reading Strategy
Previewing Text (Strategy 1)
To help students find the main idea of the selection you may wish to use Strategy 1 described in the Content-Area Reading Strategies. You may wish to provide students with a KWL Chart (Graphic Organizer 6) to help them organize their ideas about what they *know*, what they *want* to know about the topic, and eventually what they have *learned* in the process of reading the selection.

## DURING READING

### Using the Side-Margin Feature
■ Lucius Trebonius Was Here
To help students realize how large and varied the Roman Empire was, you might want to show students pictures of famous sights from the Roman Empire. You might include pictures of the Sphinx in Egypt, Greek temples in Athens, or Stonehenge

in Britain. Use a map to help students understand the distance between these attractions.

### Viewing the Art
*Roman Road* You may wish to refer students to student text page 9 and the diagram of the cross section of a Roman road such as the ones built by the Emperor Trajan. You may want to discuss what the cross section reveals about the development of Roman science and engineering.

### Differentiating Instruction
■ Learners Having Difficulty
Use a prediction-and-confirming activity by first asking students "What was the Roman Empire like?" Then, provide students with a list of words from the selection such as "caravan," "pirates," and "cinnamon," and have them create a three-column organizer with columns headed "Prediction," "Revised Prediction," and "Fact." Have students work in small groups to make predictions about how the words might relate to the selection. Provide students with new information about the words and have them revise or modify their prediction statements. Students can revise their predictions a final time after they have read the selection.

## AFTER READING

### ✔ Reading Comprehension

The following are sample answers to questions on student text page 11.

1. During peacetime, Roman legions built guard stations and signal towers to keep watch. They taught the people of Hither Asia how to build roads and bridges.

2. The Via Traiana was 400 miles long and passed through the desert between Damascus and Aqaba.

3. Petra was an important city because it was on a caravan route. When Romans took over the city to control the route, they created Roman-style streets, fountains, and theaters.

**4.** Spices were light, easy to transport, and highly profitable in Roman markets. Spices sold in Rome included cinnamon, cloves, nutmeg, mace, and gingerroot.

**5.** Only camels could make the long trips across the desert carrying heavy loads of trade goods. In desert caravans, humans used the camels' milk, dung, flesh, and hair.

## Reteaching

If students have difficulty stating the selection's main idea, have them write key words in a Cluster Diagram (Graphic Organizer 3 and Reading Strategy 3). Have students group clusters of related words and use one or two of the words to build sentences about the selection. [For example: Romans built **roads** throughout their **empire**.] Then, students can add words from other clusters to the original sentence. [Romans built **roads** throughout their **empire** to bring **spices** to **market**.] After students have built several sentences using key words, they can discuss how the different sentences reflect the text's main idea.

## Connecting to Language Arts
- Speaking and Listening

*Getting the Word Out* Have students work in groups to create a TV or radio commercial that promotes travel on the Roman roads. The commercial could promote the roads' safety and comfort, as well as the sites and scenery along the way. Students can record their commercials and play the recordings for the rest of the class.

## Connecting Across the Curriculum: Social Studies

Assign students to find out more about Roman roads: how they were constructed, what special building techniques were required, and what cities were linked by the roads. After students have completed their research, have them compare findings or work together to share the information they discovered. They could complete one of the following assignments:

- a "how-to" article explaining road-building to the people of Hither Asia
- a skit of a crew of Roman soldiers describing the secrets of road building
- a "slideshow" illustrating places that modern vacationers have traveled near or on the ancient Roman highways.

## Further Resources

The J. Paul Getty Museum offers further information about the Rome of the Emperor, Trajan, as well as materials for interdisciplinary middle school curriculum.

## Assessment

Turn to page 115 for a multiple-choice test on the selection.

*Test Answers*
**1.** c  **2.** b  **3.** d  **4.** b  **5.** d
**6.** c  **7.** b  **8.** b  **9.** a  **10.** c

# Hadrian's Wall

*from Walls: Defenses Throughout History*

by JAMES CROSS GIBLIN
*(student text page 12)*

**Reading Level:** Average

## Text Summary

In the most distant reaches of the Roman Empire, the Emperor Hadrian built a wall to protect the southern part of Britain from raiding tribes to the north. Built in the second century A.D., Hadrian's wall was 15 feet tall and 70 miles long. Until it was abandoned in A.D. 400, the wall successfully protected the Roman troops stationed in Britain. Parts of Hadrian's Wall can be seen today.

# BEFORE READING

## Make the Connection

Ask students if they have ever made their own fortifications, such as sand or snow forts. What was their purpose for building the structures? [to protect themselves from the "enemy"] What was required to build the forts? [time, materials, people, places] What elements made their defenses effective? [The walls could serve as a shield. A fort on a slick hill would be difficult to capture.] Have students consider what might have made Hadrian's wall effective as a barrier and what resources were required for early peoples to make such a large structure. [money, labor, materials]

## Build Background

■ More About the Topic

Hadrian's Wall marked the frontier between the Romans and the tribes to the north. That boundary was briefly extended by Hadrian's successor, Emperor Antonius Pius. The Antonine Wall, located about a hundred miles north of Hadrian's Wall, was built in A.D. 142 and ran across Scotland for thirty-six miles between the Clyde River and the Firth of Forth. Within twenty years, however, a revolt in the north caused soldiers to retreat southward to Hadrian's Wall.

## Vocabulary Development

The following words are underscored and defined in the student text.

**subdued:** conquered.
**recruited:** hired; enrolled.
**intervals:** spaces between objects or points.
**sector:** part of a divided area; section.
**alliance:** association or union created for a common purpose.

Before assigning the reading, you may want to introduce students to any words that could cause pronunciation or definition problems.

### Vocabulary Tip

**Using Etymology** A raid is an unexpected attack, usually by a small, armed group. This word for "attack" comes from the same root as our word *road.* The Old English word *rad* meant both "the act of riding" and "the act of raiding." *Road* is no longer used in this way, but we can still see a trace of this meaning in the word *inroad,* which means "a riding or an advance upon."

### CONTENT-AREA VOCABULARY

Although the following words are important to an understanding of the text selection, some of them may be unfamiliar to students. You may want to introduce the words to students before they begin reading. Put the words on the chalkboard or on an overhead transparency. Pronounce each word, and ask students to define the words if they can. Write their definitions and add the ones given below if students have not covered those particular meanings. You may want to assign students to groups of four to write a paragraph using the words.

**roving:** wandering.
**raiding\*:** attacking, usually by a small armed group.
**hostile:** warlike; threatening.
**sentries:** guards.

\* Although students may be familiar with other meanings of this word, the word as used in the selection has a specific meaning that pertains to the content area.

## Reading Informational Materials

### Reading Skill
Using Text Structures

Explain to students that text structures are the patterns writers use to organize their ideas. By looking at text patterns, readers can see the relationships within a text.

### Reading Strategy
Constructing Concept Maps (Strategy 4)

To help students visualize and make sense of the text you may wish to use Strategy 4 described in Content-Area Reading Strategies. Their concept maps may sketch out ideas about the wall itself, as well as about the different groups of people described in the text. [Romans, northern tribes, Goths] For a modified version of a concept map, you may wish to have students use a Cluster Diagram (Graphic Organizer 3).

## DURING READING

### Using the Side-Margin Feature
■ Holding Up the Wall

Ask students to identify places around them where concrete is used in construction. [floors, sidewalks, pillars or supports] What might their classroom look like if fireproof, waterproof concrete were not available? [The room might have a wood structure and wooden floors.]

## Reading Informational Material

▶ **Teaching Tip**

*Maps* Before students read the selection, show them maps of Europe and Great Britain. After students read, have them locate the different peoples mentioned in the text: the Scots in the west of Britain, the Saxons in the east of Britain, the Goths and Persians in the eastern part of the Roman Empire.

### Differentiating Instruction
■ English-Language Learners

Students may be unfamiliar with vocabulary in the text that relates to military matters: *forts, watchtowers, peepholes,* and *sentries.* Discuss with students the meanings of these words and other multiple meaning words, such as *barbarians, colony,* and *border.* Ask them to use as many of these words as they can to write notes as they read.

---

## AFTER READING

The following are sample answers to questions on student text page 18.

1. Hadrian's Wall is located in northern England. Soldiers built the wall in the narrowest part of the island to make the shortest possible wall.

2. The outside of the wall was made of wedge-shaped stones held together with mortar. The center of the wall was filled with small rocks and pebbles, held together with more mortar.

3. Forts that housed many soldiers and their horses were built every four miles along the wall. Smaller outposts called milecastles were positioned between forts. In the small watchtowers between each milecastle, soldiers watched for enemy invaders. Builders also dug deep ditches on either side of the wall to defend against invaders.

4. About 15,000 soldiers defended the wall's forts, milecastles, and watchtowers. The soldiers came from different parts of the Roman Empire, including Rome itself, Greece, Syria, and France.

5. When Roman emperors reduced the number of soldiers who had defended the area, allied groups attacked the wall. Then, the wall was abandoned, and local people used its stones for building materials.

### Reteaching

If students have difficulty identifying the organization of the text, you may wish to have them look for descriptive signal words. Using a blank transparency, have students mark words that are used to show the relationship of Hadrian's Wall to things around it. [*beside, between*]. Have them notice that often directions are used to indicate structures located on the north and south sides. In addition, have students mark words that indicate size, number, or distance [*every four miles*]. After students have marked signal words, have them draw a rough sketch of the wall, noting these distances, directions, and sizes.

## Connecting to Language Arts

### ▪ Writing
*Sequence or Chronological Order Graphic Organizer* The selection provides the history of Hadrian's Wall, from its construction to its abandonment and gradual decay. Have students plot the story of the wall, using a Sequence or Chronological Order Chart (Graphic Organizer 10) to mark notable dates in its growth and decline.

### ▪ Speaking and Listening
*Dramatic Monologue* Have students tell the history of northern Britain from the perspective of Hadrian's Wall. Assign students to tell a part of the wall's "life story," speaking as the wall might speak to describe the changes it has seen. Students can perform their dramatic monologues for the rest of the class.

## Connecting Across the Curriculum: Social Studies

*A Long Way from Home* The French, Greek, and Syrian soldiers stationed at Hadrian's Wall were very far from home. What sights must have seemed most odd or unusual to them? Have students work in groups to perform a historical "you are there" scene in which soldiers in a milecastle relate the events of their day guarding Hadrian's Wall. Have students find out more about the soldiers' "hometowns" in the Roman Empire to compare and contrast them with the wilds of northern Britain. You may want to give students three Venn diagrams (Graphic Organizer 11), one for each country, and have students show how temperature, climate, foods, culture, and so forth compare to those in northern England.

*On the Other Side of the Wall* Imagine the conversations that might have taken place between the tribes of northern Britain and the Roman soldiers at Hadrian's Wall. What questions might the native Britons have had about the Romans' tools, weapons, and construction techniques? What might the Romans have wondered about the Britons' religion and customs? Have students work in groups to create a dialogue in which one group meets the other and—in a friendly way—gets some answers to their curious questions.

## Further Resources
The UNESCO World Heritage Centre offers information about archaeology and research conducted at Hadrian's Wall.

The NOVA "Secrets of the Lost Empires" series on PBS television's Web site allows students the opportunity to learn more about Roman building projects; as "chief water engineer," they can build an aqueduct online on the "Roman Baths" page. The series even offers Roman recipes.

### ( Assessment )
Turn to page 116 for a multiple-choice test on the selection.

*Test Answers*
**1.** d  **2.** b  **3.** c  **4.** c  **5.** b
**6.** c  **7.** b  **8.** a  **9.** c  **10.** d

# A Persecuted Faith Becomes a World Religion

from *Calliope*

by S.E. TOTH
*(student text page 19)*

**Reading Level:** Above Average

## Text Summary

The Emperor Nero began the first widespread persecution of people who practiced the Christian religion. Persecution by Roman authorities continued until Constantine's Edict of Milan made Christianity a protected, accepted religion within the Empire. When Constantine moved Rome's capital to Constantinople, partly to get away from the many pagan rituals, he erected the Magale Ekklesia, a beautiful church later destroyed by fire.

## BEFORE READING

### Make the Connection

Ask students if they can think of any problems religions have had with governments. You might prompt them to think of groups like the pilgrims who left England to find freedom of religion or the Catholics in Ireland who fought the British for rights. Then, have students think about why a government might oppose having more than one religion or allowing the development of new faiths. [challenge to authority and tradition]

### Build Background

■ More About the Topic

Nero's persecution of Christians was only one of many infamous acts. The emperor is remembered as an inept ruler, as well as a villain who murdered two wives and his own mother. A ruler who loved composing verses and playing the lyre, he is said to have found the flames of the burning Rome so beautiful that they moved him to song. Rome's fire apparently moved Nero to an uncharacteristic act of compassion: when the flames subsided, Nero spent his own money to feed and shelter the Roman homeless.

## Vocabulary Development

The following words are underscored and defined in the student text.

**persecution:** repeated acts of torment or cruelty; harassment
**tolerated:** permitted or respected; endured
**rigor:** strictness or precision
**fervor:** intense emotion; passion
**ornate:** elaborately decorated

Before assigning the reading, you may want to introduce students to any words that could cause pronunciation or definition problems.

> ┌─ *Vocabulary Tip* ─
> **Using Related Words** Ask students to brainstorm other forms of the words in the Vocabulary Development list. [*persecute, tolerant, rigorous*] Have student volunteers use the original and the additional forms in sentences. Point out to students that the new forms of the words are different parts of speech than those in the original list.

### CONTENT-AREA VOCABULARY

Although the following words are important to an understanding of the text selection, some of them may be unfamiliar to students. You may want to write the words on the chalkboard or on an overhead transparency. Ask students to add to the list and to define other words that are connected with religion. The list might include *mass, service, atonement, beliefs, dogma.* Tell students they will be working with these words in a later assignment.

**baptism\***: a Christian ceremony in which a person is ritually purified with water before joining the religious community.

**zeal**: eagerness.

**penance**: an act of devotion performed to show sorrow for a wrongdoing.

**divinity**: a deity; a godlike being.

\*Although students may be familiar with other meanings of this word, the word as used in the selection has a specific meaning that pertains to the content area.

## Reading Informational Materials

### Reading Skill
Using Chronological Order

Explain to students that this text is organized by chronological order. Events are discussed in the order in which they happened.

### Reading Strategy
Understanding Text (Strategy 2)

To help your students follow the chronological order of the selection, you may wish to use Strategy 2 described in Content-Area Reading Strategies. You may wish to provide students with a Sequence or Chronological Order Chart (Graphic Organizer 10) to help them show the sequence of events in the selection. In addition, have them note the signal words that indicate time or sequence [A.D. 64, then, today].

▶ **Teaching Tip**

*Understanding a Magazine Selection* This selection is from a magazine. Point out to students that the shorter format of periodicals means that topics are covered in less detail than they might be in books. Point out to students that many historical characters [Nero, Diocletian, Maxentius] are discussed only briefly. For more information on these figures, students may want to consult entries in encyclopedias or biographical reference books.

## DURING READING

### Correcting Misconceptions

Students may assume that Christians were the only people persecuted for their religious beliefs. Remind students that people of many religions have suffered for their faith. Jews, for example, were killed by Nazis in Europe, a predominantly Christian area. In recent times, Serbian groups killed Muslims in the former Yugoslavia.

### Viewing the Art
*Hagia Sophia*

You may wish to refer students to student text page 24 and the photo of the Hagia Sophia. Call attention to the church's great dome. You may want to have students research the construction of the church to learn what engineering techniques were used to build the church's famous dome. Students also could research the changes that were made when the Hagia Sophia was converted from a Christian church to a Moslem mosque.

### Differentiating Instruction
▪ Learners Having Difficulty

You may wish to divide the class into study groups to summarize the different topics covered in the selection: the impact of Nero's persecutions, the rise of the Emperor Constantine, the Council of Nicaea, and the new capital of Constantinople. Each group member should summarize and explain a single portion of the text. Students can help one another understand difficult vocabulary or challenging passages.

## AFTER READING

### ✔ Reading Check

The following are sample answers to questions on student text page 25.

1. Nero blamed Christians for the fire that destroyed Rome in A.D. 64.

2. Christians often hid and held services in underground quarries called catacombs.

3. Constantine thought he saw the Greek letters *X* and *P*, the first two letters in the Greek name for "Christ." Constantine credited the Christian God for his victory, and so helped end the persecution of Christians.

4. Constantine called the first General Council of Nicaea to restore order in the empire by establishing one set of Christian beliefs.

**5.** Constantine wanted to move the center of government away from Rome's powerful ruling families and its pagan rituals. He said the Christian God ordered him to move the capital.

## Reteaching

If students have difficulty understanding the selection by graphing its chronology, model retelling a part of the story, putting events in the proper order. Then, have a student working with a partner retell a section of the text, organizing his or her paraphrase to recall the sequence in which events happened. The partner then offers suggestions as to what areas of the selection need more review. The partners then switch roles and repeat the exercise. Monitor students' work and offer suggestions and encouragement.

## Connecting to Language Arts

### ▪ Writing

***Historical Character Journal Entry*** Have students compose journal entries that might have been written by the Emperor Constantine. What were his feelings after the battle at the Milvian Bridge? What problems did he face in moving Rome's capital to Byzantium? What were Constantine's responses to some important events during his reign—and perhaps to some trivial events, also?

### ▪ Speaking and Listening

***The Emperors Speak Out*** Have students create video or live interviews with three emperors— Nero, Diocletian, and Constantine. Students can choose the emperor they would like to portray; then they can work in groups to record on video the ruler's views on the new Christian religion. Encourage students to use the selection's glossed vocabulary in their presentations. Interviewers should ask the emperors to explain decisions that affected Christians, and emperors can share their own feelings about Christianity and the ancient Roman religion. When the interviews are complete, students can perform their interviews or play their videos for the class.

## Connecting Across the Curriculum: Architecture/Science

***Building for the Faithful*** Assign students to find out more about a particular site important to early Christians: the catacombs, the Magale Ekklesia, or the Hagia Sophia. Students can work individually or in groups to complete one of the following assignments:

- act as tour guides, showing their classmates through a series of images (drawings or photographs) of the site's most interesting features
- write a memo from the site's "contractor," explaining any challenges to the construction and describing the most important tools or materials needed
- build a model of the site
- draw a floor plan or map of the site (or a section of the catacombs)

## Further Resources

A photographic tour of the Hagia Sophia is available at the site "Constantinople, Yesterday and Today." Look for the *P* button leading to the Photos page.

"Rome of the Caesars" is a site created and maintained by Woodberry Forest School that contains pages on Roman life, rulers and religions. Included is information about religions that preceded Christianity.

### ( Assessment )

Turn to page 117 for a multiple-choice test on the selection.

***Test Answers***

**1.** d  **2.** b  **3.** c  **4.** a  **5.** d
**6.** c  **7.** a  **8.** b  **9.** d  **10.** a

# The Fall and the Legacy

from *Ancient Rome*

by CHRISTOPHER FAGG
(student text page 26)

**Reading Level:** Average

## Text Summary

Rivalries among leaders, high taxes, and invaders at the frontiers all contributed to the downfall of the mighty Roman Empire. The Ostrogoths seized control of Rome in A.D. 476; the empire held together in the East until Muslims overran Constantinople in 673. Although the ruling power of the Empire disappeared, its legacy in development of government and law lives on.

# BEFORE READING

## Make the Connection

The fall of the Roman Empire shows how the weight of an accumulation of small problems can bring down a mighty government. Ask students to think about small events in their own lives that added up to serious problems. What was the situation? How could they could have prevented the situation from getting worse? Then, ask students whether they think the fall of the Roman Empire was inevitable or avoidable. Ask them to brainstorm what might have prevented the downfall. [leaders who were more willing to work together, belief on the part of would-be invaders that an invasion would not be successful] Have students consider whether every government has a life span, as a person does, or if governments can change and adapt to solve their bureaucratic problems. Ask students to support their answers.

## Build Background

■ More About the Topic

Rome's last emperor was burdened with a pretentious name that proved sadly ironic in the face of a crumbling empire. Romulus Augustus was named for Rome's legendary first king (Romulus) and its successful first emperor (Augustus). As a result of his failure, the Roman public changed Romulus to Momyllus, "little disgrace," and Augustus to

Augustulus, or 'little emperor." The taunting name "Augustulus" has stuck: many historians continue to call Rome's final emperor by a name that was meant to mock his position.

## Vocabulary Development

The following words are underscored and defined in the student's text.

**rivals:** competitors.

**treacherous:** dishonest or untrustworthy; unfaithful.

**seized:** took by force.

**deposed:** removed from power.

**convert:** to change; transform.

Before assigning the reading, you may want to introduce students to any words that could cause pronunciation or definition problems. Point out the suffix *–ous* and the prefix *de–*. Ask students to find definitions for the two affixes [full of; away from]. Discuss with them how these definitions fit in with the meanings given in their texts.

---

## Vocabulary Tip

**Using Etymology** To sack, meaning "to plunder" or "to loot," has a long pedigree arising from its association with commerce. Carrying away a sack of goods from a merchant was associated with carrying away a sack of stolen goods. Our English word comes from the Latin *sacc.* The Romans got their word from the Greeks—*sakkos*—who in turn got it from the Phoenicians. Languages as different as Hebrew, Welsh, and Albanian all share this expression.

---

### CONTENT-AREA VOCABULARY

Although the following words are important to an understanding of the text selection, some of them may be unfamiliar to students. You may want to present this list of words and their definitions to your students. Have students brainstorm any connections between the words. Encourage students to discuss other meanings they know for these words and to predict what a selection using this combination might concern.

**frontiers\*:** borders between settled regions and undeveloped territory.

**menaced:** threatened.

**sacked\*:** looted or plundered.

**refuge:** a shelter; a place of protection.

**at bay:** not able to advance; held at a distance.

\*Although students may be familiar with other meanings of these words, the words as used in the selection have specific meanings that pertain to the content area.

## Reading Informational Materials

### Reading Skill

#### Identifying Cause and Effect Text Structure

Explain to students that a **cause** makes something happen, and that an **effect** is what occurs as a result. Writers may state both the cause and the effect in their writing. Sometimes, however, they may omit part of the information, leaving the readers to use their own knowledge to infer either a cause or an effect.

### Reading Strategy

#### Understanding Text: Cause and Effect (Strategy 2)

To help students find the relationship between causes and effects in the selection, you may wish to use Strategy 2 described in Content-Area Reader Strategies. You may wish to provide students with a Cause-and-Effect Chart (Graphic Organizer 2) to help them show their ideas about how events lead to other events.

## DURING READING

### Using the Side-Margin Feature

■ SIDELIGHT

Have students consider the term *barbarian.* Is the connotation positive or negative? Would the Celts and Goths have called themselves "barbarians"? Does the author's description of the barbarians' energy and size seem negative? How do words acquire such connotations? Are those connotations always accurate?

## Reading Informational Materials

▶ **Teaching Tip**

*Map* Show students a map of Europe. Have volunteers show the paths of advancing invaders, including the Persian threat from the east. Point out the domino effect created as the Huns pushed the Vandals and Visigoths to the west.

### Differentiating Instruction

■ English-Language Learners

Build students' confidence by modeling the unfamiliar proper names found in the selection: *Diocletian, Sassanids, Rhine-Danube, Alaric, Romulus Augustulus, Suevi, Alani,* and *Saracens.* Because students may struggle over these names even in silent reading, suggest that they think of short nicknames to identify the longer names. [i. e. *Di* for Diocletian; *R-D* for Rhine-Danube]

## AFTER READING

### ✔ Reading Check

The following are sample answers to questions on student text page 30.

1. The empire was too large for one person to govern. Diocletian wanted to defend Rome's frontiers and provide for a smooth change of leadership.

2. Diocletian's two-ruler system broke down when Constantine's co-rulers betrayed him. Constantine defeated his rivals and ruled alone.

3. Constantine moved the capital to Constantinople. He increased taxes and used laws to bind people to their jobs. After Constantine's death, young, weak emperors could no longer hold back the invading barbarians.

4. The Ostrogoths invaded Italy and deposed Romulus Augustulus, Rome's last emperor.

5. Among the legacies are Roman law and government.

## Reteaching

If students have difficulty analyzing causes and effects, have them form sentences telling *who* wanted *what* and *how* the situation worked out. This formula provides motivation, conflict, and resolution. [Example: Diocletian (who) wanted to rule the empire effectively; however, the empire was too big for one person to govern, so he devised a system to divide governing responsibilities.] Students can reword this information into a concise cause-and-effect summary. [To improve the enormous Roman Empire's system of government (cause), Diocletian created a system to divide the responsibility of governing (effect).] Students can follow this formula for the different cause-and-effect patterns they find in the selection. Remind students that an effect may be the cause of the next effect.

## Connecting to Language Arts

### ■ Writing

*Complaint* Have students imagine that they live in the Roman Empire. They will write a letter to a local official complaining about how public services have declined in their neighborhoods. Letters could describe the condition of roads, aqueducts, and military defenses. In addition, students could mention how their taxes have increased. Post students' letters on the bulletin board.

### ■ Speaking and Listening

*Interview* Have students work in pairs to create a radio interview with a member of a group of Vandals or Visigoths who have settled along the Danube River. Students will research the reasons the groups made such a move, what they were expected to give back to the Empire in return, how their actions differed from those of other groups, and the type of life they lead both before and after settling. The interviewed settler will need to be ready to explain any of the above as well as answer questions about future plans or possibilities for his or her people. Students may record their interviews to share with the class.

## Connecting Across the Curriculum: Government/Architecture

*Roman Leftovers* Assign students to research what the Roman Empire left behind. Have the class work in groups to find information about the Roman artifacts, customs, architecture, or laws that remain with us today. Students can then make a "top ten" list of elements that make up Rome's legacy. Have students illustrate their "top ten" lists and post them to share with the class.

## Further Resources

The Metropolitan Museum of Art offers further information about Byzantine art and works of the later Roman Empire. Their Web site "The Glory of Byzantium" includes teacher resources and classroom activities.

## Assessment

Turn to page 118 for a multiple-choice test on the selection.

*Test Answers*

1. b    2. a    3. d    4. b    5. b
6. a    7. c    8. d    9. b    10. d

The following criteria can help you evaluate each student's success in completing the activities prompted by the Cross-Curricular Activities feature in the student textbook.

**\*Note:** Activities marked with an asterisk allow the involvement of more than one student. For these activities you may wish first to evaluate each student on his or her individual contribution and then give groups an overall rating.

## \*Geography/Speech
### Can You Get There from Here?

- Students, alone or in small groups, conduct research to investigate the Romans' network of roads and plot a trip between two cities.
- Students use the research results to create maps and itineraries of their travels, including travel conditions, terrain, and people and towns along the route.
- Students' maps are clearly drawn and labeled. Appropriate legends or keys about the map's scale and symbols are included.
- Students present maps and itinerary to the class in a clearly delivered report.

## History/Health
### Eating in the Empire

- The student conducts research to plan a typical Roman meal, noting where different kinds of recipe ingredients were grown or hunted.
- The student compares the Roman meal to the foods recommended in the modern guidelines for balanced diets.
- The student presents the findings orally, along with a Roman dish, if possible.

## Language Arts/History
### Dear Diary

- The student writes a series of diary entries describing events in the life of a person living during the fall of the Roman Empire. Perspectives may be those of a Roman soldier, a priest in a pagan temple, or a Visigoth living on the edge of the empire.
- The student addresses the changes occurring during this time and their effects on everyday life.
- The writing is relatively free of errors in spelling, grammar, usage, and mechanics.

## \*Language Arts/Drama
### Positions Available

- Assuming the role of a Roman army commander, the student writes a job description of the duties that soldiers guarding Hadrian's Wall must perform, the skills they need, and the types of situations they might encounter. Descriptions include salary and any special benefits.
- The student presents a convincing mock interview between a recruiter and a potential guard.
- The writing is relatively free of errors in spelling, grammar, usage, and mechanics.

## Art/Architecture
### Same Empire/Different City

- The student creates and presents to the class a travel brochure describing tourist attractions in Byzantium's new capital, Constantinople.
- The brochure clearly describes important buildings and works of art, and emphasizes the art and architecture at religious sites.
- The student illustrates the brochure imaginatively and creatively.

## CHAPTER 2

# Lasting Legacies
## From the Islamic World to Africa
### A.D. 600-1600

---

### *from* Travel Through the Empire

from *The Arabs in the Golden Age*

by MOKHTAR MOKTEFI
*(student text page 35)*

**CONTENT-AREA CONNECTIONS**

HISTORY ●

GEOGRAPHY ●

---

**Reading Level:** Average

### Text Summary

During the Middle Ages, Arab territory stretched from China to Spain, from Central Africa to southern France. Arab merchants carried goods across this territory, called the *dar al Islam,* by ship and camel caravan. As merchants traveled across the globe, they transported not just merchandise, but also people and their ideas.

---

## BEFORE READING

### Make the Connection

Ask students to state some reasons for traveling long distances. [to conduct business; to sightsee; to visit family or friends] Then, ask students what preparations people today make for long-distance travel. What considerations do modern travelers give to finding their food and lodging? [using travel books, packing food in a cooler, making reservations] Or, to making sure that they will be safe during their journey? [checking road conditions and weather reports, being sure their vehicle is in good repair]

### Build Background

■ More About the Topic

Contemporary Bedouins call themselves "the people of the camel" because that desert animal is vital to their culture and survival. The animal's importance is reflected in the Arabic language, which has developed about a thousand different words that

relate to "camel." Camels are such an essential part of the Bedouin economy that they are used as a measure of wealth. The worth of a bride's dowry and a sheik's wealth, for example, are calculated by the number of camels they would buy.

### Vocabulary Development

The following words are underscored and defined in the student text.

**terrain:** natural features of land.

**navigate:** to plot a course across or through; find the correct direction.

**indispensable:** required or necessary.

**convoy:** group traveling together for convenience or safety; caravan.

**communal:** shared by all; belonging to the community.

Before assigning the reading, you may want to introduce students to any words that could cause pronunciation or definition problems.

---

┌─ *Vocabulary Tip* ─

**Using Etymology** Remind students that land completely surrounded by water is an *island.* Ask what word we would use if the land is *almost* surrounded by water, perhaps with just a thin strip of ground connecting it to the mainland. [*peninsula*] Suggest that the land is *almost* an island. Explain that in Latin, the words *pene,* "almost," and *insula,* "island" put together produce **peninsula.** You may want to show students a map of the Arabian Peninsula to show them how water surrounding it *almost* makes it an island.

└─

## CONTENT-AREA VOCABULARY

Although the following words are important to an understanding of the text selection, some of them may be unfamiliar to students. You may want to present this list of words and their definitions to students.

**infertile:** unable to support growth; unproductive.

**encompassed:** included; encircled.

**collective:** characterizing a group; indicating that a number of individuals are acting as a whole.

**compatriots:** people belonging to the same country; colleagues.

**navigable:** wide and deep enough to provide passage for ships.

**peninsula:** a piece of land with water on three sides.

The content-area vocabulary words may seem familiar to students who know the following words with the same easily recognizable roots: *fertile, compass, collect, patriot,* and *navigate.* Have students make predictions about the exact definitions by looking at the words, the context of the sentences, and the words' prefixes and suffixes. You may want to give students clues to help them refine their guesses or have them look up prefixes or suffixes in a dictionary.

## Reading Informational Materials

### Reading Skill
#### Identifying Text Structure: Cause and Effect
Cause-and-effect writing often shows *why* an event happens. Some texts may state both a **cause** (what makes something happen) and an **effect** (what occurs as a result). When writers omit part of the information, readers must use their own knowledge to infer a cause or an effect.

### Reading Strategy
#### Using Graphic Organizers (Strategy 3)
To help students see how the selection is structured and find the relationship between causes and effects in the text, use Strategy 3 in Content-Area Reading Strategies. Provide students with a Cause and Effect Chart (Graphic Organizer 2) to help them organize their ideas about how certain events lead to other events. You may want to model for students how effects can have more than one cause. [For example: Cause: Deserts are harsh and dangerous.

Cause: Bandits or wild animals often attack travelers. Effect: Merchants traveled in caravans for safety.] Encourage students to make any alterations necessary to the basic design of their charts.

---

## DURING READING

### Using the Side-Margin Feature
■ A Horse for All Seasons

Although the Arabian horse was adapted to the desert, it was camels—not horses—that carried goods in caravans. Ask students to think about what resources would be needed for a horse to survive in the desert. [feed, more water than for camels, shelter from sandstorms] When might horses be more useful than camels? [when speed is the priority, as in surprise attacks or warfare]

## Reading Informational Material

▶ **Teaching Tip**

*Empires* Ask students to give examples of where they have heard the word *empire.* After they have provided examples [Roman Empire, Japanese Empire, British Empire], ask them what these different empires have in common. Discuss with students the ways in which an empire can influence the language, culture, religion, and trade practices of a large group of people. What influence would the Arab Empire have had on the people within its territory? [Nations that came in touch with the Arabs might adopt words from Arabic, foods, clothing styles, manners, and art styles or objects.]

### Differentiating Instruction
■ Learners Having Difficulty

Remind students that they can break long sentences into shorter ones that are easier to understand. Model for students a sentence in which two or more ideas are linked, and show them how they can divide it into more than one sentence.

■ English-Language Learners

Help students understand vocabulary words that are related to Arab culture: *Bedouins, caravan, Mecca, mosque.* Direct them to illustrations in the text that can give them clues to the meanings of these words.

# AFTER READING

## ✔ Reading Check

The following are sample answers to questions on student text page 39.

1. Bedouins could navigate in the desert without instruments. They used their knowledge of animals, stones, wind, and plants to find their way.

2. Escorts accompanied caravans to protect against bandits or wild animals. In addition, caravans sometimes dealt with local tribes to ensure that they could safely pass through an area.

3. Merchants could buy products with gold and silver coins, with letters of credit, or with checks, called *chakk*.

4. Arab traders sailed to China, India, and East Africa. Sometimes pirates attacked their vessels.

5. The caravansaries provided stables, sleeping rooms, offices, guard posts, and markets. In addition, larger complexes often included a mosque and a bathhouse.

## Reteaching

Students may understand causes and effects more clearly if they can look at relationships from both directions. Have students work in pairs to form *if...then* sentences that move from causes to effects. [*If* there is trouble in China, *then* the silk trade will be interrupted.] After student pairs have constructed several sentences, have them rewrite the sentences to move from effects to causes. Ask students to use *because* in their second set of sentences. [The silk trade was interrupted *because* there was trouble in China.] Discuss with students how looking at the structure of the sentence—the words following *if* or *because*—can help them pinpoint causes and effects.

## Connecting to Language Arts
■ Writing

*Easy as Falling Off a Log* Have students write a ship's log that describes an Arab merchant's journey to a distant marketplace. [You may want to provide a page from a ship's log as an example.] Before students begin writing, they can look for more information about their destination. In their

log entries, students could describe the new plants, animals, and foods they would see, as well as any difficulties—including monsoons and pirates—they encounter on the way. Have students post their logs for the rest of the class to share.

## Connecting Across the Curriculum: Geography

*Annotated Maps* Have students learn more about different caravan routes and important centers of trade. Work with students to find maps of the Arab world that show the distant lands where merchandise would be purchased and the type of terrain that would be crossed. Have students estimate the distance between trading cities, and the length of time a journey by ship or by camel might take. Then, ask students to tape a transparency over the map and plot a particular trade route on a map, jotting down notes about the goods that would be carried and the length of the trip. Students can post their annotations to share with classmates.

## Further Resources
Online

*OneWorld Magazine* is an online publication devoted to cultural and environmental issues. Its series on Arabian deserts, called "The Sands," offers photographs and articles on Mohammed, crossing the Sahara, and coping with desert sand.

## Assessment

Turn to page 119 for a multiple-choice test on the selection.

*Test Answers*
1. d  2. a  3. a  4. b  5. a
6. a  7. d  8. c  9. c  10. b

# Cordoba–Jewel of the World

from *Calliope*

by DIANA CHILDRESS
*(student text page 40)*

**Reading Level:** Average

## Text Summary

Islamic Spain flourished under Muslim rule, and the capital city of Cordoba was a center of art, medicine, and literature. Cordoba was famous for its libraries and its beautiful mosque; even after its decline in the eleventh century, the city continued to be a center of scholarship.

## BEFORE READING

### Make the Connection

Ask students to think about the qualities that make a city special. What makes their community special? [good schools, athletic opportunities, theaters, museums, religious centers, job opportunities, natural beauty] Tell them that many trading centers might have had the same advantages as Cordoba, yet this city became famous for its art and scholarship. Tell them that as they read they should consider why leaders might want to invest money in "minor" elements such as a library, a place of worship, or a park. You may want to return to this topic after students have completed the reading so they can discuss what they have learned.

### Build Background

■ More About the Topic

Cordoba became a famous center of learning because of the Islamic emphasis on scholarship: Muslims believe that the search for knowledge leads to a greater understanding of Allah. At a time when European learning was at its lowest point, Muslim scholars kept alive the knowledge of ancient Greek science and philosophy, which they had learned from the Byzantines. Arab scholars added their own commentary to the ancient texts and eventually transferred this important information to the West, where it became the basis of western intellectual tradition. Today, graduates everywhere don the robes that were once worn by Islamic scholars.

## Vocabulary Development

The following words are underscored and defined in the student text.

**metropolis:** large center of population.
**artisans:** workers skilled in a particular trade or art.
**mosaics:** images or patterns made from small pieces of colored stone, tile, or glass set in mortar.
**textiles:** woven fabrics.
**conservative:** wanting to keep things as they have been; against change; traditional.

Before assigning the reading, you may want to introduce students to any words that could cause pronunciation or definition problems.

### ⎡ *Vocabulary Tip* ⎤

**Using Context Clues** Review with students how to use context clues to determine a word's meaning. They should remember that clues to unfamiliar words may be found in surrounding sentences and paragraphs. Clues may include synonyms, antonyms, restatements, or general content. For example, "gold" and "silver" on page 42 indicate that *minted* might relate to money. On page 43, *splendor* appears related to the words "beauty," "gracious," and "sweet."

### ⬭ CONTENT-AREA VOCABULARY ⬭

Although the following words are important to an understanding of the text selection, some of them may be unfamiliar to students. You may want to present this list of words and their definitions to students.

**magnificence:** greatness; richness.
**minted\*:** coined by government authority.
**luxurious:** rich; costly.
**splendor:** brilliance; grand appearance.

\*Although students may be familiar with other meanings of this word, the word as used in the selection has a specific meaning that pertains to the content area.

Ask students to list words that have the same roots as those in this list. [examples: *magnificent*, *mint*, *luxury*, *splendid*] What part of speech is each of these words? [Of the sample words, *mint* is a verb while *minted* is a participle form; *magnificent* is an adjective while *magnificence* is a noun; *luxury* is a noun while *luxurious* is an adjective; *splendid* is an adjective while *splendor* is a noun.] Have students work in pairs to write sentences using each of the pairs of words with the same root.

## Reading Informational Material

### Reading Skill
#### Identifying Author's Purpose
Authors may write a text in order to entertain, to inform, to persuade, or to stir readers' emotions. Identifying the author's purpose can help readers approach and evaluate a text more appropriately.

▶ **Teaching Tip**
*Magazine Article* This selection is from a magazine article. Remind students that because of its length, a magazine article will focus closely on one subject or idea. Ask students what ideas are referred to but not developed further. Are there any topics in the selection that they would like to explore at greater length?

### Reading Strategy
#### Visualizing Information (Strategy 5)
To help students preview visual information in the selection and ask why the author (or the textbook) included this information in the text, use Strategy 5 in Content-Area Reading Strategies. How does it fit in with the author's purpose? To help students monitor their reading and ask themselves questions about the selection as they read, have them create and complete a three-column PIC organizer with columns labeled: *"Purpose of the Reading," "Important Ideas,"* and *"Connection to Prior Knowledge."* (See discussion of PIC in Strategy 1.) Direct them to the text's illustrations and features, having students link the visual information to information in the text.

# DURING READING
## Correcting Misconceptions
Students may think that slavery took place only in the New World. However, slavery has been practiced by many peoples at various times over the course of human history and was once common in parts of Europe, including Islamic Spain.

## Using the Side-Margin Feature
■ The Art of the Arabesque
To show students the distinctiveness of arabesque decorations, bring examples of different types of religious art for comparison. Show how Islamic art contrasts with that of other religions that permit the use of the human form for illustration—for example, the Christian Sistine Chapel, or Buddhist or Hindu art.

## Differentiating Instruction
■ Learners Having Difficulty
As students read the selection, have them jot down words and phrases that describe the city of Cordoba. After they have finished reading, have them review their notes and make a generalization about why the city was considered important. You may want to have students work in pairs to compare lists and form generalizations.

# AFTER READING

## ✔ Reading Check

The following are sample answers to questions on student text page 43.

1. Cordoba was centrally located on a river that could be used for travel and trade. Nearby mountains contained valuable minerals, and the city was close to good farmland.

2. The columns used in the mosque were found in ancient ruins in the area.

3. Mosaics were used in the mosque; the ruler of Cordoba brought a craftsman from Constantinople to teach local artisans.

**4.** The use of silver coins, an inspector to control the quality of goods, artisan representatives to settle disputes, and the warehouse and stable space provided by caravanserais—all encouraged trade.

**5.** During the Crusades, Christian scholars found translations of Greek philosophy and science in the libraries of Arab rulers. As the Crusades brought Christians into contact with the Muslim world, people in the West learned about Islamic technology and science.

### Reteaching

If students have difficulty identifying the author's purpose, brainstorm with them to develop examples of words and phrases that would be used to inform (facts or details), to persuade (ideas that help sway one's opinion), to entertain (humorous, moving, or exciting examples), and to describe (sensory details). You may want to list students' examples on the board. Then, have students analyze a short section of the text and determine what words in the selection indicate author's purpose. You may want to provide students with a Cluster Diagram (Graphic Organizer 3) to help them organize their examples of informative, persuasive, entertaining, or descriptive words and phrases. Have students discuss their examples and then determine the author's purpose.

### Connecting to Language Arts
#### ▪ Writing
*Tourist Trade* The writer describes the beauties of medieval Cordoba. Ask students to pick out three or four of Cordoba's attractive characteristics. [for example: "trade," "education," or "medicine"] Then, have students work in small groups to create travel brochures that summarize the wonders of this Islamic Spanish city. Have students illustrate their brochures with photographs, maps, or drawings. [You may want to divide tasks into writing, illustrating, proofreading, and producing.] Display the completed brochures on the class bulletin board.

#### ▪ Speaking and Listening
*City Planners* Have students conduct a mock "medieval town meeting" to debate how to best maintain Cordoba's unique beauty. Should the city continue its generous policy toward international scholars, or should scholars have to pay for the city's facilities? Has the Great Mosque finally gotten too big to maintain, or should it be expanded once again? Have students acting as the Cordoba "town council" discuss how to preserve "the jewel of the world."

### Connecting Across the Curriculum: Social Studies

How does one tell an *emir* from a *caliph*? A *dirhem* from a *dinar*? A *mihrab* from a *minaret*? Have students create a lexicon of Arabic terms, recording special words they may wish to learn more about. Have students scan dictionaries or encyclopedias to get illustrations or fuller definitions of these Arabic words. Students can also research English words based on Arabic. [Many words with Arabic roots start with *a* or *al.*] Encourage volunteers to share new information with the class. Students may want to add to their lexicon as they read other selections in this chapter.

### Further Resources
#### Online
ArtServe, Australian National University's art and architecture Web site offers surveys of art history and allows users to search by country, site, or type of art.

In the *National Geographic* magazine's Web site, Islamic Cordoba is compared to two other great cities—Alexandria, Egypt in A.D. 1 and contemporary New York City. The site includes a list of Web links and additional resources.

> ### Assessment
>
> Turn to page 120 for a multiple-choice test on the selection.
>
> *Test Answers*
> **1.** b  **2.** b  **3.** a  **4.** c  **5.** d
> **6.** c  **7.** b  **8.** a  **9.** a  **10.** b

# *from* The Magic of Mathematics

from *Science in Early Islamic Culture*

by GEORGE BESHORE

*(student text page 44)*

**Reading Level:** Average

## Text Summary

The Islamic religion encouraged scholars to learn more about their world. Moslem scholars advanced the scientific knowledge of mathematics and astronomy, building on the information found in ancient texts. Baghdad's House of Wisdom became a major center of medieval scholarship.

# BEFORE READING

## Make the Connection

Tell students they will be reading about a culture that contributed heavily to the system of mathematics we use today. Show students a column of Roman numerals and ask them to add the numbers quickly. Ask them how they were able to add the numbers, if they were. [They will probably say they had to change the numbers into the Arabic system they use daily.] Ask them what common mathematical computations are aided by the Arabic system of numerals and decimals. [computer programming, any computations with money] Tell students that as they read they should think about what elements of the modern world have been made possible by the development of Arabic numerals and advanced calculations.

## Build Background

■ More About the Topic

The Islamic culture of learning was helped enormously by one simple invention: paper. Introduced from China in A.D. 751, paper allowed a cheap and plentiful supply of book-making materials. Books in Europe were written on parchment, and a single book could cost the same amount as 120 acres of land. Not surprisingly, the largest European library in the ninth century contained only thirty-six books. At the same time, libraries in Cordoba contained half a million volumes. Because of Islamic scholarship,

Arabic replaced Latin as the international language of science. A prominent medieval bishop complained about so many Christian men studying Arabic.

## Vocabulary Development

The following words are underscored and defined in the student text.

**decimals:** fractions with unwritten denominators of ten, which is indicated by a decimal point before the numbers.

**calculations:** acts or processes of figuring or computing, usually with numbers, as in addition or subtraction.

**ratios:** comparisons of two numbers by division; for example, a ratio of one to two is one divided by two, or one half.

**compute:** to use arithmetic to find a number or amount; to work out an answer to a math problem.

**procedures:** usual methods or series of steps.

Before assigning the reading, you may want to introduce students to any words that could cause pronunciation or definition problems.

┌─ *Vocabulary Tip* ─────────

**Investigating Etymology** The development of the science of numbers involved three seemingly unrelated interests: knowledge, triangles, and rocks. **Mathematics,** which includes arithmetic, algebra, and geometry, comes from the Greek word *mathematikos,* which means "inclined to learn." The root of **trigonometry,** which investigates the relationships between the sides of a triangle, clearly reflects that function—the Greek word *trigonon,* or "triangle." The word **calculate** reveals perhaps the simplest beginnings of our use of numbers. The Latin *calculus* means "pebble," in particular, those used as arithmetic aids. This word is now the name of the branch of mathematics called *calculus.*

## CONTENT-AREA VOCABULARY

Although the following words are important to an understanding of the text selection, some of them may be unfamiliar to students. Discuss with students how examining word parts can help them determine the meanings of the content-area words. Together the Latin prefix **ob–** and the root **servare** mean "about keeping," something an observer intends when making an observation. From *astron,* the Greek word for star, we get a clue that *astronomers* look at the sky. We can anticipate that a *manuscript* is a type of a document when we look at the word parts *manu–* (by hand) and *–script* (written). Have students work in pairs to see how many other words they can find that use the word parts *deci–, astri–, manu–,* or *–script.*

**observe:** to watch; to pay great attention.
**astronomers:** experts who study celestial bodies such as stars and planets.
**manuscripts:** articles or documents, especially those written by hand.

## Reading Informational Material

### Reading Skill
#### Developing Vocabulary Knowledge
Explain to students that we use our knowledge and experience to figure out the meanings of words and word parts. We may use context clues to determine the meanings of unfamiliar words, or we may study a word's prefixes, suffixes, and roots.

▶ **Teaching Tip**
*Using Common Roots* You may wish to help students to develop a list of common roots, prefixes, and suffixes that they can keep in their Reader's Logs. Include *act–, aud–, man–; il–, mal–, pro–,* and *–ful, –less,* and *–ment.* Assign groups of students a particular word part, such as prefixes, and ask them to find as many examples as they can in the selection. Students should write down the word part, the word in which it occurs, and the definition of the prefix, suffix, or root word. When students are finished, combine their examples and definitions into one long list that can be used as a resource.

### Reading Strategy
#### Building Background Information (Strategy 6)
To help students build background information before they begin to read, use Strategy 6 in Content-Area Reading Strategies. Provide students with a list of words containing the selection's important concepts. You may wish to have students use PACA (Graphic Organizer 8) or to create a three-column organizer with the columns labeled "clues," "inferences," and "predictions" to help them clarify information about the word lists.

▶ **Teaching Tip**
*Numbers* Review with students the difference between Roman and Arabic numerals, explaining that the "Indian numbers" referred to in the selection are the numbers we use today.

# DURING READING

## Using the Side-Margin Feature
■ Poet and Astronomer
Read students some short selections from *The Rubaiyat of Omar Khayyám.* Ask them whether they find it unusual that a poet would want to watch the stars. Do they think there is a connection between mathematics and poetry? [Students may say that mathematical formulas have a rhythm and can tell a story, just as poems can. The challenge of writing and understanding a poem can be similar to the challenge of discovering stars or unlocking mathematical secrets.]

## Differentiating Instruction
■ English-Language Learners
The selection contains descriptions of many different types of mathematical terms and equations. While the English vocabulary may be unfamiliar to students, they may recognize the mathematical concept if they see an example of it. You may want to write examples of the different types of equations on the board to allow students to compare and contrast arithmetic, algebra, fractions, decimals, and trigonometry.

## Reading Informational Material

▶ **Teaching Tip**
*Understanding Instructions* Students may more fully understand the instructions for measurements across a river or swamp, described on student text page 46, if they plot the directions on a flowchart. Have students use a Sequence or Chronological

Order Chart (Graphic Organizer 10) to break down the instructions into a series of steps. When students have finished plotting their information, display their graphic organizers.

## AFTER READING

 **Reading Check**

The following are sample answers to questions on student text page 48.

1. Algebra is used to solve problems in which some information is provided but other information remains unknown.

2. Surveyors and astronomers use trigonometry to measure distances. To measure a distance, they mark points that form an imaginary right triangle. They can compute an unknown distance using information from trigonometry tables.

3. Eratosthenes determined that the earth was round. Both scholars calculated the circumference of the earth to a very accurate degree, but Eratosthenes' figure was closer to the measurement that scientists accept today.

4. The Greek astronomer and geographer Ptolemy used Posidonius's smaller number for creating his maps.

5. The ruler Al-Ma'mun wanted scholars to measure the earth, and accounts of ancient procedures helped them with the task.

### Reteaching

If students have difficulty with the vocabulary and concepts in the selection, you may want to discuss different types of context clues found in the selection. A *definition/explanation clue* provides the exact meaning of the word within a sentence. A *restatement/synonym clue* restates an idea in other words, often using signal words such as "for example" or "especially." A *contrast/antonym clue* gives the opposite meaning of an unfamiliar word, sometimes using signal words such as "despite," or "however." Tell students that *inference/general context clues* are not as obvious as the other types of context clues discussed. A reader must infer an unfamiliar word's meaning from other details within a passage. Have students look for different types of context clues within the selection. What context clues did they use to determine the meanings of words such as *algebra, surveyors,* or *circumference?*

### Connecting to Language Arts
▪ Writing

*And the Winner Is . . .* Posidonius! No, it's Eratosthenes! Tell students there will be an awards ceremony for the two early astronomers who calculated the distance around the earth. Have them decide what award would go to Eratosthenes, whose numbers were more accurate, and what to Posidonius. Then, ask each student to assume the role of either Eratosthenes or Posidonius and write an acceptance speech in the voice of the astronomer chosen.

### Connecting Across the Curriculum: Social Studies

Assign students to learn more about "Indian numbers," Al-Khwarizmi, surveying, or the House of Wisdom. Have students work in pairs to create a brief radio infomercial about their topic. They may want to present their information through a question-and-answer dialogue, or with short interviews with their subjects. Have students present their infomercials to the class.

### Further Resources
#### Online

The Internet has numerous Muslim Web sites, some of which include information about individual Muslim mathematicians, scientists, and astronomers. You can even find audio readings from the Koran. You may want to preview any sites you find before students use them. (Individual pages can be printed out for classroom use).

**Assessment**

Turn to page 121 for a multiple-choice test on the selection.

*Test Answers*
1. b  2. c  3. d  4. a  5. d
6. b  7. a  8. b  9. a  10. c

# The Coming of Islam

from *The Royal Kingdoms of Ghana, Mali, and Songhay: Life in Medieval Africa*

by PATRICIA AND FREDRICK McKISSACK
*(student text page 49)*

---

**Reading Level:** Average

### Text Summary

The Islamic religion profoundly shaped the Middle East and Africa. From its beginnings in Mecca with the revelations of the prophet Muhammad, the religion spread through holy wars to North Africa. Muslim traders and missionaries carried the tenets of Islam's five "pillars", or obligations, across the desert to West Africa, introducing the new religion to the kingdoms of Ghana, Mali, and Songhay.

---

## BEFORE READING

### Make the Connection

Ask students to brainstorm how they learned about a new idea, song, or style. Where did the new idea start, and how many people did it pass through to get to them? Tell students they will be reading about the spread of Islam outward from Mecca. What barriers hindered the spread? [The Sahara created a physical barrier, dangerous to cross. Local spiritual practices were another hindrance.]

### Build Background
■ More About the Authors

Patricia McKissack was a teacher; her husband, Fredrick, was a civil engineer. Then in 1975, Patricia decided that there weren't enough books for young people about African Americans, and she began to write them. Later, she and Fredrick collaborated; he did the research, while she did the writing. Their system works—they have won numerous awards for their fiction, nonfiction, and biographical writings on the African American experience. The tradition of family collaboration continues as Patricia writes books with her son, Fredrick L. McKissack Jr.

### Vocabulary Development

The following words are underscored and defined in the student text.

**revelation:** a revealing or understanding of something not known before.

**sacred:** holy; from or belonging to a god or religion.

**destiny:** fate; events that are certain to occur.

**obligations:** duties.

**testify:** to declare; bear witness.

Before assigning the reading, you may want to introduce students to any words that could cause pronunciation or definition problems.

┌─ *Vocabulary Tip* ─

**Evolving Meanings** Discuss with students how a word can begin as a proper noun denoting a person or place and take on a figurative, or more general meaning. Mecca, Saudi Arabia, is a prime destination for Muslims, who consider the city to be sacred. From Mecca's special significance, the word *Mecca* has come to mean "a place where many people go or where one may long to go"; "a goal or ideal." [An art museum is a mecca for art lovers.] Ask if students can think of other proper nouns that have evolved into common nouns. [China, china]

( **CONTENT-AREA VOCABULARY** )

Although the following words are important to an understanding of the text selection, some of them may be unfamiliar to students. You may want to present this list of words and their definitions to your students. Have students show the connection between the words by putting all the words into one clear sentence. [The purpose of the *pilgrimage* to *Mecca* was for *devout* followers to meet the *prophet*.]

**pilgrimage\*:** a journey to a holy place.

**prophet\*:** one who is regarded as speaking for God through holy inspiration.

**devout:** faithful to one's religion.

**Mecca\*:** a city holy to those who follow Islam

\*Although students may be familiar with other meanings of these words, the words as used in this selection have a specific meaning that pertains to the content area.

## Reading Informational Material

### Reading Skill

**Identifying Text Structure: Chronological Order**

Explain to students that this text is arranged in chronological order. Events are discussed in the order in which they happened.

### Reading Strategy

**Understanding Text (Strategy 2)**

To help students follow the chronological order of the selection, use Strategy 2 in Content-Area Reading Strategies. Provide students with a Sequence or Chronological Order Chart (Graphic Organizer 10) to help them show the order in which events in the selection occurred. In addition, have students mark the signal words that indicate time. [*during, now, eventually*]

▶ **Teaching Tip**

*Reading a Map* Show students a map, with a transparency overlay, of the Middle East and North Africa to follow as they read the selection. Have volunteers use colored markers to mark the spread of Islam at different times in history. Ask them to vary the colors to indicate how Islam spread from its beginnings in Mecca to North Africa and West Africa.

## DURING READING

### Using the Side-Margin Feature

▪ **Sacred Stone**

After students have read the feature and looked at a picture of the Ka'aba, point out that the most sacred part of the monument is a black stone. Have them brainstorm other natural features that are sacred to other cultures. [Examples: The Holy Land is sacred to both Christians and Jews; the Ganges River in India is sacred to Hindus.]

### Differentiating Instruction

▪ **Learners Having Difficulty**

Review the footnotes and vocabulary words with students. Point out that even though reading marked words interrupts the story, they can re-read a passage after they have learned the meaning of an unfamiliar word. Students could look at the footnoted words as a preview before they begin reading.

▪ **English-Language Learners**

Some English-language learners may not understand the allusion to the American west on student text page 51. You may want to explain further why the author would compare Arab traders in Africa to the missionaries and traders in the territory that became the United States. [In both North America and West Africa, the culture and language of native peoples was changed when travelers introduced new customs, goods, and ideas.]

## AFTER READING

### ✔ Reading Check

The following are sample answers to questions on student text page 52.

1. The Koran was written by only one person, Muhammad, rather than by many different people, as were the Bible and the Torah.

2. The five pillars are praying, giving to the poor, fasting during Ramadan, making a pilgrimage to Mecca, and professing one's faith. The profession of faith is the most important pillar.

3. The Islamic religion spread through holy wars, trade, and cultural exchanges.

4. Merchants and travelers brought Islam to the area of West Africa. The enormous Sahara protected Ghana from invasion.

5. The writings of scholars, or *ulama,* who came to Ghana to convert the people to Islam, provide a record of life in the kingdom.

## Reteaching

If students have difficulty understanding the selection's chronology, you may want to have them create a time line by answering *before, after,* or *then* questions. First, have students work in groups to answer questions such as: *What happened to Muhammad before he wrote the Koran? **After** holy wars, what happened to North Africa? Sultans heard about riches south of the Sahara—**then,** what happened? **Before** Islam came to Ghana, what was the empire's culture like?* Then, have students chart their answers on a time line, arranging their answers in sequential order. After they have answered the questions, have students scan the selection for dates and times. [A.D. 611, 22 years, between 639 and 708] Have students use the context of the selection to insert the dates and times in the proper places on their time lines. Have students compare their time lines when they have finished.

## Connecting to Language Arts

### ▪ Writing

*Keeping a Diary* Have students write diary entries that might have been composed by a person in Mecca, in North Africa, or in West Africa. The entries should describe the thoughts and feelings of a person who has just learned about the religion of Islam. How does Islam compare to their current beliefs? Why might Islam be appealing or unappealing to the writer?

### ▪ Speaking and Listening

*Let Me Tell You* Assign students to learn more about medieval Africa and the Arab merchants who traveled there. Then, have students work in pairs to present mock conversations that might have taken place in a marketplace of ancient Ghana, Mali, or Songhay. What might the merchants have shared about their countries and the new religion of Islam? And what could the people of Africa have revealed about their kingdom and its own ancient religions? Encourage students to create costumes and goods to "sell."

## Connecting Across the Curriculum: History/Architecture

*All the Way to Timbuktu* When Islam arrived, what did it find in the cities of Africa? Have students work in groups of four or so to explore an ancient city that became part of the Islamic Empire. Each group should choose one of the following cities: Timbuktu, Mali; Algiers, Algeria; Tunis, Tunisia; or Tangier, Morocco. What did the city look like? What were its notable features? How did it change after the coming of Islam? Have students find illustrations of the city they are examining and write a brief report of their findings.

## Further Resources

### Online

The Annenberg/CPB Web site has an interactive exhibit that compares the decline of the Mali and Songhay empires with that of three other ancient empires: the Mayan, the Mesopotamian, and the Copan Valley. The exhibit includes hands-on activities and links to related resources.

The Kennedy Center's Web site includes *African Odyssey Interactive,* offering arts and education resources for teachers, as well as cultural and historical information about the empires of West Africa.

### ( Assessment )

Turn to page 122 for a multiple-choice test on the selection.

*Test Answers*

**1.** b  **2.** d  **3.** c  **4.** a  **5.** c
**6.** c  **7.** d  **8.** a  **9.** d  **10.** b

# *from* Mali: Empire of the Mandingoes

from *A Glorious Age in Africa: The Story of Three Great African Empires*
by DANIEL CHU AND ELLIOT SKINNER
*(student text page 53)*

**Reading Level:** Average

## Text Summary

The empire of Mali produced fabulous riches and, consequently, fabulously extravagant rulers. Mansa Musa's pilgrimage to Mecca, a journey of thousands of miles, famously displayed Mali's wealth to Africa and the Middle East. The peoples of Egypt and other areas long remembered Mansa Musa's enormous caravan carrying hundreds of pounds of gold dust and accompanied by thousands of followers.

# BEFORE READING

## Make the Connection

Ask students to brainstorm the kinds of news events they remember. [natural disasters such as hurricanes, tornadoes, floods, deaths of famous people, presidential elections] What historic events are recorded and remembered? [disasters such as wars and plagues, scientific discoveries, technological advances] Why would historians, hundreds of years later, still remember a king's pilgrimage to Mecca? [The king must have done something notable or conducted his journey in a special way.]

## Build Background

■ More About the Topic

Twelfth-century Mali was an enormously wealthy state, since two thirds of the world's gold came through it. With all its riches, Mali valued scholarship; indeed, two of its cities, Djenne and Timbuktu, were considered the world's greatest centers of learning. When the ruler Mansa Musa returned from his famous pilgrimage to Mecca, he brought back with him scholars and architects who built a new university in Timbuktu, the University of Sankore. In its native language, the name *Mali* means *hippopotamus* and the capital city's name means *crocodile.*

## Vocabulary Development

The following words are underscored and defined in the student text.

**pilgrimage:** journey to visit a holy place.
**diplomacy:** talks and negotiations between nations.
**commerce:** buying and selling of goods between large groups, such as cities or nations.
**descendants:** offspring; children and their children.
**elaborate:** having many parts or details.

Before assigning the reading, you may want to introduce students to any words that could cause pronunciation or definition problems.

┌─ *Vocabulary Tip* ─────────────

**Using Knowledge of Parts of Speech and Context Clues** Four of the words above are nouns. Have students determine which word is not a noun. [elaborate] Does a context clue suggest what part of speech *elaborate* is here? [*Elaborate* describes characteristics of a noun, which is what an adjective does.] What other common meaning does *elaborate* have, how is the word pronounced, and what part of speech is it? [The verb form is pronounced ē·lab´ə·rāt´ and means "to give more details."] What similarity do you find between these two words? [Both involve detail.]

└──────────────────────────────

( CONTENT-AREA VOCABULARY )

Although the following words are important to an understanding of the text selection, some of them may be unfamiliar to students. You may want to present this list of words and the definitions to your students.

**succeeded\*:** followed; came next in line.
**promoted\*:** helped to establish or grow.
**observances\*:** customary ceremonies; traditional rites.

\*Although students may be familiar with other meanings of these words, the words as used in this selection have a specific meaning that pertains to the content area.

Discuss with students how the content-area vocabulary words can have more than one meaning, depending upon how they are used in a sentence. *Succeeded* means "followed" in the selection, but it can also mean "turned out well." Have students create sentences in which *succeeded, promoted,* and *observances* each has a meaning other than the one in the selection.

## Reading Informational Material

### Reading Skill
#### Determining the Main Idea
Explain to students that the main idea is what the writer wants us to remember about the subject. Supporting details help illustrate or further explain the main idea.

### Reading Strategy
#### Making Predictions (Strategy 7)
To help students determine the main idea of the selection, use Strategy 7 in Content-Area Reading Strategies. After presenting students with pictures or other information to help them generate word lists, you may wish to provide them with a Cluster Diagram (Graphic Organizer 3) to help them divide the word lists into different concepts or categories.

▶ **Teaching Tip**

*Reading a Book Excerpt* The selection begins with a reference to Ghana, but it does not offer more information about that empire. Tell students that this selection is an excerpt from a book and was written as a longer discussion about African empires. You may want to ask students to find more information about the empire of Ghana and share it with the class.

## DURING READING

### Using the Side-Margin Feature
- Timbuktu U.

After students have read the feature about Timbuktu U., tell them that people sometimes use the name of the city to refer to a place far away or inconveniently located. [Example: Of course we'll still see you; we're just moving to the suburbs—not Timbuktu.] Have students find Timbuktu on a map, noting its proximity to the Sahara, as well as to major roads, railways, and airports. Then, ask them to speculate about why Timbuktu acquired this connotation.

### Differentiating Instruction
- **Learners Having Difficulty**

The list of Mali's rulers, given at the beginning of the selection, may intimidate some readers. Students could use a Sequence or Chronological Order Chart (Graphic Organizer 10) to create a "genealogy chart." Students could list the rulers in chronological order and draw lines to show the order of the leaders' succession. Students may want to jot down notes to indicate who was related to whom.

- **English-Language Learners**

In the selection, rulers adopt the title of *Mansa;* the ruler of Cairo is known as a *sultan*. Have students share other titles of respect or honor from their first languages and explain when these titles are used. They may also share the words used to politely address adults or other people in authority.

## AFTER READING

### ✔ Reading Check

The following are sample answers to questions on student text page 57.

1. Mansa Musa ruled Mali for twenty-five years.

2. Accept any three: As a ruler, Mansa Musa enlarged the country of Mali, encouraged trade and commerce, and promoted the spread of learning. He loved the arts and was devoutly religious.

3. Mansa Musa was a religious man, and the pilgrimage to Mecca is a basic observance of Islam.

4. Accept any three details, or parts of details: For months, officials and servants collected supplies for the Mansa Musa's pilgrimage; provisions included up to one hundred camel-loads of gold dust weighing up to three hundred pounds each; the enormous caravan included perhaps sixty-thousand people; those accompanying Musa included local chiefs, friends and family, doctors, and teachers.

5. Because of his generosity, Mansa Musa used all his money and had to borrow more. Because he

had given away such quantities of gold as gifts, the Cairo gold market was depressed, causing the price of gold to fall sharply.

## Reteaching

If students have difficulty determining the selection's main idea, suggest that they focus on a text by looking for its most important words. Have them review the text and write down three words they think are important to understanding its meaning. [*empire, pilgrimage, gold*] They should then write a brief reason for each choice, explaining its importance to the main idea. Students can discuss their choices in small groups, narrowing down their lists to one word. Then, have students use this word to write a statement expressing the main idea of the selection. [Mansa Musa's **pilgrimage** to Mecca showed the world Mali's wealth.] Emphasize to students that their explanation is as important as the word they choose. You may want the entire class to work together and vote on which word they think is most important. Be sure to have students explain the reasons for their answers.

## Connecting to Language Arts

### ▪ Writing

*What About the Camels?* The sight of Mansa Musa's caravan must have been awe-inspiring. Nevertheless, such a huge caravan from Mali to Mecca was an enormous undertaking, and there must have been some grumbling. Divide the class in half, and have students learn more about the workers or animals that made the caravan possible. What difficulties did they have to prepare for? Encourage students to use their imagination and sense of humor to write a short account from the point of view of their assigned category: human (a camel driver, a foreman, a teacher, a family member, and so forth) or animal (goats for milk or meat, a camel, the sultan's horse).

## Connecting Across the Curriculum: Geography

Encourage students to learn more about Mansa Musa's pilgrimage and to create a presentation of their findings for the class. Suggest that they research some of the following information: What route would the ruler have taken? What flora, fauna, and terrain did he see on the way? What would the city of Cairo have looked like when he arrived? As part of their presentation, students might want to include videos or images showing the landscape from the Western Sudan and modern Mali.

## Further Resources

### Online

The Internet Puppet Theater's Web site re-creates history in its Global Studies Series. "The Great Civilizations of Africa" offers facts about ancient Mali and the Songhay Empire, including images of Timbuktu and an ancient salt market.

### Museum

The Smithsonian Institute has a permanent exhibition that focuses on the art of sub-Saharan Africa. Its section on the Western Sudan provides information on many artifacts from the kingdoms of Ghana, Mali, and Songhay.

### Assessment

Turn to page 123 for a multiple-choice test on the selection.

*Test Answers*

1. d  2. c  3. b  4. a  5. a
6. c  7. a  8. b  9. c  10. d

# Talking Drums and Talking Gongs

from *Faces*

by ENID SCHILDKROUT
*(student text page 58)*

**Reading Level:** Average

## Special Considerations

The text indicates that many drums can be made and played only by men. You may want to discuss with students why women are sometimes not allowed to play talking drums or talking gongs. [Traditional African societies may view women's roles more narrowly than our industrial society does; the traditions that have grown up around talking drums may be hundreds of years old.]

## Text Summary

Long before modern technology evolved, the people of West Africa learned to send messages long distances by using drums. Two-tone gongs and "talking drums" continue to be created and played following traditional ceremonies and rites. Even today, their complicated rhythms continue to spread news of events both large and small across the west African countryside.

## BEFORE READING

## Make the Connection

Ask students to list ways they could send messages from one city to another. [*telephone, e-mail, letter*] Then ask them which messages could be sent without modern technology. You may need to define what is included in the term *modern technology*. [The message would have to be carried, as by courier or carrier pigeon; or sent visually, as with smoke or a bonfire; or sent by sound, as with a horn or whistle.] Conclude by asking what limitations these methods would create.

## Build Background
■ More About the Topic

Bata drums, which imitate the tonal language of the Yoruba people, are often played for the orishas, or the Yoruban gods. These Nigerian peoples believe that praising something helps them gain influence with it, so many people have "praise poems" played on the drums to things they want to influence. When the slave trade brought the Yoruba to Cuba, they took with them their knowledge of Bata drums. In Cuba, however, authorities often prohibited the use of these talking drums, afraid that they would spread messages of revolt.

## ― Vocabulary Tip ―

**Using Context Clues** Tell students that they are probably familiar with the content-area vocabulary words but that they may not recognize the manner in which they are used in the selection. If they know that *bush* means "shrub," for example, they might think that a "bush telegraph" would be able to send messages across country covered with trees and shrubs. Ask students how they used context clues and previous knowledge of these words to determine their meaning in the selection.

## Vocabulary Development

The following words are underscored and defined in the student text.

**emphasis:** special stress given to make something stand out.

**variables:** things that can change.

**convey:** make known; communicate.

**repertoire:** group of songs or musical pieces ready to be performed.

**commemorate:** to honor an act or event.

Before assigning the reading, you may want to introduce students to any words that could cause pronunciation or definition problems.

### ( CONTENT-AREA VOCABULARY )

Although the following words are important to an understanding of the text selection, some of them may be unfamiliar to students.

**bush\*:** sparsely settled land
**set\*:** established deliberately or by convention
**summons\*:** an order or command to appear

*Although students may be familiar with other meanings of these words, the words as used in the selection have a specific meaning that pertains to the content area.

## Reading Informational Material

### Reading Skill
Identifying Text Structure: Comparison and Contrast
Explain to students that *comparing* means discovering the ways in which things are similar. *Contrasting* means finding the differences between things. Readers often compare and contrast ideas, opinions, and examples within a text.

### ▶ Teaching Tip
*Using Signal Words* Provide students with a list of signal words that indicate when ideas are being compared or contrasted. [*different from, same as, although, however*] Have the class scan the selection looking for signal words, and then list their words on the chalkboard under the headings "Compare" and "Contrast."

### Reading Strategy
Anticipating Information (Strategy 9)
To help students find ideas that compare and contrast within the selection, use Strategy 9 in Content-Area Reading Strategies. You may wish to provide students with a Venn Diagram (Graphic Organizer 11).

## DURING READING

### Using the Side Margin Feature
■ "Ear" Witnesses
The feature includes a British traveler's description of how quickly a message could be sent by drumming. Ask students to think of examples of traditional products that fit into modern society. [Medicines of indigenous peoples often are effective; reinterpretations of pieces of ancient music, such as Gregorian chants, have been radio hits.]

### Differentiating Instruction
■ Learners Having Difficulty
Use a Think-Pair-Share strategy to help students find similarities and differences. Begin having students choose partners; then ask the student pairs questions such as "What are the most important differences between the talking drums and the

talking gongs?" Give the student pairs a time limit, for example, five minutes, to formulate and discuss their answer. After they have reviewed their answer mentally and verbally, they can share it with the class.

## AFTER READING

### ✔ Reading Check
The following are sample answers to questions on student text page 62.

1. A talking drum can call troops into battle, request goods, or announce births and deaths.

2. Accept either one of the following: The Asante use an hourglass drum with two skins, one at each end. The *fontomfrom* has thongs that can be loosened or tightened. It may have bells attached. The *ntumpane* is a large drum with skin over one end. *Ntumpanes* come in pairs called the husband and the wife.

3. Rules about drums include the following: Drummers must never carry their own drums; women must not touch the drums; a drummer should not teach his own son to drum; and a drummer must always walk behind the chief.

4. Drum language uses more syllables than regular speech to deliver a message because it can convey ideas only through tone.

5. The author thinks that modern technology will make talking drums obsolete. Drumming may be kept alive because it is needed but also because people are proud of their traditions.

### Reteaching
If students have difficulty comparing and contrasting ideas in the selection, have them list descriptive details in a series of Venn Diagrams (Graphic Organizer 11). Have students start with two concepts or items that are entirely covered in the text, such as hourglass drums (*fontomfrom*) and *ntumpane* drums. Ask students to list the similarities [*both are used as talking drums*] and differences [*one drum has two skins, while the other has only one; one drum is played alone, while the other is played in pairs*]. Students also might compare and

contrast African tonal language and talking drum language, or talking drums and talking gongs. When students are familiar with the Venn Diagrams, ask them to work in pairs to compare and contrast ideas that require them to make inferences and draw their own conclusions, such as telephones and talking drums, or technology workers and drum makers. Before they begin these more complex comparisons, have students discuss the points they will use for comparing and contrasting. When they have finished, ask volunteers to share their diagrams with the rest of the class.

## Connecting to Language Arts

▪ Writing

*Job Application* Have students write applications for the job of drummaker in an imaginary village. Their letters should be addressed to the village chief and should show their knowledge of different types of drums and drum-making techniques.

## Connecting Across the Curriculum: Art/Music

Assign students to learn more about the different types of drums and musical instruments in West Africa. How are the instruments made, and how is music performed? Have students locate illustrations and, if possible, audio recordings of these instruments. Have them share the sounds of West Africa with the rest of the class.

## Further Resources
### Online
The Kennedy Center's Web site offers educational resources for African music, including links to related Web sites.

### Assessment

Turn to page 124 for a multiple-choice test on the selection.

*Test Answers*

**1.** c  **2.** c  **3.** b  **4.** d  **5.** a
**6.** b  **7.** a  **8.** a  **9.** c  **10.** d

The following criteria can help you evaluate each student's success in completing the activities prompted by the Cross-Curricular Activities feature in the student textbook.

**Note:** Activities marked with an asterisk allow the involvement of more than one student. For these activities you may wish first to evaluate each student on his or her individual contribution and then give groups an overall rating.

## Science/Music/Speech
### The Science of Drumming

- The student conducts research on how drums work, based on the science of sound waves.
- The student uses the research to prepare a brief oral presentation.
- The student uses props that clearly support the discussion.
- The student's report is informative and clearly delivered, giving the audience a better understanding of the topic.

## History/Drama
### Griots Live!

- The student selects a scene from history and performs it the way a griot might.
- If the student includes music, dance, or visual images, these are appropriate for the story and are creatively integrated.
- The student uses gestures and voice in imaginative and creative ways to tell the story.
- As performed, the student's story effectively portrays a historical event, leaving the audience with a clear historical perspective.

## Language Arts/Geography
### The View from a Camel's Back

- The student writes a series of journal entries describing a caravan journey.
- The student includes where the caravan starts and ends, what items the camels carry, and how someone can survive desert travel and raiders.
- The student creates a clearly drawn and labeled map showing the cities where the caravan stops.
- The writing is relatively free of errors in spelling, grammar, usage, and mechanics.

## Art/Architecture
### The Beauties of Al-Andalus

- The student conducts research on a palace or religious building in Andalusia.
- The student presents information about the building to the class, pointing out interesting works of art and construction techniques.
- The student sketches designs particular to Islamic art or draws blueprints of buildings, showing locations of courts and fountains.
- The writing is relatively free of errors in spelling, grammar, usage, and mechanics; illustrations are neat and appealing.

## *Mathematics/Science
### Whose Discovery?

- The student conducts research on a historical Islamic mathematician, astronomer, doctor, or geographer and role-plays that person in a round-table discussion.
- The student creates a diagram, chart, or map (if appropriate) to illustrate the contribution of that person.
- The student debates whose findings were most important and who had the biggest impact on history.
- The student successfully and accurately answers questions from the class.

## CHAPTER 3

# Looking to the East
## China and Japan A.D. 618–1500

### Land of Discovery

from *Scholastic Update*

by PHIL SUDO AND JEAN CHOL
(*student text page 67*)

**Reading Level:** Average

### Text Summary

Many of the "Western" technologies we rely on today come from ancient Chinese culture. From paper to petroleum, from plows to gunpowder, China's philosophers and inventors are the source of many insights and inventions that modern people find fundamental to daily life.

## BEFORE READING

### Make the Connection

Have students perform a few simple actions such as working a math problem using decimals or looking at a classroom clock to check the time. Ask students to think about the technology that made these actions possible. Who thought of creating paper, a decimal system, or a mechanical clock? Tell students that all of those things were created by Chinese inventors. Ask students what life would be like without these creations. [Students may say that without paper they would have no homework assignments. Without clocks they would not be tardy to class. Without decimals the money system would change.]

### Build Background

▪ More About the Topic

Many Chinese discoveries seem so basic that their true origins may not be known to many people today. For example, English physician William Harvey has often been credited with discovering the circulatory system of the blood, since he published his findings in 1628. However, circulation of the blood had been a well-known part of Chinese medicine since the second century B.C. The famous voyage of Christopher Columbus was made possible by borrowing two basic elements of Chinese nautical technology: the rudder and the compass. Evidence of steering rudders first appears in Europe in 1180—more than a thousand years after the first evidence of use of the rudder in China. Without rudders to steer a ship and a compass to determine location, Europeans could not have made their long voyages of discovery.

### Vocabulary Development

The following words are underscored and defined in the student text.

**adhere:** to hold fast; firmly support.

**surge:** sharp increase; something that moves forward like a wave.

**legitimate:** something that is true, logical, or reasonable.

**rigorous:** strict or difficult.

**pervades:** spreads throughout.

Before assigning the reading, you may want to introduce students to any words that could cause pronunciation or definition problems.

## Vocabulary Tip

**Using Word Parts** To help students work out each word's meaning, ask students to look at the roots and prefixes of the content-area vocabulary. To work out the meaning of *propel*, ask students to think of other words that use the prefix *pro–* (meaning "before" or "forward") [*promote, proceed, protrude*]; students also may be familiar with another form of the word. [an airplane's *propeller*] To help students get a better sense of the words *definitive* and *expertise*, have them work with the related forms *define* and *expert*.

### CONTENT-AREA VOCABULARY

Although the following words are important to an understanding of the text selection, some of them may be unfamiliar to students. Present this list of words and the definitions to students. Encourage students to discuss other meanings they know for these words.

**propel:** to push forward.
**definitive:** final or comprehensive; decisive.
**expertise:** a specialist's skill or knowledge.

### Reading Informational Material

## Reading Skill
### Making Generalizations

Explain to students that we make generalizations when we form general ideas or principles based on the details we read. A generalization requires a reader to examine textual clues, combine them with prior knowledge of a topic, and infer an explanation that applies to the situation explained in the text.

## Reading Strategy
### Taking Effective Notes (Strategy 10)

To help students organize the selection's details as they form a generalization, use Strategy 10 in Content-Area Reading Strategies. First, introduce students to the note-taking symbols. Then, make sure students clearly understand the difference between important concepts and the supporting details that are used to illustrate these concepts. If you want students to use a divided-page note-taking system, provide them with a Key Points and Details Chart (Graphic Organizer 5).

▶ **Teaching Tip**

*Investigating Martial Arts* Have students look up some of the martial arts discussed in the selection to see how their names describe their subtle differences. Students should make a two-column chart, labeling the columns "Translation of Name" and "Description of Martial Art." After students work individually to fill out this chart, they should work in pairs to write a sentence or two to describe each martial art.

## DURING READING

### Using the Side-Margin Feature
■ **You Read It Here First . . .**

To put the side-margin feature (student text page 69) in context, help students familiarize themselves with different types of predator insects. Have students look up information about the "good guy" insects—the praying mantis, the ladybug, and the common lacewing—to see how they are used today to control pests.

### Differentiating Instruction
■ **Learners Having Difficulty**

Emphasize to students that the selection makes its point by providing numerous examples of Chinese discoveries. Help students chart the text's details using the Cluster Diagram (Graphic Organizer 3) that allows them first to list the types of discoveries discussed [medicine, agriculture] and then to jot down specific details about each of these discoveries.

■ **English-Language Learners**

Language learners may be confused by the paragraph in the middle of page 67, in which sentence fragments are used in a list of inventions. Ask students when they make lists in their own lives. [shopping lists, to-do lists] Ask them if they usually use complete sentences when they write their own lists, and then discuss why the answer is probably no. [The sentences would be repetitious and unnecessary.] You may want to work with students to rewrite part of the paragraph in complete sentences to illustrate this point.

# AFTER READING

##  Reading Check

The following are sample answers to questions on student text page 72.

1. Some Chinese inventions were thought to have been created by Europeans because sometimes Europeans made the same type of invention at a later date.

2. Doctors in China use acupuncture for a variety of reasons, including pain relief. Western medical experts have been skeptical about acupuncture because there is no explanation for why it works.

3. Crops planted in rows have more room to grow, so they mature more quickly than crops planted in other ways.

4. Martial arts are practiced in order to develop strength, self-discipline, and self-knowledge.

5. Confucius wanted to help Chinese society overcome its corruption and become more harmonious through the principles of respect, kindness, selflessness, and obedience.

## Reteaching

Help students make generalizations using the following technique. Have students create a five-column organizer, labeling the columns "Question," "Text's Answer," "My Take," "This Suggests," and "I Conclude." Then, provide students with a question that requires an inference. [For example, Why would the Chinese have planted their crops in rows?] In the "Text's Answer" column, have students write what the selection says about the subject. [The selection says that the Chinese started planting crops in rows in the sixth century B.C. It says that crops in rows grow faster because they have more space.] In the "My Take" column, have students write their responses to the text's information. [How did the Chinese figure out that crops grow faster in rows? There must have been a lot of trial and error before they learned that.] In the "This Suggests" column, have students make an inference. [The Chinese must have spent a lot of time experimenting and watching in order to learn that crops grow faster in rows.] When students have completed the chart, have them use the "I Conclude" column to form a generalization statement. [Chinese agricultural developments must have evolved slowly, requiring great patience and lengthy observation.]

## Connecting to Language Arts
- Writing

*A Letter Home*  Have students imagine that they are traveling in China in ancient times and seeing the developments of the Chinese. Have each student write a letter home explaining a new Chinese discovery to people who have never seen it. Have students include examples or illustrations and give the reader instructions on how to use the item. The instructions should compare the new discovery to a similar device, such as the one it improves upon—paper, for example, is a cheaper alternative to the expensive silk or fragile bamboo previously used for writing.

## Connecting Across the Curriculum: Health/Science

*Healing*  Assign students to compare Chinese healing techniques with Western ones. Have one group of students find out how ancient Chinese medicine treats a common ailment, such as a fever, a cold, or a broken bone. Then, have another group research how Western medicine treats the same ailment. Have students share their results with the rest of the class, comparing the techniques' similarities and differences.

## Further Resources
- Web Sites

"China's Gifts to the West," the Asiatic Studies in American Education Web site, provides information on numerous Chinese inventions.

The Franklin Institute's "China: Ancient Arts and Sciences" Web site provides further details about papermaking, printing, gunpowder, and compass making.

## Assessment

Turn to page 125 for a multiple-choice test on the selection.

*Test Answers*

1. b  2. d  3. a  4. d  5. c
6. a  7. b  8. c  9. d  10. c

# The Biggest Wall of All

from *National Geographic World*

by MARGARET McKELWAY

*(student text page 73)*

**Reading Level:** Average

## Text Summary

About two thousand years ago, settlers in what is now China erected barriers of earth and stone to protect their villages from the attacks of mounted invaders. Gradually, those earthen barriers were combined with other local fortifications to create a wall that stretched a thousand miles. In the 1300s, the wall was expanded and rebuilt into what we recognize as China's Great Wall, the longest structure ever built.

# BEFORE READING

## Make the Connection

Ask students to describe the biggest human-made structure they have ever seen. [Students may describe a bridge, an airport terminal, or a highway.] Then, ask students to describe the oldest building they have seen or have read about. [Students may describe an old church or municipal building, or an ancient structure such as the Egyptian pyramids.] Tell students that China's Great Wall is both ancient and huge; the wall dates back to 221 B.C. and is considered the world's largest human-made structure.

## Build Background

■ More About the Topic

China's Great Wall is really a number of "great walls" that have been built and rebuilt over the ages. The wall that we recognize today was built during the Ming dynasty, when the defensive structure became much bigger and fancier than its earlier versions. The construction secret was the use of brick. While Europeans of this time were using hard-to-handle stone, the Chinese developed sophisticated kilns that allowed them to make great quantities of strong, sturdy bricks. The Chinese spent an estimated $360 billion on the wall in today's terms; in comparison, the United States has spent about that sum of money on its interstate highway system over the last forty years.

## Vocabulary Development

The following words are underscored and defined in the student text.

**loot:** stolen goods.

**invaders:** those who enter forcibly; intruders.

**plagued:** troubled.

**continuous:** unbroken; attached together.

**gorges:** narrow, deep passages, with steep sides; ravines.

Before assigning the reading, you may want to introduce students to any words that could cause pronunciation or definition problems.

### Vocabulary Tip

**Recognizing Words with Multiple Meanings** Talk with students about the multiple meanings for the content-area vocabulary words. In the selection, *wore away* describes how the wall eroded, becoming smaller. Students may be more familiar with *wore* used in relationship to clothing. Have students look up dictionary entries for the content-area vocabulary to see the many meanings for *common* and *dash*, and discuss with them how they would use context to determine the word's use in a sentence.

### CONTENT-AREA VOCABULARY

Although the following words are important to an understanding of the text selection, some of them may be unfamiliar to students. You may want to present this list of words and their definitions to students.

**dash\*:** to move quickly; to rush.

**common\*:** shared by two or more; mutual.

**wore away\*:** made smaller by use or handling; eroded.

\*Although students may be familiar with other meanings of these words, the words as used in the selection have a specific meaning that pertains to the content area.

## Reading Informational Material

### Reading Skill

**Identifying Text Structure: Cause and Effect**

Discuss with students how a **cause** makes something happen, and an **effect** occurs as a result of that cause. Tell students that writers may include in their writing both the cause and effect of a situation. Sometimes, however, a selection may omit part of the information, leaving the readers to infer a cause or effect by using their own knowledge.

### Reading Strategy

**Understanding Text Structure: Cause and Effect (Strategy 2)**

To help students find the relationship between the selection's causes and effects, use Strategy 2 in Content-Area Reading Strategies. You may wish to provide students with a Cause and Effect Chart (Graphic Organizer 2) to help them organize their ideas about how certain events lead to other events.

▶ **Teaching Tip**

*Tracking the Warriors* The selection's first paragraph refers to fierce, nomadic warriors who attacked settlers in what is now China. Tell students that these nomadic tribes, which continued to plague China for more than fifteen hundred years, included the Mongols and their leader Genghis Khan. For a quick description of these warrior peoples, students can skim features in the selection *"from* The Search for Genghis Khan." Students can look at the "You Need to Know…" feature (page 77) or "Rules for a Warrior People" (page 79) to get a fuller picture of why the Chinese needed protection from their neighbors.

## DURING READING

### Viewing the Art

▪ **The Great Wall of China**

You may wish to refer students to page 74 and the map that shows the Great Wall's length. Ask students to find information that puts the wall's length in perspective. For example, have students investigate the number of time zones the wall passes through, the number of mountain ranges and rivers it crosses, or the length of time it would take to drive from one end to the other.

### Differentiating Instruction

▪ **Advanced Learners**

Have students find out more about how walls have been used as defensive devices. Direct them to walls in other cultures and times [Rome, Berlin], and ask them to make comparisons with "Hadrian's Wall" (page 12).

▪ **English-Language Learners**

Students who are learning English may have some knowledge of China's history and geography, especially if their background is Asian. Pair English-language learners with native English speakers, and have students share what they each know about China. Have each pair study the maps and art, which can help them better understand the selection.

## AFTER READING

### ✔ Reading Check

The following are sample answers to questions on student text page 75.

1. Settlers in early China built fortifications as protection from invading nomadic tribes.

2. The Chinese Empire was formed when Qin Shi Huangdi, the ruler of a small state in eastern Asia, combined his state with several other states in 221 B.C.

3. The Great Wall linked existing local fortifications together to form one long barrier.

4. Signal platforms and towers for troops and supplies are built into the Great Wall.

5. The Great Wall was sometimes overrun and did not always protect the Chinese people.

### Reteaching

If students have difficulty analyzing the selection's causes and effects, ask them to answer the following questions:

Who did something that started an action? [Mounted warriors wanted to raid Chinese villages.]

What did this first action lead to? [Villagers tried to protect themselves.]

What did this response lead to? [Villages built barriers to protect themselves.]

Explain to students that their first answer is a cause. Their second answer is the effect of that cause. Their second answer also becomes a cause that leads to the third answer, another effect.

Have students work in pairs to repeat the process throughout the selection.

## Connecting to Language Arts
▪ Writing

*Whose Idea Was This, Anyway?* Have students find out more about Qin Shi Huangdi, China's first emperor. Ask them to write a thumbnail sketch describing the ruler who started construction on the Great Wall. Did he have other interests or major accomplishments? What kind of ruler was he? Have students present a picture of the leader who began such a huge construction project.

## Connecting Across the Curriculum: Geography

*Following the Great Wall of China* Have students journey through China by taking an imaginary trip along the Great Wall. Tell them that they will record an imaginary hike of about a hundred miles anywhere along the wall's length. Ask students to mark their trips on a map and to do research on the area. Then, have them write a brief description of the cities the wall passes through, the terrain in the area, and the mountains or rivers within their hundred-mile area. When students have finished the descriptions of their journeys, post their maps in geographical order on the bulletin board so that students can follow the Great Wall's route.

## Further Resources
▪ Web site

The Discovery Channel's "Secrets of the Great Wall" Web site offers satellite photos and information about the wall's construction history. Students will enjoy finding little-known facts about the wall using the site's "Random Factoid Generator."

### Assessment

Turn to page 126 for a multiple-choice test on the selection.

*Test Answers*

**1.** a  **2.** d  **3.** a  **4.** c  **5.** d
**6.** b  **7.** c  **8.** d  **9.** b  **10.** c

# *from* The Search for Genghis Khan

from *Current Events*
(student text page 76)

**Reading Level:** Above Average

## Special Considerations

Genghis Khan's military tactics were disciplined and ruthless. You may want to lead a discussion about the conditions that could lead to the type of large-scale, merciless slaughter described in the selection. Ask students to compare Genghis Khan's strategies with those of other effective but cruel leaders with which they may be familiar. [Hitler and Stalin]

## Text Summary

Genghis Khan united the nomadic tribes north of China into a fearsome fighting force. Under his leadership the Mongol army conquered vast portions of Asia and Eastern Europe, creating an enormous empire. The Mongol leader was buried amid great secrecy, and the location of his tomb has remained a secret since his death in 1227. Scientists and historians believe that Genghis Khan was buried with a wealth of artifacts, and the search for his tomb continues.

# BEFORE READING

## Make the Connection

Ask students what qualities make a great leader. [Students may say a great leader is brave or enthusiastic or focused on his or her purpose.] Then, ask students whether it would be easy to be around a person with these qualities. [Students may say that a leader focused on his or her work might be demanding or impatient.] Tell students that while Genghis Khan may be considered a national hero to the Mongolian people, in other parts of the world, he is often associated with ruthlessness and savagery.

## Build Background

■ More About the Topic

The Mongols had no written language to record the victories of the mighty Genghis Khan. How did their history come down to us today? Conquered peoples recorded the Mongols' tales. The writer Ata-Malik Juvaini, who worked for the Mongol governors, is an important source of information. His task was to praise the very Mongol rulers who had murdered many people and destroyed their culture of learning. Juvaini drew on stories told by his father and grandfather to present the chronicle of Genghis Khan. At the same time, Juvaini mourned the nations that the leader had conquered.

## Vocabulary Development

The following words are underscored and defined in the student text.

**resounding:** echoing; making a loud sound.
**plunder:** goods or belongings taken in warfare.
**encountered:** met unexpectedly or accidentally.
**reputation:** public opinion about someone's character.
**renounced:** gave up, or disowned.
**delegation:** collection of people sent to speak for others.
**eminent:** distinguished; outstanding in character or performance.
**fending:** resisting.
**tactic:** special military arrangement.
**realm:** kingdom or region.

Before assigning the reading, you may want to introduce students to any words that could cause pronunciation or definition problems.

┌─ *Vocabulary Tip* ─────────────

**Recognizing Words for War** Talk with students about the use of the content-area vocabulary words to describe strategies and situations that relate to war. Ask students whether they have heard the word *ruthless* before and, if so, in what context. Determine whether students have heard the word *siege* used in other contexts. Then, have them look at a dictionary entry to learn more about its military meaning.

Although the following words are important to an understanding of the text selection, some of them may be unfamiliar to students. Present this list of words and definitions to students. Have students brainstorm the connection between the words.

**ruthless:** without pity or mercy; cruel.

**siege\*:** a military strategy of surrounding a city in order to force its surrender and prevent any people or goods from entering.

*Although students may be familiar with other meanings of this word, the word as used in the selection has a specific meaning that pertains to the content area.

## Reading Informational Material

### Reading Skill
#### Using Word Parts

Discuss with students how identifying the prefixes, suffixes, and roots of unfamiliar words can help them use what they already know to unlock a word's meaning. Students can more easily identify vocabulary words when they break the words into recognizable parts.

### Reading Strategy
#### Developing Vocabulary Knowledge (Strategy 11)

To help students when they encounter unfamiliar words, use Strategy 11 in Content-Area Reading Strategies. Provide students with the Contextual Redefinition Chart (Graphic Organizer 4) to organize their thoughts when using this strategy. Students may prefer to create a chart using the CSSD strategy, labeling the columns "Context," "Structure," "Sound," and "Dictionary."

▶ **Teaching Tip**

*Names for a Mongol* Perhaps because of their enormous empire, the Mongols were known by many names. In India and Persia, they were called Moguls. When the Russians saw the Mongols' gleaming, golden tents, they called these people the Zolotaya Orda, or "The Golden Horde." The word also means "a swarm" or "a large, moving mass of people."

## DURING READING

### Using the Side-Margin Feature
▪ **Dressed for Success**

After students have read the feature about Mongol battle gear, ask them to think about how soldiers probably would have acquired their silk shirts. Remind students that nomadic people would not have had the resources for silk production. [China is famous for its silk. The Mongols must have, in some way, acquired the silk from the Chinese or other people who learned the silk-making process. Ironically, the Mongols used silk as a defense against the very people who made the cloth.]

▶ **Teaching Tip**

*Using Roots and Affixes* Provide students with lists of common roots, prefixes, and suffixes. The lists should include the definition of the word part, as well as sample words. You can also have the class work together to compile their own root word and affix list. As they read, have students jot down word parts that they recognize. Students can work in groups to divide the list by word part, to write down the word part's definition, and to provide sample words.

### Differentiating Instruction
▪ **English-Language Learners**

English-language learners may have difficulty understanding the meanings of idioms such as "suicide corps," "long shot," or "gates of Europe." Pair English-language learners with native English speakers and have each pair review the English-language idioms and discuss how their usage differs from the literal meaning of the words in the idiom.

## AFTER READING

### Reading Check

The following are sample answers to questions on student text page 83.

1. According to legend, Genghis Khan's burial site remains a secret because any person who might have known of the site was killed so the location could not be revealed.

**2.** The Tatars poisoned young Genghis Khan's father and stole his family's animals. When he grew older, Genghis Khan defeated the Tatars.

**3.** The conflict began when Genghis Khan sent a caravan of merchants to Muhammed, proposing trade between the two empires. However, a city governor accused the merchants of being spies and killed them.

**4.** People in Europe as far away as England were terrified of the news of the Mongol defeat of Russian armies.

**5.** After Genghis Khan's death, his son Ogadei inherited the empire. However, by the next century, the Mongol Empire disappeared.

## Reteaching

To help students analyze word parts, show them how to create vocabulary "trees" to help recognize Greek and Latin roots. First, select a root word or affix for students to examine. [*re–:* back] Have students sketch the outline of a tree and write this word part and its definition in the roots. Have students write in the tree's trunk a word from the selection that contains this affix or root and the definition of the word [*resounding:* echoing, making a loud sound]. Ask students to write in the tree's upper "branches" two other words that have the same root or affix. [examples from the selection: *retracing, renounced, returned, remained, rejoined, remarkable*] Have students jot down beside these additional words the words' definitions and an example of how each word is used. [*retracing:* going back over again; "retracing her steps"] Provide students with another affix or a root [*pro–:* forward (*procession*); *loc–:* place (*location*); or *–ful:* full of (*powerful*)], and have students work in pairs to build another vocabulary tree. Tell students that words for the tree's branches should come from the selection if possible; otherwise, their examples may come from their background knowledge.

## Connecting to Language Arts

### ▪ Writing

***Don't Go to the Funeral!*** Since attending the funeral of Genghis Khan would have been a fatal mistake, how else could people living in the Mongolian Empire have marked his passing? Have

students write a funeral speech for the late leader. Their remarks about him should note what he accomplished, the way he affected people's lives, and what he will be remembered for. Stage a mock memorial service, and have students read their eulogies to the rest of the class.

### ▪ Speaking and Listening

***I Remember Little Temujin When . . .*** The Mongol emperor came a long way from his days as a poor, fatherless child. Have students stage a "This Is Your Life" program that recalls incidents marking Genghis Khan's rise to fame. Have students learn more about the ruler's life so they can include anecdotes from the khan's early, pre-empire days, as well as later battlefield tales. Have students present their stories aloud; ask for a volunteer to act as Genghis himself and to respond to their recollections.

## Connecting Across the Curriculum: History

***Creating a Family Tree*** Genghis Khan's descendants continued to rule for a time after his death. Have students create a family tree that charts the great khan's family. When students have finished researching Genghis Khan's family, have volunteers share with the class the rest of the story of the Mongol Empire.

## Further Resources
### Magazine Online

*National Geographic* featured Mongolia in its December 1996 and February 1997 issues. *National Geographic's* Web site "The Land of Genghis Khan" offers a time line of biographical information about the military leader, as well as maps of the Mongol Empire. The site includes classroom ideas and additional resources for teaching about Genghis Khan.

---

### ( Assessment )

Turn to page 127 for a test on the selection.

***Test Answers***

**1.** a  **2.** c  **3.** b  **4.** d  **5.** c
**6.** b  **7.** a  **8.** a  **9.** b  **10.** b
**11.** b  **12.** a  **13.** a  **14.** a  **15.** b

# The Paper Revolution

from *Faces: The Magazine About People*

by JOHN S. MAJOR

*(student text page 84)*

**Reading Level:** Average

## Text Summary

The invention of paper allowed people to abandon the clumsy, inconvenient, and expensive methods of writing that had been used in earlier times. Using paper for writing encouraged the development of the printing press and led to great changes in education. Today, the uses of paper have multiplied in homes, businesses, and schools.

# BEFORE READING

## Make the Connection

Ask students to list ways they have used paper since waking up in the morning. [Students may have read a newspaper or book, written a letter or assignment, eaten from a paper plate, carried their lunch in a paper sack, or drunk milk from a paper carton.] Then, ask students to think of how they would have accomplished those tasks without the use of paper. What products would have been used instead? [Reading material could have been on parchment or a computer screen; meals could have been eaten from china plates or carried in canvas sacks; milk could have arrived in glass bottles or from a cow to a pail to a glass.] How would the tasks have changed without the use of paper? [The tasks might have been harder or taken longer; some tasks would per-haps not have been possible, since books made of parchment would be very expensive.]

## Build Background

■ Write It Down

Silk was used as a writing material before the invention of paper; part of the Chinese character for *paper* means "silk." When the court official Ts'ai Lun was later credited with creating China's paper-making process, his discovery was so important that China's emperor made him a noble. His paper, which was thin, yet strong and flexible, was called *Ts'ai Ko-Shi,* or "Distinguished Ts'ai's Paper." The

Chinese continued to improve the quality of their paper. For example, they added dye that served as a preservative against insects.

## Vocabulary Development

The following words are underscored and defined in the student text.

**perishable:** easily spoiled.

**imperial:** related to an empire; having supreme authority.

**fibers:** threadlike tissue from plants or animals.

**luxurious:** expensive; costly.

**spur:** to urge to action.

Before assigning the reading, you may want to introduce students to any words that could cause pronunciation or definition problems.

---

## *Vocabulary Tip*

**Using Context Clues** Discuss with students how the content-area vocabulary words are used to describe different writing materials. Have the class work together to find context clues that can help reveal the words' meanings. For example, the use of contrasts in the selection's first sentence indicates that *clumsy* and *elegant* have opposite meanings. Ask students how important the words are to understanding the text. Discuss with students when it might be appropriate to skip over an unfamiliar word, looking it up *after* finishing the reading.

---

### CONTENT-AREA VOCABULARY

Although the following words are important to an understanding of the text selection, some of them may be unfamiliar to students. Present this list of words and the definitions to students. Have students brainstorm the connection between the words. Encourage students to discuss other meanings they know for the words.

**clumsy:** awkward; not graceful.

**elegant:** graceful or beautiful; of a high quality.

**fragile:** delicate; easily broken.

## Reading Informational Material

### Reading Skill
Identifying Text Structure: Problems and Solutions
Discuss with students how writers may organize ideas to focus on problems and their solutions. Tell students that identifying a text's structure can help them make predictions, recognize relationships, and make inferences about a selection.

### Reading Strategy
Activating and Using Prior Knowledge (Strategy 8)
To help students ask questions about problems developed in the selection and present their possible solutions, use Strategy 8 in Content Area Reading Strategies. Provide students with a KWLS chart (Graphic Organizer 7). You may want to show students pictures of modern papermaking techniques to help them build background information about the process of creating paper.

▶ **Teaching Tip**
*Taking Notes* As students read, have them take notes about the papermaking process described on page 86 and enter them into a flowchart. When students have completed the reading and filled in the steps, ask volunteers to explain to the class the process of turning rags and plant fibers into paper.

## DURING READING

### Correcting Misconceptions
Students who are unfamiliar with cold climates may not understand the selection's comparison of bamboo slats to snow fences. Discuss with students how slatted fences are designed to keep snow from drifting across roads.

### Using the Side-Margin Feature
■ Sidelight
Bring one hundred pennies to class, and have students compare the weight and size of the coins to that of a dollar bill. Ask students to brainstorm how business transactions would be different if all purchases were made in gold and silver coins. [Purchases would be time-consuming and troublesome because of the weight of the money. People would not want to carry much money unless they were going to buy something immediately.]

## Reading Informational Material

### Viewing the Art
■ Japanese Woodcuts
You may wish to refer students to the pictures of Japanese woodcuts on student text page 86. Why might an artist have chosen papermaking as a subject for art? [The artist may have wanted to record specific papermaking techniques. Making paper must have been considered an important activity.]

▶ **Teaching Tip**
*Block Printing* Some students may be unfamiliar with block-printed designs and the use of wooden blocks for printing type. You may wish to have students work in groups to find illustrations of these prints and explain their basic techniques to the class.

### Differentiating Instruction
■ Learners Having Difficulty
If students have difficulty understanding the different types of early writing materials discussed in the selection, help them plot the information in a two-column chart. Have groups of students label the columns "Writing Materials" and "Problems." When students have completed the chart, have them compare how writing developed in different parts of the world.

## AFTER READING

### ✔ Reading Check

The following are sample answers to questions on student test page 88.

1. Wood and bamboo slats were inexpensive; however, they were awkward to carry. If the strings connecting them broke, they could become mixed up.

2. Other early civilizations wrote on materials including stone, clay tablets, bone, tree bark, palm leaves, papyrus, and parchment.

3. People wanted improved writing materials in China because they had to know how to read and write to have a successful career.

**4.** The Chinese began to color the paper and decorate it with block-printed designs.

**5.** People in Baghdad in present-day Iraq were making paper by A.D. 750. The practice later spread to Egypt, Spain, Italy, and the rest of Europe.

## Reteaching

Have students use the Problem and Solution Chart (Graphic Organizer 9) to organize their ideas about the number of difficulties faced by people developing writing materials. You may want to have students read the selection through once and list only problems [bamboo is clumsy to write on; wooden strips can be easily mixed up; silk is very expensive] and read it through again to list solutions only [paper can be made from rags]. Discuss how some solutions develop problems of their own. [Paper made from rags is strong but also expensive.] Suggest to students they may have to set up a series of Problem and Solution Charts to trace fully the author's argument. Discuss with students that not all problems will have several solutions, as illustrated by the chart. Sometimes there will be one solution to many problems. Tell students that they may want to modify the chart depending on the evidence they find in the selection.

## Connecting to Language Arts

### ▪ Writing

*No More Bamboo Slats!* Have students tell the ancient world about the advantages of paper. Ask them to write an advertisement explaining how the new invention improves on the old-fashioned techniques. They may also want to preview upcoming improvements and predict the types of paper products that will soon be available.

### ▪ Speaking and Listening

*Can You Tell Us How You Did It?* Have students work in groups to learn more about papermaking techniques. Then, have them conduct an imaginary interview with the man who helped create the paper we use today. Have students prepare questions to ask Ts'ai Lun about how he became interested in papermaking and how his improvements changed reading and writing for the Chinese people. Students can take turns asking questions as reporters and answering them as the inventor Ts'ai Lun.

## Connecting Across the Curriculum: Science/Technology

*Producing Paper* The Chinese made paper from fishnets and tree bark, but much paper today is made from wood pulp. Have students research the types of materials that have been used for making paper. Ask them to compare the quality of different papers and to find out what materials are used to achieve different effects. They can share their results in short reports to the class.

## Further Resources
### Online

The Institute of Paper Science and Technology provides information about the development of paper and its history. Its Web site also describes the writing materials used in early cultures before the invention of paper.

### Assessment

Turn to page 128 for a multiple-choice test on the selection.

*Test Answers*

**1.** c    **2.** c    **3.** a    **4.** c    **5.** a
**6.** d    **7.** b    **8.** b    **9.** c    **10.** d

# from **Prince Taishi Shōtoku**
# Japan, A.D. 574–622

from *Heroes: Great Men Through the Ages*
by REBECCA HAZELL
*(student text page 89)*

**Reading Level:** Average

## Text Summary

Prince Taishi Shōtoku modernized the Japanese government and supported the development of its arts. In both these areas, he looked to China as a model. His changes in government were based on the teachings of Confucius. He brought Chinese artists and craftspeople to Japan so his people could learn their techniques. With the prince's support and encouragement, Japanese people blended and adapted Chinese ideas to create their unique culture.

# BEFORE READING

## Make the Connection

Have students brainstorm examples of changes they have witnessed in school or city policies. [A school might change its dress code, its absentee policy, or its schedules for lunches or vacations. A city might change the fees for garbage collection, the hours for parks and museums, or the price of public transportation.] How did people adjust to these new rules? Have students discuss how people react to changes—both big and small—in their schools and their government.

## Build Background

■ More About the Topic

Among Prince Taishi Shōtoku's accomplishments is the Seventeen Article Constitution, a code for reorganizing the Japanese government according to the Chinese system. The Seventeen Article Constitution emphasized that rulers were responsible for their subjects, and that people should be obedient to their rulers. Following the Chinese system, the Seventeen Article Constitution selected government workers according to their merit. To emphasize this idea of merit, Prince Shotoku devised a system of twelve court ranks, with each rank identified by a cap of a different color. The colorful ranking system was a visible reminder of Japan's break with the old method of inheriting one's post.

## Vocabulary Development

The following words are underscored and defined in the student text.

**rustic:** rural; unsophisticated.

**rival:** competitive with another.

**influential:** able to exert power over someone or something else.

**prosperity:** wealth; good fortune.

**adapted:** adjusted to new circumstances; made to fit.

Before assigning the reading, you may want to introduce students to any words that could cause pronunciation or definition problems.

┌─ *Vocabulary Tip* ─────────────────

**Finding Out Word History** For thousands of years, builders carved decorations on the front of their ships. This type of ornament, called a *figurehead,* could take the form of a dragon, a lion, the head of a god, or a human figure. These carved figures made vessels look impressive, but they were only decorations, unnecessary for sailing a ship. Similarly, a person is called a *figurehead* when he or she holds a position of leadership without having actual power or authority—he or she merely looks good, while others do the work.

└──────────────────────────────────

( **CONTENT-AREA VOCABULARY** )

Although the following words are important to an understanding of the text selection, some of them may be unfamiliar to students. Present this list of words and the definitions, and have students brainstorm what connection there is between the words.

**nobles:** people with high ranks or titles.

**figurehead:** someone given a position of leadership without real authority.

**clan\*:** a group of people descended from a common ancestor.

**sage\*:** a person who has gained wisdom through experience.

**commoners:** people without rank or title.

\*Although students may be familiar with other meanings of the word, the words as used in the selection have a specific meaning that pertains to the content area.

## Reading Informational Material

### Reading Skill
Summarizing

Elicit from students the idea that a summary restates the main events and ideas of a text in only a few words. Tell students that being able to summarize can help them understand and remember what they read.

### Reading Strategy
Previewing Text (Strategy 1)

To help students identify and remember the selection's most important ideas, use Strategy 1 described in Content-Area Reading Strategies. Provide students with a KWL chart (Graphic Organizer 6). You may want to direct students to the selection's illustrations and graphic features to help them build background information about the culture of Japan.

▶ **Teaching Tip**

*Cloze Concept Mapping* Draw a Cloze Concept Map for students on the chalkboard or on a handout to distribute. Help students chart the details of Prince Shōtoku's changes. You will want to provide students with a general heading, such as "Shōtoku's Influence on Japanese Culture," and then make suggestions about the categories of innovations that the prince introduced. Start students out by filling in some subheadings and details in the Cloze organizers. For example, under the subheading "religion," you could list the details "Buddhism," "compassion," "respect for people," and "reduced amount of violence."

## DURING READING

### Using the Side-Margin Feature
■ Would You Believe?

Tell students that the carp's gold color was just one of the hidden traits that blossomed under selective breeding. Other abnormalities that became prized include the shape of the tail fin, protruding eyes, and the lack of a long dorsal, or top, fin. Have students discuss why such abnormalities would be seen as attractive or desirable. [The hidden traits would be unusual and different. Rare traits are often seen as valuable.]

### Differentiating Instruction
■ Learners Having Difficulty

To help students better understand Prince Shōtoku's contributions, ask them as they read to make notes in a Before-and-After Chart. Have them create a two-column chart, labeling the columns "Japan Before Prince Shōtoku" and "Japan After Prince Shōtoku." After students have read the selection and completed their notes, have them review the chart and write a couple of sentences summarizing the Before and After differences.

■ English-Language Learners

English-language learners may have difficulty understanding the selection's discussion of Japanese art and culture. Encourage them to keep track of the ideas that are unclear. When they have finished reading, pair language learners with native English-speakers and see how many of these ideas they can figure out through the selection's context. If students want further explanation of particular concepts, have them work in groups to find more information in reference books or from Internet sources.

## AFTER READING

### ✔ Reading Check

The following are samples to questions on student text page 92.

1. Because there was not a clear way to choose a new ruler when an emperor or empress died, civil war often broke out between rival clans.

2. Prince Taishi Shōtoku centralized and reformed Japanese government based on the teachings of Confucius. Because of changes, nobles gave up some of their power to commoners.

3. Prince Shōtoku sent messengers to China to study Chinese culture. The messengers returned with Chinese artists, craftspersons, and scholars, who shared their skills with the Japanese.

4. Prince Shōtoku helped spread Buddhism, a religion that was practiced in addition to Shinto.

5. Origami (the art of paper folding), the tea ceremony, flower arranging, and archery all were developed by Japanese artists.

## Reteaching

To help students summarize the selection, have them focus on it by looking for its most important words. Have students review the text and write down three words they think are important to understanding its meaning. [Shōtoku, reformed, society] Students should then write a brief explanation of each choice, explaining its importance to a summary. Have students discuss their choices in small groups Then, have students use these words to write a statement summarizing the selection. [Prince **Shōtoku reformed** Japanese **society** by introducing many new ideas.] Emphasize to students that their explanation is as important as the words they choose.

## Connecting to Language Arts
### ▪ Writing

*Poetry* Have students find examples of haikus, the seventeen-syllable Japanese poems that developed during Prince Shōtoku's time. Then, have students write their own haikus about the prince, about Japan's rapid changes, or about the country's new-found peace and prosperity.

### ▪ Speaking and Listening

*Job Interview* Prince Shōtoku determined that government jobs would be awarded by merit, rather than inherited by nobility, which must have made for some interesting job interviews. Have students stage a mock job interview in which a person who has inherited his job tries to keep it, while a supervisor tries to explain how Prince Shōtoku's new system has changed the requirements of the position. Before they begin, you might want to have students research the kind of government jobs that were available at this time in Japan's history.

## Connecting Across the Curriculum: Arts/Music

*Cultural Connections* Have students learn more about some of the art forms described in the selection: the gagaku dance, the tea ceremony, calligraphy, origami, or flower arranging. Have students work in groups to find examples, illustrations, videos, or descriptions of one of these types of Japanese art. They can share their findings through an informational poster or in a short report to the class.

## Further Resources
### Online

Kids Web Japan offers information about Japanese history and culture. The Web site also includes an atlas of the country.

> ## Assessment
>
> Turn to page 129 for a multiple-choice test on the selection.
>
> *Test Answers*
> **1.** d  **2.** b  **3.** a  **4.** d  **5.** b
> **6.** a  **7.** b  **8.** c  **9.** d  **10.** c

# *from* **Murasaki Shikibu**

from *Outrageous Women of the Middle Ages*
by VICKI LEÓN
*(student text page 93)*

**Reading Level:** Average

## Text Summary

The brilliantly talented Murasaki Shikibu was discouraged from pursuing an education or her dream of becoming a writer. Nonetheless, she educated herself and became a teacher for the young empress Akiko. During this time she continued working on her secret project, the lengthy novel *The Tale of Genji,* her romantic masterpiece that readers have enjoyed for a thousand years.

## BEFORE READING

### Make the Connection

Have students brainstorm how they might write in secret. What would they have to do to ensure that no one knew they were composing a story or poem? [To keep their composition a secret, they might have to write late at night or early in the morning. They might have to go to a quiet library or schoolroom. They might have to hide their notebooks.] How do they think Murasaki Shikibu may have tried to keep her book a secret? [She might have made excuses for her absence or invented a story about a time-consuming activity.]

### Build Background

■ **More About the Topic**

Murasaki Shikibu wrote during the Heian period of Japanese history, a time of security and peace in which the arts flourished as never before. During this time the Japanese court developed a cultural life different from its earlier Chinese model, one that expressed the Japanese values of *miyabi,* "courtliness"; (politeness, elegance, formality) *makoto,* "simplicity"; and *aware,* "sensitivity." A form of Buddhism called Shingon, or "True Words," was popular at the Japanese court and added to its emphasis on art. True Words' followers believed that beauty revealed Buddha's truth, and believers cultivated the arts of painting, music, and gesture.

## Vocabulary Development

The following words are underscored and defined in the student text.

**modest:** humble; quiet.
**conceited:** vain; having too high an opinion of oneself.
**elegance:** gracefulness; refinement.
**prestige:** impressive reputation.
**prompt:** prod into action; remind.

Before assigning the reading, you may want to introduce students to any words that could cause pronunciation or definition problems.

─ *Vocabulary Tip* ─────────

**Tracing a Word's Etymology** It once was a compliment to be called a *prude femme,* a phrase that meant "wise woman" in Old French. By the time the word was first recorded in English in 1704, it had been transformed from praise of a person's integrity to a criticism of his or her excessive modesty. Today, to call a person "a prude" is to imply that he or she ought to loosen up a little, have some fun, and stop worrying so much about proper behavior.

**Using Word Connotations** Discuss with students circumstances in which the content-area vocabulary words could have either positive or negative connotations. How are the words intended to be understood in the selection? When is it a compliment to be considered "stubborn"? Could an "unsociable" person also be "reserved" or just "shy"? Have students look for context clues that indicate whether the description is a form of practice or criticism.

─────────────────────────

( **CONTENT-AREA VOCABULARY** )

Although the following words are important to an understanding of the text selection, some of them may be unfamiliar to students. You may wish to present this list of words and the definitions to students. Have students brainstorm connections between the words.

**unsociable:** not friendly; reserved.

**eggheads:** a mildly negative word to describe intellectual people.

**stubbornly:** in a way resistant to change.

**prude:** a person overly concerned with modesty.

## Reading Informational Material

### Reading Skill

#### Analyzing Text Structure: Chronological Order

Make sure students understand that the terms *chronological order* and *sequence* mean the order in which events happen. Explain that as they analyze a text's chronological order, they can learn more about how an author organizes ideas and can gain insight into the purpose of a text.

### Reading Strategy

#### Understanding Text (Strategy 2)

To help students follow the chronological order of the selection, use Strategy 2 described in Content-Area Reading Strategies. You may wish to provide students with a Sequence or Chronological Order Chart (Graphic Organizer 10) to help them show the order in which events in the selection occurred. In addition, have students mark the signal words that indicate time in the selection. [back then, young Shikibu, about 978, later recalled]

#### ▶ Teaching Tip

*Cultural Classics* The Tale of Genji is a famous text in the Japanese literary tradition. Discuss with students how different cultures have pieces of classic literature that are respected and widely read. Have students talk about examples of classic texts in the English language, as well as famous pieces from other literary traditions with which they might be familiar.

## DURING READING

### Differentiating Instruction

#### ■ Advanced Learners

Advanced learners may want to see examples of Shikibu's famous novel, excerpts of which are available in translation in anthologies. Have students look at a short selection from *The Tale of Genji* and discuss in groups the story's setting and Shikibu's writing style.

#### ■ English-Language Learners

English-language learners may have difficulty understanding the author's casual writing style, particularly her use of idioms. [*stubborn as a mule, eggheads, a good catch*]. Have more confident speakers explain the literal meaning of some of the English-language idioms; if possible, have them sketch a picture of what the phrase describes literally. Have students then try to figure out the phrase's figurative meaning from this literal one, using the selection's context, and write down the definition of the idiom. Have student pairs discuss their definitions with the class.

## AFTER READING

### ✔ Reading Check

The following are sample answers to questions on student text page 98.

1.  Japanese girls might be taught to read and write Japanese; however, they were forbidden to learn Chinese, which was considered a more prestigious language.

2.  She learned Chinese by listening to her older brother's lessons.

3.  Shikibu hid her knowledge because she was afraid her education would make her unpopular.

4.  Shikibu taught the young empress Chinese.

5.  Shikibu continued to work on her book, *The Tale of Genji*. Although she completed fifty-four chapters, her book appears unfinished.

### Reteaching

If students have difficulty understanding the selection's chronology, you may want to have them create a time line by answering "before," "after," or "then" questions. First, have students work in groups to answer questions such as "What studies did Shikibu conduct before she was married?" "After her husband died, how did Shikibu's life change?" "After the emperor heard about Shikibu's novel—then what happened?" Then, have students chart their answers on a time line, arranging their answers in sequential order. After they have answered the questions, have students scan the selection for dates and times [from 800 to 1100, about 978, in 1001]. Have students use the context of the selection to insert the dates and times in the proper spots on their time lines. Have students compare their time lines when they have finished.

## Connecting to Language Arts
### ▪ Writing

*Adding a Chapter* Murasaki Shikibu's life remains cloaked in mystery, just as her masterpiece remains unfinished. Have students write the last chapter in the life of Murasaki Shikibu. Based on the information presented in the story, have students imagine how she spent her final years. Did she find romance? Did she happily finish her novel while living in a nunnery? Or did she unwisely anger an important person with an unflattering portrait in *The Tale of Genji*? Let students decide.

### ▪ Speaking and Listening

*Interview with the Author* Have students work in small groups to research what Murasaki Shikibu's life might have been like at the royal palace. Then, ask them to conduct an imaginary interview in which the author answers questions about her life as a teacher, as well as about her own writing and studies. Students may also want to expand their interviews into a round table discussion in which the emperor, the empress, and members of Shikibu's family review *The Tale of Genji*.

## Connecting Across the Curriculum: History

*Postcards of Kyoto* The ancient city of Kyoto has been recognized as a cultural and religious center of Japan for more than a thousand years. Have students find out more about Japanese gardens and architecture by reporting on a famous site or monument in the city. Then, have them create a postcard and write a message home about what they have seen. Create a bulletin board display of the cards.

## Further Resources
### Online

Read Murasaki Shikibu's diary at the University of Pennsylvania's Celebration of Women Writers Web site. Her diary is part of a grouping titled "Diaries of Court Ladies of Old Japan," a Web site that includes numerous illustrations of court costumes and buildings of the period. Be advised that the diaries sometimes record adult situations and themes.

## Assessment

Turn to page 130 for a multiple-choice test on the selection.

*Test Answers*

**1.** b  **2.** b  **3.** b  **4.** a  **5.** c
**6.** d  **7.** a  **8.** d  **9.** c  **10.** b

The following criteria can help you evaluate each student's success in completing the activities prompted by the Cross-Curricular Activities feature in the student textbook.

**\*Note:** Activities marked with an asterisk allow the involvement of more than one student. For these activities you may wish first to evaluate each student on his or her individual contribution and then to give groups an overall rating.

## History/Art
### Mongolian Graffiti
- The student conducts research on how the Mongols would have depicted themselves, Genghis Khan, or the Chinese emperor.
- The student creates two or three examples of Mongolian art that might have appeared on the Great Wall.
- The student's illustrations are appropriate.
- The student presents the mural to the class, clearly explaining how it reflects ideas or information from research sources.

## Language Arts/Science
### Try It—You'll Like It!
- The student conducts research on a Chinese invention or discovery, such as paper, acupuncture, or row planting.
- The student designs a brochure with pictures and an explanation of how the invention works, how it will make life different, and why Chinese citizens should try it.
- The writing is relatively free of errors in spelling, grammar, usage, and mechanics.

## \*Health/Drama
### Medicine in the Empire
- The student researches medieval Chinese medical treatments and medicines.
- In pairs, students role-play the parts of a doctor and patient in an original dialogue based on the research.

- As performed, the dialogue effectively conveys a diagnosis and treatment for a common ailment, such as a broken leg, a cold, or an infected finger.

## \*Science/Media
### Get Out Your Papers
- The student researches the materials and equipment used to make paper today.
- The student videotapes a demonstration of the steps, showing how raw materials become a finished product.
- The demonstration might show someone making paper or explaining the industrial papermaking process.
- The videotape is relatively free of technical errors.

## Science/Art
### Smooth as Silk
- The student conducts research on the life cycle of the silkworm.
- The student creates a "how-to" manual on raising silkworms, with drawings and time lines of each stage of the cycle and details on how the silk is subsequently unwound from the cocoon and spun into thread.
- The writing is relatively free of errors in spelling, grammar, usage, and mechanics; illustrations are neat and clear.

## Art/Mathematics
### The Empress's New Clothes
- The student researches designs for tenth- and eleventh-century Japanese kimonos.
- The student creates a colorful pattern for a kimono, including measurements for the parts of the garment.
- The student draws and colors the design on graph paper.

## CHAPTER 4

# The Making of the Middle Ages
## Europe and Japan A.D. 500–1500

---

### *from* Viking Luck

from *Accidental Explorers*
by REBECCA STEFOFF
*(student text page 103)*

**CONTENT-AREA CONNECTIONS**

GEOGRAPHY •
HISTORY •

---

**Reading Level:** Average

### Text Summary

With the help of bad weather and good luck, Viking sailors sighted the North American continent. Without the help of maps or advanced technology, the Vikings returned to the area and set up a colony, probably on Newfoundland. The Vikings' luck did not hold, however, and the Norse colonists failed to establish a permanent settlement.

## BEFORE READING

### Make the Connection

Ask students to recall a trip, an experiment, or a cooking or building project that did not go quite as they originally planned. Ask students what they found out when they took a wrong turn, did not follow directions exactly, or added a wrong ingredient. Have students brainstorm about the ways in which explorers and scientists can learn from their mistakes.

### Build Background
▪ More About the Topic

In their highly efficient longships, the Vikings sailed large expanses of the North Atlantic, navigating with simple techniques—for example, steering by the sun and stars, and noting the birds and whales that signaled the position of land. From the eighth to the eleventh centuries, Norsemen raided cities from Paris to Baghdad, from Dublin to Constantinople. The Vikings made such an impact on the areas where they traded and plundered that the place names still conjure up memories of the Vikings: The Slavic

peoples called the Vikings *Rus*—a name that eventually was given to the country of Russia.

### Vocabulary Development

The following words are underscored and defined in the student text.

**dispose:** distribute or transfer; sell.
**exploited:** made use of; used to advantage.
**sojourn:** visit; temporary stay.
**ancestry:** line of family members.
**receded:** became fainter or more distant.

Before assigning the reading, you may want to introduce students to any words that could cause pronunciation or definition problems.

---

### *Vocabulary Tip*

**Discovering Words with Multiple Meanings**
Have students discuss the multiple meanings of the content-area vocabulary words. The selection describes how Vikings *settled* the area of Vinland. Students may more often use *settled* in the context of "settling a disagreement"; they probably do not use the noun *settle*, referring to a type of bench, but they will find that meaning when they look at dictionary definitions of the content-area vocabulary. Have them discuss the many listings they find for these common words. Discuss with students how they regularly use context to determine which of a word's meanings makes sense.

---

Although the following words are important to an understanding of the text selection, some of them may be unfamiliar to students. Present this list of words and the definitions to students. Encourage them to discuss other meanings they know for these words.

**course\***: the path followed by a ship or plane.
**settle\***: to make a permanent home.
**touch\***: being in communication; having contact with.

\*Although students may be familiar with other meanings of these words, the words as used in the selection have a specific meaning that pertains to the content area.

## Reading Informational Material

### Reading Skill
#### Making Generalizations

Explain to students that generalizations are broad ideas or principles based on the specific information we gather. To form a generalization, readers examine textual clues, combine them with what they already know about a topic, and then infer an explanation about the situation explained in the text.

▶ **Teaching Tip**
*Previewing Illustrations* You may help students build background by having them preview the illustrations in the selection, by having them view videos, or by providing them with additional illustrations of Viking relics.

### Reading Strategy
#### Activating and Using Prior Knowledge (Strategy 8)

To help students activate their knowledge of Vikings and make generalizations about exploration, use Strategy 8 in Content-Area Reading Strategies. Provide students with a KWL Chart (Graphic Organizer 6), and ask them to fill in the first two columns now. Tell students they will be filling out the last column when they have finished reading the selection.

# DURING READING

## Using the Side-Margin Feature
- No Wonder Vikings Were Scary

Have students read the feature about Vikings and the St. Cuthbert monastery. Then ask them to describe a stereotype of the Vikings, such as the one that appears in cartoons or comic strips. [In cartoons, Vikings are usually bearded and often wear horned helmets on their heads. They may be portrayed as savage or ruthless.] How does the information about Viking farming and government challenge the stereotype of "savage" Norsemen? [Information about the Vikings' government and agricultural practices gives a more balanced view of Viking life and culture.]

## Viewing the Art
- The Viking Longship

You may wish to refer students to text page 104 and the illustration of a Viking longship. Have students discuss reasons Vikings might have decorated ships with shields, colorful flags and sails, and carved animals. [Vikings might have wanted to impress or frighten the people they encountered.] What might the longships' decorations reveal about the Vikings' strategy? [Students might conclude that the decorations indicate that Vikings did not want to hide from the people they attacked. They must have attacked boldly in battle.]

## Differentiating Instruction
- Learners Having Difficulty

Students may need help visualizing the Vikings' westward progression. Provide students with maps of the North Atlantic Ocean, and have students locate the place names mentioned in the selection: Norway, Iceland, Greenland, and Newfoundland. Have students take notes on the maps or on plastic overlays on the maps indicating which Vikings arrived in these places and when they landed.

# AFTER READING

## ✓ Reading Check

The following are sample answers to the questions on student text page 107.

1. The flat, wooded land that Bjarni Herjolfsson saw did not match the descriptions he had heard of Greenland.

2. Reports of someone seeing an area with trees would have interested people in Greenland because there was a shortage of wood in that area.

**3.** Leif Eriksson and his thirty-five men were the first Europeans in North America.

**4.** The Viking colonists fought with the native inhabitants of North America; they also fought among themselves.

**5.** Vinland was remembered because people in Iceland, England, and northern Europe continued to tell stories about it.

## Reteaching

Help students make generalizations with the following technique. Have students fold a piece of paper to create five columns and label the respective columns: *Question, Text's Answer, My Take, This Suggests, I Conclude.*

In the first column have students write a question that you provide to prompt a response about the selection. [For example, *Why would Vikings have wanted to make dangerous explorations from the settlement on Greenland?*] In the *Text's Answer* column, have students write what the selection says about the subject. [The selection says that people in Greenland never had enough wood.] In the *My Take* column, have students write their personal interpretation of the text's information. [If Greenland didn't have enough wood, the people might have cut down most of the existing trees. The island may have been crowded. Plus, the map shows that Greenland is close to the Arctic Circle, and trees may not grow well there.] In the *This Suggests* column, have students make an inference. [The Vikings must have moved to Greenland and cut down all the trees for housing and fuel. Because Greenland is so cold, they needed to burn a lot of trees to keep warm, and trees probably don't grow in the northernmost part of the island.]

When students have completed the chart, have them use the *I Conclude* column to form a generalization statement. [Because Greenland's harsh climate provided few resources, Vikings were always on the lookout for areas with sources of fuel and building materials.] If students need more practice forming generalizations, provide more questions for them to work with and have them repeat the process. Have them share the information from their charts in a class discussion.

▶ **Teaching Tip**

*Literature Connection* Introduce students to a Norse saga, such as the Erik the Red saga men-

tioned in the selection. Discuss with students how this type of Old Norse literature, which could be either prose or poetry, recorded biographical and historical information in ancient times.

## Connecting to Language Arts
▪ Writing

*Newsletter from Vinland* Have each participating student contribute to a newsletter for the Vinland colony, *The Vinland Chronicle.* Students can report on the colony's activities, including illnesses, the building and repair of houses, the birth of children, the Vikings' relations with the inhabitants of North America, and so forth. Ask volunteers to illustrate the newsletter with drawings.

## Connecting Across the Curriculum: Archaeology

*Digging Up the Facts* Have students learn more about what artifacts can reveal about Viking culture. Ask students to find out what digs have taught archaeologists about Viking boats or villages. Students can share an illustration of a particular artifact with the class, reporting on where it was found and how it was used during the Vikings' time.

## Further Resources
Online Resource

The PBS Web site, NOVA "The Vikings," provides information about Viking ships, gives a virtual tour of a Viking village, and maps the range of the warriors' travel. The site also includes teacher resources for class projects.

Video

*Nova—The Vikings.* WGBH Pubns., 2000, Not Rated.

*Secrets of the Dead— The Lost Vikings* (vol. 2). PBS Home Video, 2000, Not Rated.

### ( Assessment )

Turn to page 131 for a multiple-choice test on the selection.

*Test Answers*

**1.** d   **2.** b   **3.** c   **4.** d   **5.** a
**6.** c   **7.** b   **8.** d   **9.** b   **10.** b

# *from* Plague

from *Invisible Enemies: Stories of Infectious Disease*
by JEANETTE FARRELL
*(student text page 108)*

**Reading Level:** Above Average

## Text Summary

In the fourteenth century, a deadly disease moved west from Asia to Europe. Spread primarily by flea-infested rats, the bubonic plague moved along trade and shipping routes. Only one quarter to one half of the people who contracted the disease would survive. The deaths of such a large percentage of the population greatly disrupted the society of the Middle Ages, causing people to wonder if the plague would stop or whether the end of the world had arrived.

# BEFORE READING

## Make the Connection

Divide the class into two groups, either by having students count off or by separating the group down the middle of the room. Now ask students to imagine that one half of the class is suddenly gone. How will that loss affect the rest of the group? Who will take care of the responsibilities of the people who have left without warning? Have students discuss the deaths experienced by people of the Middle Ages, and how they could have coped with such enormous losses.

## Build Background

■ More About the Topic

The plague that struck Britain, beginning in 1348, respected no class distinctions. Archbishops, nobles, the Duke of Lancaster, and even one of the daughters of King Edward III died from the disease. Rural peasants, however, suffered the highest mortality rate, and their deaths greatly affected the upper classes. Medieval accounts repeatedly note that peasants' rents are unpaid *defectus causa pestilencie*, that is, "because of the plague." The great reduction in the population gave workers an enormous bargaining chip, allowing ordinary peasants to demand higher wages and to choose where they would work.

## Vocabulary Development

The following words are underscored and defined in the student text.

**stench:** foul odor; stink.

**calamities:** great misfortunes; disasters.

**stupefied:** stunned; astounded.

**chaos:** disorder; confusion.

**appeased:** satisfied or calmed; bought off.

**quarantined:** isolated from human contact for a required period of time to prevent spread of disease.

**epidemic:** rapid spread of contagious disease.

**disperses:** spreads widely.

**toxin:** poison.

**inexplicable:** not easily explained.

Before assigning the reading, you may want to introduce students to any words that could cause pronunciation or definition problems.

## *Vocabulary Tip*

**Noting Etymology** Two important words in this selection have their roots in numbers. *Quarantine* comes from the Italian *quarantina*, which means "a space of 40 days." People in port cities once believed that they could protect themselves from catching any diseases that might be aboard an arriving ship by isolating the ship for *quaranta*, or 40, days. Only after that time were the people and goods aboard ship allowed to enter the city. *Decimate* is based on the Latin word for 10, *decem*. Today, the word can mean "wide-scale destruction" or "killing a great number of." In Roman times, however, the word was much more specific. It meant "killing every tenth person." When a legion of the Roman army rebelled, the group was *decimated*, that is, punished by the death of one tenth of its soldiers.

## Vocabulary Tip

**Using Word Parts** Have students look at the prefixes and roots of the content-area vocabulary to help figure out the words' meanings. To find the meanings of *beneficial* and *multitudes*, ask students to think of other words that use the prefix *bene– (well)* [benefit, benediction, benefactor] or *multi– (many)* [multiply, multi-purpose]. Then have students look up the meanings of these Latin prefixes and roots and find other words containing these word parts. You may want to have students keep their lists and continue adding Latin word parts as they encounter them in other selections.

### CONTENT-AREA VOCABULARY

Although the following words are important to an understanding of the text selection, some of them may be unfamiliar to students. Present this list of words and the definitions to students. Encourage students to discuss other meanings they know for these words.

**beneficial:** positive; to one's advantage.
**mortality\*:** death in great numbers.
**multitudes:** great numbers.

\*Although students may be familiar with other meanings of this word, the word as used in the selection has a specific meaning that pertains to the content area.

### Reading Informational Material

#### Reading Skill
Identifying Text Structure: Cause and Effect
Explain to students that a cause makes something happen and that an effect results from that cause. Writers often state both cause and effect in their writing. Sometimes, however, they may omit part of the information, leaving the readers to use their own knowledge to infer a cause or an effect.

▶ **Teaching Tip**
*Creating Sub-headings* Have students divide the selection into shorter sections and create additional headings for each section. For example, the first six paragraphs might be headed "From Asia to Europe." The next three paragraphs might be headed "Death and Social Disorder." Have students work

their way through the entire selection, writing brief summary headings as they go.

### Reading Strategy
Understanding Text (Strategy 2)
To help students find the relationship between causes and effects in the selection, use Strategy 2 in Content-Area Reading Strategies. You may wish to provide students with a Cause-and-Effect Chart (Graphic Organizer 2) to help them organize their ideas about how certain events lead to other events. Emphasize to students that some effects are the result of many causes. Tell students that they may illustrate a chain of events by linking their cause-and-effect charts.

## DURING READING

### Using the Side-Margin Feature
▪ "Ring Around the Rosey"
After students have read the feature about the plague and nursery rhymes, ask them why they think such a frightening image could have been turned into a children's game. [By acting out effects of the Black Death in a game, children and others could poke fun at the disease and perhaps make the plague seem less frightening.]

### Viewing the Art
▪ The Dreadful Plague
You may wish to refer students to the illustration on page 110. Discuss with students how such a deadly epidemic could change people's views of themselves and their world order. [The loss of so many people could make the survivors feel vulnerable and threatened. The plague might have leveled the social classes, because no one was too rich or too poor to contract the disease.]

### Differentiating Instruction
▪ Learners Having Difficulty
Students may have difficulty keeping track of ideas because of the selection's length. Have students create a concept map as they read to help them focus on important points. The map can note the selection's boldfaced headings as well as key words and phrases from each paragraph, such as "Florence, 1348," or "begins in Mongolia, 1330."

■ **English-Language Learners**

English-language learners may need assistance with the many medical and scientific terms used in the selection: *buboes, bacilli, toxin, lymph, sputum, pneumonic.* Have English-language learners make lists of unfamiliar medical words and then work in pairs with native speakers to find context clues relating to them and to look at dictionary definitions for clarification.

# AFTER READING

## ✔ Reading Check

The following are sample answers to the questions on student text page 115.

1. Sufferers of the Black Death experienced painful lumps in their groins or armpits, black splotches on their skin, and a horrible smell from their sweat and urine. They could die within a day of contracting the disease.

2. During the Middle Ages, people also faced starvation, unsafe living conditions, and the constant fear of robbers.

3. The plague lives in fleas, which in turn live on rats. Fleas carry the disease from animal to person.

4. The plague seems to have come from the burrows of wild rodents that lived in the mountainous area near China, India, and Burma.

5. The plague spreads through the body's lymphatic system. It collects in the lymph nodes, the lymph's filtering centers.

## Reteaching

Help students identify causes and effects by having them make a list of statements: either *Look What They (It) Did!* (causes) or *See What Happened!* (effects). Divide the class into two groups. Have each group read through the text finding information to create one of the statements. [*Look What They (It) Did!* Rats ran off ships at harbor cities; *See What Happened:* Rats spread the plague to the port of Messina.] After the groups have completed their lists, copy the lists on an overhead transparency. Then see how many of the statements can

be logically combined into a sentence using the word *because* before the cause statement. [*Because* rats ran off ships at harbor cities, the plague spread to the port of Messina.] When statements can be combined, have students draw lines connecting them. If any of the cause or effect statements cannot be completed, have students revise the statements or look in the text again for further information.

## Connecting to Language Arts
■ **Writing**

*Dramatic Monologue* The rats of the Middle Ages experienced an epidemic, just as the humans did. Have students write dramatic monologues that give a rat's perspective of the bubonic plague. Student monologues should trace the rat's activities as the rat boards the ship, travels with cargo, or moves from house to house. Have students perform their monologues, compile them into a booklet, or post them on a class Web page.

## Connecting Across the Curriculum: Health/Science

*Fighting Epidemics* How do officials contend with epidemics in modern times? Have students find out more about how doctors have dealt with communicable diseases such as smallpox, tuberculosis, the Spanish Flu outbreak of 1918, or AIDS. Have student groups research a particular disease and present reports on how much public health guidelines and sanitation practices have or have not changed since the time of the Black Death.

## Further Resources
Online

The Discovery Channel has a Web site in its *Time Travel* section on "The Black Death." The site has information about the fourteenth century's bubonic plague, including an interactive map and audio clips.

The Web site for the Museum of Medicine and Health has links to other sites about the plague.

## Assessment

Turn to page 132 for a multiple-choice test on the selection.

*Test Answers*
**1.** b  **2.** c  **3.** a  **4.** d  **5.** c
**6.** a  **7.** b  **8.** a  **9.** a  **10.** b
**11.** a  **12.** b  **13.** b  **14.** b  **15.** a

# Brother Sun . . . Sister Moon

*from Brother Sun, Sister Moon:*
*The Life and Stories of St. Francis*
by MARGARET MAYO
*(student text page 116)*

**Reading Level:** Average

## Text Summary

At the end of his life, St. Francis of Assisi, a thirteenth-century Italian monk, composed a song praising the beauties of nature. The canticle, or praise song, "Brother Sun . . . Sister Moon" encourages people to give thanks to God for the Earth's creations.

# BEFORE READING

## Make the Connection

Ask students to describe the last time they admired a work of nature, for example, by watching a beautiful sunset or by gazing at blooming flowers. Have students explain why they stopped to examine this natural beauty, and have them describe how the experience of viewing it made them feel.

## Build Background

- **More About the Author**

The scene was dramatic. Francesco di Pietro di Bernadone, the son of a rich cloth merchant, was accused of selling his father's goods without permission and giving the money to the poor. In front of his father and a church bishop, the young man removed all his clothes and returned them to his father. With this gesture, the young man gave up all his material goods and family ties and lived among his followers. These followers of St. Francis became called the Gray Friars because their habits, or robes, were made of inexpensive cloth that had not been dyed. St. Francis's own simple gray habit is displayed at his basilica in Assisi.

## Vocabulary Development

The following words are underscored and defined in the student text.

**nourish:** feed; support or help develop.
**humility:** lacking pride; the quality of being humble.

Before assigning the reading, you may want to introduce students to any words that could cause pronunciation or definition problems.

## Vocabulary Tip

**Considering Etymology** Two of St. Francis's words for expressing joy have their roots in words for money. Both *precious* and *praise* come from the same Latin word—*pretium*, or "price." Have students discuss the connection between our words for "approval" and "beloved" and the connotation of money.

### CONTENT-AREA VOCABULARY

Although the following words are important to an understanding of the text selection, some of them may be unfamiliar to students. Present this list of words and the definitions to students. Encourage students to discuss other meanings they know for these words.

**precious\*:** valuable; treasured.
**joyful:** showing extreme happiness.
**praise\*:** to admire; to worship.

\*Although students may be familiar with other meanings of these words, the words as used in the selection have a specific meaning that pertains to the content area.

### Reading Informational Material

## Reading Skill
### Identifying Author's Purpose

Authors may write a text in order to entertain, to inform, to persuade, or to move readers' emotions. Identifying the author's purpose helps readers approach and evaluate a text more appropriately.

## Reading Strategy
### Previewing Text (Strategy 1)

To help students familiarize themselves with the poem's format and begin thinking about the author's purpose, use Strategy 1 in Content-Area

Reading Strategies. To use the PIC strategy, provide students with a KWL organizer (Graphic Organizer 6). Since the poem illustrates the author's spiritual beliefs, emphasize to students that previewing the selection's biographical materials will put the poem in context.

▶ **Teaching Tip**
*Combining Music and Poetry* Help students appreciate St. Francis's "praise song" by allowing them to hear it sung. Bring in recordings of "Brother Sun" or other canticles by the saint to share with students, showing them how music contributes to the poetry's message of praise and thanks.

# DURING READING

## Differentiating Instruction
■ **Learners Having Difficulty**
The poem's repetition may be confusing to some students. Have students work in pairs to recite the poem aloud, exploring how certain repeated words can receive different emphasis (*praise*, for example).

■ **English-Language Learners**
Some English-language learners may need clarification about the purpose of "Brother Sun . . . Sister Moon." Explain that the poem is a prayer of praise and, as a *canticle*, it was intended to be sung. Ask students to describe similar songs from their own traditions and to share them if possible.

# AFTER READING

 **Reading Check**

The following are sample answers to the questions on student text page 117.

**1.** St. Francis praises things found in the natural world, which he describes as God's creations.

**2.** Francis's song asks people to be thankful for nature's works and to serve God.

## Reteaching
If students have difficulty identifying the author's purpose, brainstorm with them to develop examples of words and phrases that would be used to inform (facts or details), to persuade (ideas that

help sway your opinion), to entertain (humorous, moving, or exciting examples), and to describe (sensory details). In addition, you may focus on verbs in which the author encourages action [praise, bless, thank, serve], having students analyze how these actions indicate the author's purpose.

List students' examples on the board. Then, have students analyze a short section of the poem and determine what words in the selection indicate the author's purpose. You may want to provide students with a Cluster Diagram (Graphic Organizer 3) to help them organize their examples of informative, persuasive, entertaining, or descriptive words and phrases. Have students discuss their examples and then determine the author's purpose.

## Connecting to Language Arts
■ **Writing**
*Poem* "Brother Sun . . . Sister Moon" describes the beauties of medieval Italy. Have students write a poem praising the beauties of a contemporary setting. They might want to praise the excitement of an urban street or the wonder of technology that makes their homework easier. Have them model their poems on St. Francis's simple style and language, and invite students to read their finished poems aloud to the class.

■ **Speaking and Listening**
*Interview with the Author* Imagine that St. Francis's book has been selected by a television book club. Have students find out more about St. Francis's life and then work in groups to plan an interview with the author. One student can portray a television host who can ask Francis questions about his life and how he came to write his beautiful poem. Another student can play the role of Francis and explain the meaning of his poem. Members of the television audience can ask additional questions and offer their own readings of the poem. The groups may want to videotape their performance and replay their "television" interview.

## Connecting Across the Curriculum: Art
*Portrayals of St. Francis* Have students find out how artists perceived and depicted St. Francis. Many portraits of the saint can be found at his basilica in Assisi, and students may want to learn more about that famous church. Have students find pictures of statues or paintings in art books or

on the World Wide Web, and have students select one representation of the saint to share with the class. Students should explain what aspect of his life is portrayed and give a short description of its artist.

## Further Resource
### Online
The Franciscan site offers a virtual tour of Assisi, St. Francis's hometown. The tour includes a stroll through the city, as well as a visit to the Basilica of St. Francis. The site also offers a short biography of the Italian saint and a complete translation of his "Canticle of Creatures" (Brother Son . . . Sister Moon) in both English and Latin.

## Assessment

Turn to page 133 for a multiple-choice test on the selection.

*Test Answers*

**1.** d  **2.** b  **3.** b  **4.** a  **5.** c
**6.** d  **7.** c

# Anna Comnena

from *Outrageous Women of the Middle Ages*
by VICKI LEÓN
*(student text page 118)*

**Reading Level:** Average

## Special Considerations

The text refers to Muslims as "infidels" and discusses how Jerusalem must be taken back by the Christians. Discuss with students the tensions between Muslim and Christian religions in this geographic area, and emphasize that Muslims experienced the "holy wars" as a time of brutal invasion.

## Text Summary

The educated daughter of Emperor Alexius was for a short time intended to rule the Byzantine throne. When her fortunes were reversed, Anna Comnena turned her talents toward recording the historic events she witnessed during her lifetime. Her history, *The Alexiad*, describes the effect of the Crusades on Constantinople and the Byzantine Empire's response to crusaders from the West.

# BEFORE READING

## Make the Connection

Ask students if they have ever wanted to write down memorable events in their lives—for example, meeting an important person, visiting a notable site, or experiencing a flood or tornado. Have students discuss why people would write their memoirs and what purpose such writing would serve. [Memoirs could help the writer remember events clearly, even after much time has gone by. Memoirs can serve historical purposes by recording events that future generations may want to study.]

## Build Background

■ More About the Topic

The Emperor Alexius helped start the Crusades by asking the Pope in Rome for help in defending his empire from the invading Turks (the Infidels, or non-Christians). When the crusaders arrived, however, their help was offset by their own looting and destruction of Byzantine riches. Anna Comnena observed that the crusaders, or Franks, were always looking for money, and that they seemed to abandon their agreements at the least provocation. She also cites the bad manners of a crusading prince, perhaps Count Robert of Paris, who had the impudence to sit on Emperor Alexius's throne. In 1204, after Anna's death, crusaders sacked Constantinople, the very city they had been asked to defend.

## Vocabulary Development

The following words are underscored and defined in the student text.

**penance:** an act of devotion done to show sorrow for a wrongdoing.
**fanatic:** extremely devoted to a cause.
**destitute:** poor; lacking basic necessities.
**formidable:** impressive; awe-inspiring.
**momentous:** important; significant.

Before assigning the reading, you may want to introduce students to any words that could cause pronunciation or definition problems.

---

### Vocabulary Tip

**Brainstorming Connotations** Before introducing the content-area vocabulary, ask students to brainstorm about the meaning of the word *eyewitness*. Students may think of *eyewitness* in relation to a crime or an accident. Explain that in this selection, Anna Comnena is an *eyewitness* to historic events.

---

### CONTENT-AREA VOCABULARY

Although the following words are important to an understanding of the text selection, some of them may be unfamiliar to students. Present this list of words and the definitions to your students. Have students brainstorm any connection between the words. Students might try putting the three words into one sentence.

**eyewitness:** a person who reports on what he or she has seen.

**document\***: to provide with supporting information; to back up.

**keen-eyed**: perceptive; able to see sharply or sensitively.

[The reports **document** the details of the accident in the words of a **keen-eyed eyewitness**.]

\*Although students may be familiar with other meanings of this word, the word as used in the selection has a specific meaning that pertains to the content area.

## ( Reading Informational Material )

### Reading Skill
Finding the Main Idea

Explain to students that the main idea is the topic, and the author's primary message, developed in an article or in a section of an article. Sometimes this idea is stated directly; other times it is implied through important details.

▶ **Teaching Tip**
*Creating Visuals* Have students create visuals to help organize their information about Anna Comnena. A family tree can help them see relationships among the people named in the story. Students also can compare important events in Anna's life with events of the First Crusade by plotting the events on a time line.

### Reading Strategy
Building Background Information (Strategy 6)

To help students gain information they will need when reading about Constantinople and the Crusades, use Strategy 6 in Content-Area Reading Strategies. To complete the Prediction and Confirming Activity, have students use the PACA organizer (Graphic Organizer 8).

## DURING READING

### Using the Side-Margin Feature
■ "Lightning from Heaven"

*A Medieval Secret Weapon* After students have read the feature about Greek fire, ask them to brainstorm and identify other "secret weapons" that have been used in both real and legendary warfare. What makes a "secret weapon" so effective? [Students may cite the Trojan horse, poison gases of World War I, or the atomic bomb. A "secret weapon" often depends upon surprising the enemy before it can prepare for an attack. The "secret weapon" also may depend upon superior technology that the enemy cannot neutralize.]

### Viewing the Art
■ Illustrations of Crusaders

You may wish to refer students to text pages 119 and 121 for the illustrations of crusaders on the way to the Holy Land. Refer students to the selection "Getting Dressed" (page 131) and have them compare the crusaders' armor they can see in these illustrations to the parts visible in the suit of armor on page 131.

### Differentiating Instruction
■ Learners Having Difficulty

Students may have difficulty keeping track of the many people named in this long selection. As students read, have them jot down historic characters' names and briefly note an important fact about each person. When students have finished listing the people in the selection, they can draw lines connecting those historical figures that have important relationships.

■ English-Language Learners

English-language learners may need assistance with the many terms that relate to Christianity and the Crusades. Have them work together in groups with native speakers to list these terms. [pilgrimages, crusaders, infidels, papal, monk] If the meanings are not explained within the selection's context, have native speakers explain a dictionary definition.

## AFTER READING

## ( ✔ Reading Check )

The following are sample answers to the questions on student text page 123.

1. The First Crusade began on August 15, 1096. Emperor Alexius asked the pope to send troops to drive the non-Christian peoples from Christianity's holy places.

2. Anna and her family thought the "Franks" were barely civilized; in addition, the emperor was disappointed to have received untrained peasants instead of trained soldiers.

3. Anna observed that the crusaders included both soldiers and civilians; in addition, she saw that women and children made the journey to Constantinople.

4. Anna received an excellent education and followed the teachings of Galen, an important physician.

5. At age eight, she became engaged to a boy who was to inherit the Byzantine throne. However, her brother was named as heir and her engagement was broken off. When Anna was sent into exile, she began to write an important history of her father and the Crusades.

## Reteaching

If students have difficulty stating the selection's main idea, have them write key words in a Cluster Diagram (Graphic Organizer 3 and Strategy 3). Have students group clusters of related words and use one or two of the words to build sentences about the selection. [For example: **Crusaders** arrived in **Constantinople**.] Then, students can add words from other clusters to the original sentence. [**Anna Comnena** wrote a **history** of the **Crusaders'** arrival in **Constantinople**.} After students have built several sentences using key words, have them discuss how the different sentences reflect the text's main idea.

## Connecting to Language Arts

### ▪ Writing

***Writing a Marriage Proposal*** Ask students to consider the difficult position of Nicephorus Bryennius and to write a marriage proposal to the unwilling Anna Comnena. Tell students to write a letter that acknowledges Anna's predicament, as well as that of the potential groom's, and tries to persuade the Byzantine princess to marry the man who is everyone's second choice.

### ▪ Speaking and Listening

***Mock Hearing*** The residents of Constantinople have had enough of the lawless crusaders. Ask students to stage a hearing before a Constantinople justice of the peace in which Byzantine citizens complain about the actions of their western "guests." Tell them to give the accused crusader an opportunity to respond to the charge, and then have a judge rule on the case and, if necessary,

impose a punishment. Students may perform their case before the rest of the class; the audience also may serve as a jury.

## Connecting Across the Curriculum: Geography

***Constantinople: Gateway to the Holy Land*** Have students investigate the geography of the Crusades to see why Constantinople was the gateway to the Holy Land for western crusaders. Ask students to find maps of medieval Europe and Asia and chart the route of the First Crusade from the West to Jerusalem. Have students annotate their maps, noting other cities on the route and physical features that would have created problems for the crusaders. Post the completed maps to share with the class.

## Further Resources

### Online

The Medieval Sourcebook, sponsored by Fordham University, offers a complete translation of *The Alexiad.*

### Assessment

Turn to page 134 for a multiple-choice test on the selection.

***Test Answers***
**1.** b  **2.** a  **3.** c  **4.** d  **5.** a
**6.** b  **7.** a  **8.** d  **9.** b  **10.** c

# The Children's Crusade

from *Renaissance*
by CRISTINA PELAYO
*(student text page 124)*

**Reading Level:** Average

## Text Summary

Medieval religious enthusiasm affected many European children in a tragic way. In the thirteenth century, two youthful leaders—one in Germany and one in France—convinced thousands of young people to undertake a crusade to the Holy Land. Few, if any, of the children reached Jerusalem. Many died from exposure or drowned at sea. Thousands more may have been sold into slavery.

# BEFORE READING

## Make the Connection

Ask students if they have ever been caught up in a cause—either a march, a protest, or a celebration—that involved many other people. Have them discuss the experience of being involved with many people who believe strongly in an idea. [Students may say that a large group of people creates a great deal of energy and enthusiasm.]

## Build Background

■ More About the Topic

The Children's Crusade arose in part from European shame over the dreadful Fourth Crusade, begun by Pope Innocent III in 1202. Crusaders agreed to pay the city of Venice for their transportation to the Holy Land. At the end of their journey, however, they had no money. The Venetians proposed that crusaders attack Zara, a rival city located in present-day Croatia, and pay their debt with the spoils. The sack of Zara in 1202, the first attack on a Christian city, set a precedent, and the crusading army subsequently looted Constantinople, the Byzantine capital, in 1203. Westerners were horrified at the attack on this venerable Christian city. The innocent appeals of the Children's Crusade must have seemed like a perfect answer to their elders' greed and savagery.

## Vocabulary Development

The following words are underscored and defined in the student's text.

**zeal:** enthusiasm; eagerness.
**redeem:** take back; restore.
**deplored:** disapproved of; regretted.
**impressionable:** easily influenced.
**horde:** traveling crowd; large throng.

Before assigning the reading, you may want to introduce students to any words that could cause pronunciation or definition problems.

┌─ *Vocabulary Tip* ─────────────┐

**Considering Etymology** The word *sinister*, with its threatening connotations, comes from the Latin word meaning "on the left side." Ancient Greek prophets thought that east, the direction of the rising sun, was lucky, while the direction of the setting sun was unlucky. As religious officials faced north during their rituals, any signs that appeared to the west, their left side, were considered unlucky. The source of bad news, to the Greeks, was always the *sinister* side.

**Using Context Clues** Have students examine the selection to find context clues for the meanings of the content-area vocabulary words. For example, the sentence (on page 125) stating that the route is *treacherous* also includes the word *difficult*. The paragraph later states that children traveling on the route were exhausted. How does this information provide clues about the definition of *treacherous*? In addition, have students check to see whether the vocabulary words are similar to other, more familiar words [treachery, reputation].

└────────────────────────────┘

─────( **CONTENT-AREA VOCABULARY** )─────

Although the following words are important to an understanding of the text selection, some of them may be unfamiliar to students.

**treacherous:** not to be trusted.

**disreputable:** having a bad reputation; lacking in character.

**sinister:** suggesting trouble; threatening or menacing.

Present this list of words and the definitions to your students.

## Reading Informational Material

### Reading Skill
#### Summarizing
Discuss with students how a summary gets to the heart of a text: It restates the main events and ideas of a piece of writing in only a few words. Tell students that summarizing can help them understand and remember what they read.

#### ▶ Teaching Tip
*Using Plural Terms* Students may want to know why the selection refers to the Crusades, a plural term. Tell them that there were many military expeditions during the Middle Ages, and historians generally divided the Crusades into eight different campaigns, referring to them as the First Crusade, the Second Crusade, and so on.

### Reading Strategy
#### Constructing Concept Maps (Strategy 4)
To help students focus on the most important parts of the Children's Crusade selection, use Strategy 4 in Content-Area Reading Strategies. You may want to have students draw their own concept maps, or you may provide a Cluster Diagram or a Sequence or Chronological Order Chart (Graphic Organizers 3 and 10) that students can modify with lines or arrows to create a concept map. Model for students how they can take information for their maps from the text's headings and general structure.

## DURING READING

### Using the Side-Margin Feature
#### ▪ Sidelight
After students have read the Sidelight, have them think about what might have sparked the sudden departure of so many children. Ask them what incidents mentioned in the text might have contributed to the children's sense of mission and urgency. [The boys began to leave about Easter time, which is an important Christian holiday. The boys left their work for the crusade; they might have felt that a crusade would be more exciting than plowing or herding animals.]

### Viewing the Art
#### ▪ Child Crusaders
Refer students to the illustrations of child crusaders on pages 125 and 126. Have them compare these illustrations to one of adult knights and crusaders in "Getting Dressed" (page 131) or "Anna Comnena" (page 119). What contrasts do they see? [Knights and adult crusaders would have the money to travel with many helpers and quantities of supplies. They could travel on horseback, and their expensive armor would protect them. By contrast, the children would look poor and unprotected.]

### Differentiating Instruction
#### ▪ Learners Having Difficulty
Pair a student having difficulty reading with a more experienced reader. Have the students take turns reading short sections of the text aloud and discussing what they have read at the end of each section. Model for students the kinds of questions they could ask for clarification.

#### ▪ English-Language Learners
Model the unfamiliar place names found in the selection to build students' confidence about their pronunciation. [Jerusalem, Mainz, Marseilles, Venice, Alexandria, Algeria] If students' native languages are spoken in any of these areas, have students pronounce the place names as people living there would say them.

## AFTER READING

### ✔ Reading Check
The following are sample answers to the questions on student text page 127.

1. A German boy named Nicholas eventually convinced about 20,000 other children to travel to Jerusalem to defend the Holy Land.

2. When they reached Genoa, the children were refused passage to the Holy Land, so they had to give up their crusade. Many scattered across Italy; most disappeared.

3. Stephen said that he had a vision in which Christ ordered him to help the crusaders in the Holy Land.

4. The French king refused to approve of the young people's crusade, and he suggested that the crusaders return home.

5. The children who reached Marseilles might have been aboard ships that were sunk in a storm. They might have reached Alexandria and Algeria and have been sold as slaves.

## Reteaching

To help students summarize the selection, have them focus on a text by looking for its most important words. Have students review the text and write down six words they think are important to understanding its meaning. [children, crusade, Jerusalem, religion, slaves, tragic] Students should then write a brief explanation of each choice, describing why they think it should be included in the summary. Have students discuss their choices in pairs, narrowing their lists down to one word. Then, have students use this word to write a sentence or two summarizing the selection. [most important word: tragic. Thousands of young people in the Middle Ages were caught up in a religious crusade. Their crusade was **tragic** because most of the children were lost or killed, and they never returned home. You may want to have the entire class work together and vote on which words they think are most important. Be sure to have students explain the reasons for their answers, and emphasize that students' explanations are as important as the words they choose.

## Connecting to Language Arts

- Writing

*Have You Seen This Child?* With all those lost children, there were sure to be parents searching the countryside to find them. Have students create a Wanted poster such as a parent might have made to look for a lost child. The poster should describe the child's age and appearance and how he or she became part of the Children's Crusade. The poster also could offer suggestions about which direction the child went and where he or she might be found. Display the Wanted posters on the class bulletin board.

- Speaking and Listening

*Nicholas Wants You* What kind of arguments could have persuaded 30,000 children to leave their homes on a trip to Jerusalem? Ask students to work in groups to create a rousing speech of the sort Nicholas or Stephen might have made to European youth in the thirteenth century. Have students consider what types of promises or incentives would have been most persuasive to children, and how they might have countered any objections. Have one "Nicholas" and one "Stephen" character present their arguments to the class.

## Connecting Across the Curriculum: Geography

*Creating an Annotated Map* Have students learn more about the terrain and climate of Europe and the Holy Land. Then, ask them to create an annotated map that follows a route of the doomed Children's Crusade. The maps should mark the physical features, such as mountains, rivers, and seas, and note how those features would hamper the group's progress. The maps also could indicate how weather conditions could have affected the crusaders' progress. Have students calculate how many miles the children might have traveled before they reached their final destination, and then note that figure on their maps. Post maps of different routes for students to compare.

## Further Resources
### Online

The Manchester Medieval Sources Web site includes artwork, original documents, and maps illustrating the Crusades, as well as links to further information about the city of Jerusalem and important historical figures.

> ## Assessment
>
> Turn to page 135 for a multiple-choice test on the selection.
>
> *Test Answers*
> 1. c   2. d   3. b   4. a   5. d
> 6. c   7. b   8. a   9. a   10. d

# The Sword of the Samurai

from *Calliope*
by CAROLYN GARD
*(student text page 128)*

**Reading Level:** Average

## Text Summary

The sword of a samurai warrior was a deadly weapon—and also a piece of art. The swordsmith who created a samurai's sword as a valued artisan who had perfected the craft of forging a strong yet flexible blade. Swordmaking was an exacting, time-consuming process that was bound up with religious rituals.

## BEFORE READING

### Make the Connection

Ask students to think of a time when they watched a craftsperson—such as a potter, carpenter, or weaver—making a product. What did students notice about the craftsperson's work? What did his or her techniques or attitude reveal about the artist's approach to the art? [Students may say that the craftspeople were very familiar with their tools or that they seemed very relaxed as they worked. They may say that a craftsperson's attitude reveals that he or she is confident in the techniques needed to create a work of art.]

### Build Background

■ **More About the Topic**

Swords are an important part of Japanese mythology and culture and are thought to have lives of their own. Shinto tradition says that the storm god Susanoo discovered the first sword. Susanoo later gave his sword to his sister, the Sun Goddess. The Sun Goddess, in turn, gave the weapon to her grandson to allow him to reign on earth. This weapon was thought to be Japan's first sword.

### Vocabulary Development

The following words are underscored and defined in the student text.

**obedience:** willingness to obey authority.
**virtue:** honor; respectability.
**esteem:** favorable opinion; high regard.

**fasted:** ate very little or no food at all.
**purified:** made clean by special rituals or ceremonies.

Before assigning the reading, you may want to introduce students to any words that could cause pronunciation or definition problems.

## Vocabulary Tip

**Recognizing Specialized Language** The content-area vocabulary words describe the construction and special qualities of samurai swords. Discuss with students that certain trades, businesses, or sports may have a specialized language, or jargon, that applies to just one subject. Have students brainstorm to think of terms that have a special meaning when applied to a particular area. [Example: The words *dribble, screen,* and *foul* have special meanings to basketball players.]

### CONTENT-AREA VOCABULARY

Although the following words are important to an understanding of the text selection, some of them may be unfamiliar to students.

**welding:** uniting by heat or pressure; fusing together.
**tempered:** strengthened a substance by heating and cooling.
**flexible:** able to bend without damage.

Present this list of words and the definitions to your students.

### Reading Informational Material

**Reading Skill**
**Using Sequential Order**
Discuss with students that the selection describes the swordmaking process as a series of steps that must be done in a particular order. Explain the

importance of following directions in a sequence when constructing, cooking, or assembling items: If actions are not taken in proper order, the results may not be satisfactory.

## Reading Strategy
### Constructing Concept Maps (Strategy 4)
To help students understand the development of the text by examples, use Strategy 4 in Content-Area Reading Strategies. Have students create a concept map to show what examples are used to describe the armor. Some students may prefer to use a Cluster Diagram (Graphic Organizer 3) to show how descriptions support the main idea.

► **Teaching Tip**

*Discussing Status Items* In Japanese society, a samurai gained status from a well-made sword. Discuss with students how particular items illustrate status in different cultures. Ask them to give examples with which they are familiar. [Students may say that bicycles, televisions, or automobiles can be status symbols in the culture of the United States. In agricultural or nomadic cultures, horses, cattle, or camels may be signs of status.]

# DURING READING

## Using the Side-Margin Feature
- Samurai Goes Hollywood

After students have read the feature "Samurai Goes Hollywood" on text page 130, ask them to think about the connections between samurai culture and the culture represented in westerns. [Students may say that westerns often feature lone gunmen who try to save a town, or who fight for honor. They may say that honor is important in both cultures.] Have students think of examples of movies with strong heroes and ask them to describe how samurai fighters might portray them.

## Viewing the Art
- Samurai Armor

Refer students to the illustration of the samurai on page 129. Ask students to identify the basic parts of the samurai's armor. [helmet, sword, and protective coverings] Ask students to compare the samurai's armor with that of warriors in other cultures (for example, on text page 131). In what way is it similar or different? [Students may say that soldiers

in all cultures protect themselves in basic ways. Because available materials and technologies are different, these basic types of protection may look very different.]

## Differentiating Instruction
- **Learners Having Difficulty**

Discuss the text's organizational structure with students, explaining that only the section discussing swordmaking is written in sequential order. Have students review the opening and closing sections of the text, and have them explain how information in those sections is presented. [The opening and closing sections provide details and background about swords and swordmaking.]

- **English-Language Learners**

Some English-language learners may have difficulty understanding the words and concepts describing Japanese culture. Have students make a list of some of the Japanese terms mentioned in the selection and the side-margin features. [*katana* (long sword), *kaji* (swordsmith), *meijin* (master swordsmith), *daimyo* (lord)] Then, pair language learners with more proficient readers and have the pairs discuss how these words and their concepts are used in the selection.

# AFTER READING

## ✔ Reading Check

The following are sample answers to the questions on student text page 130.

1. A samurai slept with his sword under his pillow because he could not risk losing it. If he lost his sword, he would also lose his honor.

2. The swordsmith prayed, fasted, and purified himself before making a sword.

3. The swordsmith formed a blade by putting steel strips together, then repeatedly heating them, folding them over, and beating them together. The process created many layers of steel.

4. The swordsmith covered the sword in clay, then removed the clay from the sword's edge. The sword was then heated in a fire and put into

cold water. The quick change in temperatures made the edge hard; the area covered by clay cooled slowly and so remained soft.

5. Masamune's swords were thought to have power over their owners' enemies; in addition, Muramasa's swords were thought to cast evil spells.

## Reteaching

If students have difficulty understanding the selection's sequence, you may want to discuss with them some words commonly used to indicate the order in which events happen. Ask volunteers to perform simple tasks while describing what they are doing. [for example, tying a shoe, starting a videotape, writing an e-mail] Ask members of the class to listen for words they say when something happens, and to jot them down. As volunteers complete their tasks, compile a list of common sequence words on the chalkboard for students to use as a reference. [before, prior to, during, since, beginning, now, soon] Tell students that verb tenses also indicate the sequence of events and should be closely observed. Finally, have students scan the selection for words that indicate order or sequence. [started, again, repeated, after]

## Connecting to Language Arts

### ▪ Writing

***Samurai Sword Sale*** Have students create an illustrated advertisement for a well-made samurai sword, written as the swordmaker might have described it. The ad should describe the sword's appearance and the special techniques that went into its construction. In addition, it should note any special characteristics or powers that the sword might possess. Combine the ads to make a sword "catalog" for the class.

### ▪ Speaking and Listening

***A Two-Edged Sword?*** Ask students to conduct a debate that will decide once and for all whose swords are better: Muramasa's or Masamune's. Have students find out more information about these swordmakers and their works, and then ask the class to discuss the swords' different qualities and strengths. In addition, you may wish to ask volunteers to pose as the two famous craftsmen and explain their work to the class.

## Connecting Across the Curriculum: Art/History

***Choose Your Weapons*** Have students learn more about famous Japanese swords and swordmakers. Ask them to research samurai swords and find one weapon that is especially notable for its strength, age, or beauty. Then, have students create an illustrated fact sheet to present the most important information about the sword and the artist who made it. Post the fact sheets to let students compare the appearance and history of the different weapons.

## Further Resource

### Online

The Texas Humanities Resource Center includes images of samurai culture and armor, as well as games, lesson plans, and teaching resources.

## Assessment

Turn to page 136 for a multiple-choice test on the selection.

***Test Answers***

1. d   2. b   3. a   4. d   5. c
6. c   7. a   8. d   9. b   10. c

# Getting Dressed

from *Armor*
by CHARLOTTE AND DAVID YUE
*(student text page 131)*

**Reading Level:** Average

## Text Summary

Preparing for battle was a complicated process in the Middle Ages, requiring the work of many skilled craft workers. To protect themselves, knights wore heavy, intricately designed suits of metal that protected them from blows. Donning the armor was an art in itself and required careful attention to a number of detailed parts.

# BEFORE READING

## Make the Connection

Ask students what experience they have had with puzzles or puzzling processes. Have them describe their experience putting together a model plane, a jigsaw puzzle, or a toy with a large number of parts. Discuss with them how a suit of armor is similar to a puzzle. [Students may say that a suit of armor, like a puzzle, is made of many small pieces. They also may say that armor, like a puzzle, will look very different before and after assembly.]

## Build Background

▪ More About the Topic

All armor was not created equal, since it developed in response to various types of terrain and styles of fighting. The most beautiful, best-developed plate armor was made in the Holy Roman Empire and in Italian city-states, where the art of crafting metal reached its peak. In these regions, fighting was based around cities and sieges, and plate armor was created to protect knights from the heavy blows of crossbow bolts. Such heavy armor would not have been practical in the harsh climate of the Iberian Peninsula, where mules were more popular than horses, or in the eastern parts of Europe, where battles were usually fought by light cavalry armed with bows and arrows.

## Vocabulary Development

The following words are underscored and defined in the student text.

**vulnerable:** easily injured or hurt.

**wield:** use a weapon or tool with skill.

**agile:** able to move quickly and easily.

**hoisted:** lifted into place, especially with the help of a pulley or other apparatus.

**impairing:** hindering or undermining.

Before assigning the reading, you may want to introduce students to any words that could cause pronunciation or definition problems.

### Vocabulary Tip

**Examining Context** Ask students to look at the context of the content-area vocabulary and determine whether these adjectives are positive or negative. Have students examine how the words are used in the sentence and decide whether or not a *secure* defense is beneficial. Then, have them think of situations in which a *stout* or *sturdy* garment would and would not be desirable. [*Stout* and *sturdy* are desirable qualities for clothes worn in combat, but probably not for party clothes.]

### CONTENT-AREA VOCABULARY

Although the following words are important to an understanding of the text selection, some of them may be unfamiliar to students. Present this list of words and the definitions to students and have them brainstorm connections between the words. [All words can be used to describe people or things. All of them relate in some way to strength.] Encourage students to discuss other meanings they know for these words.

**sturdy:** well-built; strong.

**stout\*:** strong; substantial.

**secure:** not likely to fail; fixed in place.

## Reading Informational Material

### Reading Skill

Monitoring Reading Comprehension

Talk with students about why they would want to monitor their comprehension during the act of reading. [By thinking about the reading process and recognizing when they have trouble with a text, they can look for methods to help us improve our understanding.]

### Reading Strategy

Taking Effective Notes (Strategy 10)

To help students use symbols to indicate places in the text that may require extra attention, such as re-reading or asking questions, use Strategy 10 in Content-Area Reading Strategies. If you would like students to take notes in a divided-page system, provide them with a Key Points and Details chart. (Graphic Organizer 5)

▶ **Teaching Tip**

*Identifying Pieces of Armor* Tell students that the unfamiliar names applied to armor can make the part of the selection starting on page 132 appear especially confusing. [greaves, cuisses, and so forth] Draw, or have a volunteer draw, on an overhead transparency an illustration of a suit of armor to which students can refer without turning pages and losing their place in the text. Tell them the text will discuss the main armor pieces shown in the illustration, starting at the bottom and going to the top.

## DURING READING

### Using the Side-Margin Feature

- Designer Armor

After students have read "Designer Armor," talk with them about the types of work that bear the names of the people who created them. [Students may say that news articles are printed with the name of the person who wrote them, or that artists sign their works of art.] What does the name of the

person who made the item, such as an armor's signature mark, imply about the work? [A signature may imply that the person is proud of his or her work. It may indicate a guarantee, or a promise to stand behind the truth of a piece of writing or the craftsmanship behind a tool or weapon.]

### Viewing the Art

- Medieval Armor

Refer students to the illustration of medieval armor on page 131. Ask them to think about what parts of a knight's armor are with us today, in updated or modified forms. [Students may say that soldiers wear helmets, or that police often wear bulletproof vests, which are similar to breastplates.]

### Differentiating Instruction

- Learners Having Difficulty

The sequence of donning the pieces of armor may seem confusing to some students. Provide students having difficulty with a Sequence or Chronological Order Chart (Graphic Organizer 10) to help them plot the order in which a knight put on the different parts of his armor.

- English-Language Learners

English-language learners may have understanding the individual parts of a medieval suit of armor. Have them work in pairs with more confident English speakers to draw comparisons between a suit of armor and the protective equipment used in familiar sports. [They may say that greaves are similar to shin guards used in soccer. The helmet covering a knight's face might be compared to a hockey face mask.]

## AFTER READING

### ✔ Reading Check

The following are sample answers to the questions on student text page 134.

1. An arming doublet was a close-fitting jacket. It needed to be made of tough material to avoid being worn through by the metal armor. It was lined with a softer fabric, however, to prevent the doublet from chafing the wearer.

2. Additional mail was attached in places that might not be fully protected by armor, for example, at armpits, elbows, and knees.

3. If a knight's plate armor was not properly attached, it could break or work improperly, leaving the knight vulnerable to attack.

4. The knight dressed himself from bottom to top. He started with foot armor and worked his way up to his helmet and gauntlets.

5. When knights were fully dressed, their mobility varied. Because of their extensive training in armor, however, most knights could move around easily.

## Reteaching

Tell students that taking notes is one way to have a figurative discussion about a text and to monitor their understanding of its meaning. Another method is to discuss the text aloud with a partner. Have pairs of students take turns reading short sections of the text aloud. Tell students that they will stop at regular intervals to discuss the material—they can make a comment, ask a question, or connect one idea in the text to another. [*Comment:* I don't think they could move with all those clothes on. *Question:* What's the difference between armor and pieces of mail? *Connection:* This description seems to be describing a football player getting dressed.]

Have students create a three-column chart with the respective headings: *Comment, Question, Connection.* Then, tell them to put their notes in the appropriate columns and to put a check mark by the note when they have completed reading that section and feel they understand it. If they do not feel comfortable that they understand the material for each column, then they need to re-read the passage. Students may find that questions they raised earlier in their notes can be answered by their partners.

## Connecting to Language Arts

### ▪ Writing

*Write and Sketch* Ask students to research armor and find out about a well-known piece of armor, a famous armorer, or a knight who wore an especially beautiful suit of armor. Have students write thumbnail sketches about their findings, including an illustration of the piece or the person associated with it. Post the sketches so students can compare information about well-made armor.

### ▪ Speaking and Listening

*Role-Playing* Have two students act the roles of a knight and an armorer. The knight is interested in ordering a new suit of armor and wants to find out what he can expect about the safety and durability of this armorer's work. The armorer, in turn, should ask the knight about his likes—and dislikes—in armor. Have the pair decide on a style and a price to be paid for the armor.

## Connecting Across the Curriculum: History

*Creating Flashcards* Have students learn more about the individual pieces of armor by creating flashcards. On the front of the card, students should draw or paste an illustration of one part of a knight's armor. On the back of the card, they should write the piece's name and any interesting facts they discover about how it was made or worn. Have students test one another with the flashcards until they can easily name all the parts of a suit of armor.

## Further Resources

### Online

The Metropolitan Museum of Art in New York City has a Web site showing its extensive collection of armor and weapons—approximately fifteen thousand pieces covering many historical and geographic regions—with links to other online armor sites.

The German Historical Museum in Dresden has an armory site showing armor, weapons, and uniforms from the Middle Ages to World War I.

### Assessment

Turn to page 137 for a multiple-choice test on the selection.

*Test Answers*

1. b  2. c  3. c  4. a  5. d
6. b  7. d  8. b  9. c  10. a

# from The "Little Ice Age"

from *The Ice Ages*
by ROY A. GALLANT
*(student text page 135)*

**Reading Level:** Average

## Text Summary

A slight change in precipitation and temperature led to major changes for many people during the "Little Ice Age" of the Middle Ages. People fled their villages as glaciers threatened to cover their homes. The minor change in climate shortened the growing season in some areas; many people starved because of crop failures.

# BEFORE READING

## Make the Connection

Ask students to describe a period of unusual weather—a long, hot summer, or an especially cold winter. What did they do to cope with periods of severe weather? What would have happened if the weather had continued for many years? [Students may say that water was rationed during a drought or that extra insulation was added during a cold spell. Students may say that an extended period of severe weather could cause people to change the way they live, or perhaps even move away from the area.]

## Build Background

■ More About the Topic

The colony of Greenland was settled near the end of the tenth century. It eventually flourished to boast a cathedral, a monastery, a nunnery, and three thousand colonists living on three hundred farms. Eventually, many of those farms were abandoned because of the advancing ice and colder weather. The last winter in the Norse settlement of Nipaatsoq must have been grim: Scientists found that only the hooves remained from butchered dairy cows. Today, archaeologists in Greenland date colonists' remains based on the depth of their graves; as the Arctic permafrost advanced and the Little Ice Age advanced, the graves became increasingly shallow.

## Vocabulary Development

The following words are underscored and defined in the student text.

**glacier:** large mass of ice and snow that flows slowly over land.
**rubble:** rough, loose fragments of rock and debris.
**sown:** scattered for planting.
**rioted:** participated in a violent public disturbance.
**severe:** extremely intense; harsh.

Before assigning the reading, you may want to introduce students to any words that could cause pronunciation or definition problems.

### ⌐ *Vocabulary Tip* ─────────

**Understanding Connotations** Students may be familiar with the content-area vocabulary words used in other contexts to describe urgent or extreme circumstances. Have them give examples of other usages, and then discuss with students why the writer chose words showing intensity for this selection. How does the meaning of the text change if you substitute *held* for *gripped* or *bad* for *fierce*? [Students may say that the vocabulary emphasizes the danger and difficulty of the Ice Age and the problems it created.]

### CONTENT-AREA VOCABULARY

Although the following words are important to an understanding of the text selection, some of them may be unfamiliar to students. Present this list of words and the definitions to students, and encourage them to discuss other meanings they know for these words.

**fierce\*:** violent; intense.
**gripped\*:** seized; held firmly.
**rigor\*:** harsh condition; a difficult circumstance.

\*Although students may be familiar with other meanings of these words, the words as used in the selection have a specific meaning that pertains to the content area.

## Reading Skill

### Identifying Text Structure: Cause and Effect

Discuss causes and effects with students, explaining that a **cause** makes something happen, and an **effect** occurs as a result of that cause. Tell students that writers may not explain every cause and effect; sometimes readers may have to make inferences using their own knowledge.

## Reading Strategy

### Making Predictions (Strategy 7)

To help students activate their knowledge about glaciers and make predictions about what events could have triggered a mini Ice Age, use Strategy 7 in Content-Area Reading Strategies. As you share word lists or illustrations with students, you may want to provide them with a Cause-and-Effect Chart or Cluster Diagram (Graphic Organizers 2 and 3), or suggest they create a Concept Map.

## ▶ Teaching Tip

*Linking Cause and Effect* The selection describes several effects of the Little Ice Age: increasing size of glaciers, lower temperatures, harsh winters, crop loss, starvation, and destruction of homes. Show students how they can link together the Cause-and-Effect Chart (Graphic Organizer 2) to illustrate these more complex causal chains.

# DURING READING

## Using the Side-Margin Feature

### ▪ What If the Gulf Stream Moves Again?

After students have read "What If the Gulf Stream Moves Again?" have them compare the latitude of Scandinavian countries with that of Greenland. To emphasize the benefits of the Gulf Stream for Norway and Sweden, tell students that Greenland is covered by an ice sheet with an area of about 400,000 square miles and a maximum thickness of around 11,000 feet.

## Viewing the Art

### ▪ Glacier

Refer students to the illustration of a glacier on page 136. Tell them that most glaciers move very slowly; the motion, only a few inches per day, can-

not be seen. Ask students what the illustration reveals about a glacier's power. [Students may say that the glacier's power lies in its size, not its speed. Glaciers are so big that they can knock down anything in their path, even if they do it slowly.]

## Differentiating Instruction

### ▪ Learners Having Difficulty

Pair students needing assistance with learners who are comfortable using graphic organizers to interpret information. Have the struggling student read a paragraph aloud while the partner fills in a graphic organizer—perhaps a Cluster Diagram or Cause and Effect Chart (Graphic Organizers 2 and 3) or creates an original one. Then, have the partners explain their graphic and the reasons they organized their material in that way.

### ▪ English-Language Learners

The climate and agricultural practices of northern Europe may be very unfamiliar to some language learners. Help students understand terms related to this climate and agriculture, such as mountain glacier, mist, sleet, partridges, and barley. You may want to provide additional illustrations for students who have trouble understanding these concepts.

# AFTER READING

## ✔ Reading Check

The following are sample answers to the questions on student text page 138.

1. The Little Ice Age came into evidence about 1400. Snow, rain, and hail increased and accumulated in the mountains, increasing the size of glaciers. The larger glaciers, in turn, lowered temperatures slightly.

2. The change in temperatures shortened the growing season by about two weeks in the mid-latitudes, long enough to prevent some crops from maturing.

3. During the Little Ice Age, many homes in the Chamonix Valley were crushed by the oncoming glacier. Many people starved to death because the growing season became shorter.

**4.** In 1739, there was no spring season in Belgium. Bad weather lasted until May.

**5.** People in Iceland once grew a number of grains. As the weather became colder, only barley withstood the cold temperatures. Finally, even barley could not survive.

## Reteaching

Have students fill in the blanks in the following sentence to show a cause-and-effect relationship. *Who* or *What* (moving force) _____ wanted (cause of conflict)_____; however (change) _____ happened, so (conflict's result) _____. [People in Chamonix (Who) *wanted* to live in their houses, *however*; glaciers came close to their villages, *so* the villagers moved away.] After filling out the chart, students can use this information to form a sentence summarizing this causal relationship. [Because glaciers moved close to their villages (cause), many people in the Alps were forced to move away (effect).] Ask students to create several similar statements to explain the many ways that the Little Ice Age affected people of the Middle Ages.

## Connecting to Language Arts

### ▪ Writing

***Weather Reports from the Little Ice Age*** Ask students to pose as meteorologists of the Middle Ages, recording the unusual weather patterns of the Little Ice Age. Have students pretend they are writing for *The Greenland Journal-Star* between A.D. 1300 and 1400. Assign specific students each to write an article for an end-of-year summary for a specific year during the Little Ice Age. (You may want to set ten- or twenty-year intervals, depending on how many students are interested in this assignment.) Ask students to report in capsule form the weather and climate surprises for their specific year. What has changed? Why? What is the speculation about future weather? How have the changes affected living conditions? Students should find out more information about medieval weather patterns and include those details in their articles. Writers should communicate with each other to be sure that students writing about the later periods have not missed major changes reported earlier. Have students post their articles on a class Web site or compile a special fourteenth-century weather booklet.

### ▪ Speaking and Listening

***To Move or Not to Move—That Is the Question*** Have two student groups debate to determine the fate of a village in the Chamonix village. One group should argue the need to stay in the village to preserve its important history and heritage, while the other should make the case for fleeing for safety. Students may adopt the roles of important villagers—mayors, storekeepers, or ministers—to make their points. After students have made their arguments, they may want to learn more about the histories of actual villages in the French Alps to find out how many were actually destroyed or abandoned during the Little Ice Age.

## Connecting Across the Curriculum: Science

***Plotting Weather Graphs*** Have students learn more about the weather patterns in their own area. Divide the class into groups to find government weather-service records of their region and to trace climate fluctuations over the last hundred years. Have one group of students trace precipitation and another group look at temperature changes. Ask students to make a graph, plotting some of the temperature and rainfall extremes and noting any trends or marked changes in the area's weather.

## Further Resource

### Online

The National Snow and Ice Data Center Web site offers glacier facts and photos of glaciers from around the world.

### ( Assessment )

Turn to page 138 for a multiple-choice test on the selection.

***Test Answers***

**1.** c   **2.** b   **3.** d   **4.** a   **5.** d
**6.** b   **7.** c   **8.** c   **9.** a   **10.** d

The following criteria can help you evaluate each student's success in completing the activities prompted by the Cross-Curricular Activities feature in the student textbook.

**\*Note:** Activities marked with an asterisk allow the involvement of more than one student. For these activities you may wish first to evaluate each student on his or her individual contribution and then give groups an overall rating.

## Geography/Science
### Have I Got a Deal for You . . .
- The student conducts research on a country or region of southern Europe to learn about the climate, annual rainfall, and crops grown today.
- The student creates a brochure advertising the advantages of the area to people in northern Europe and explaining why they should move there.
- The writing is relatively free of errors in spelling, grammar, usage, and mechanics.

## History/Health
### Tracing the Path of the Black Death
- The student conducts research on how bubonic plague is transmitted.
- The student designs a flowchart that traces the course of the disease from animal to human.
- Playing the role of a health official in a medieval town, the student presents the chart to the class. He or she also makes suggestions on preventing the spread of the disease.
- The flowchart is neatly rendered and easy to understand.

## Language Arts/Media
### It's A.D. 986 and You Are There
- The student conducts research on the Vikings who sailed west and discovered Iceland, Greenland, and North America.
- The student writes a TV news story about a Viking sailor's experiences.

- The news report includes an account of the boat being blown off course and a description of arriving in the new land and setting up camp.
- Acting as a newscaster, the student smoothly presents the story to the class.

## History/Art
### Armor, East and West
- The student researches medieval European and Japanese armor.
- The student creates a fact sheet that lists what the knight and the samurai wore, defining each piece of armor and explaining its function.
- The student illustrates the fact sheet with pictures or diagrams comparing the two sets of armor.
- The student presents the fact sheet and illustrations to the class or posts them in the classroom.
- The writing is relatively free of errors in spelling, grammar, usage, and mechanics; illustrations are neat and clear.

## *Language Arts/Drama
### My Life as a Medieval Teen
- The student researches Anna Comnena, Joan of Arc, or Eleanor of Aquitaine.
- The student takes part in a panel discussion of the accomplishments of these women or prepares a script and dramatizes the lives of the women as teenagers.
- The student speaks clearly and uses appropriate facial expressions.

## Architecture/Mathematics
### What Has a Moat, a Bailey, and a Keep?
- The student researches how a typical European castle was constructed.
- The student constructs a model of a castle and its grounds, using balsa wood, clay, plastic foam, sugar cubes, or other suitable materials.
- The student clearly labels each part of the castle.
- The student's artwork results in an accurate representation of a European castle.

## CHAPTER 5

# Forces of Change
## Renaissance, Reformation, and Scientific Revolution 1350–1750

### *from* Leonardo da Vinci

by DIANE STANLEY
*(student text page 143)*

**CONTENT-AREA CONNECTIONS**

SCIENCE ●
HISTORY ●

---

**Reading Level:** Average

### Text Summary

This excerpt from *Leonardo da Vinci* focuses on his detailed notebooks, particularly those containing sketches of human anatomy. The excerpt also discusses da Vinci's practice of scientific observation. The focus on the notebooks supports the writer's point that da Vinci was a man ahead of his time.

---

## BEFORE READING

### Make the Connection

Invite students to identify some basic facts about the internal workings of the human body. [the heart pumps blood through the arteries and veins; the lungs draw air into the body; the brain is the center of the nervous system] Then, ask students how they know these basic facts. [from science or health class; from television] Explain that before the time of Leonardo, little was known about the way the bodies of living creatures worked.

### Build Background
■ More About the Topic

Ancient Egyptians actually had a better idea of what the inside of the human body looked like than people of da Vinci's time. Thousands of years after the Egyptians, the Greek scientist Aristotle (384–322 B.C.) and the Roman doctor Galen (A.D. 131–200) studied anatomy but never dissected a human body—only plants and animals. Their work was important, but flawed. Erasistratus

(310–250 B.C.) actually dissected human bodies, but he made mistakes, too. For instance, he thought that arteries contained only air!

### Vocabulary Development

The following words are underscored and defined in the student text.

**grotesque:** distorted; bizarre; ugly.
**moral:** relating to correct behavior or thinking; knowing the difference between right and wrong.
**dissected:** cut into pieces to be examined.
**decompose:** to rot or decay.
**hypothesis:** possible reason or explanation meant to be tested.

Before assigning the reading, you may want to introduce students to any words that could cause pronunciation or definition problems.

---

**Vocabulary Tip**

**Using Context Clues** Before students begin reading the selection, tell them that there may be unfamiliar vocabulary words that are not defined in the glossary or footnotes. Explain that clues in the sentences around these words may help students guess their meanings. For example, in the second sentence, Leonardo is described as solitary. The next sentence quotes his opinion about being alone.

---

Although the following words are important to an understanding of the text selection, some of them may be unfamiliar to students. Pronounce each word and ask students to define the words if they can. Write their definitions on the chalkboard and add the ones given below.

**scientific method:** an experiment that follows specific guidelines and is performed to test an idea. Repeating the experiment should get the same results.

**humidity:** the measurable level of moisture in the air.

**altitude:** the height of a place above the earth's surface.

**observation\*:** the careful noticing and recording of scientific data.

**cross section:** a slice, real or pictured, to reveal an interior.

*Although students may be familiar with other meanings of this word, the word as used in the selection has a specific meaning that pertains to the content area.

## Reading Informational Material

### Reading Skill

#### Identifying Text Structure: Cause and Effect

Explain to students that the relationship between a cause and its effect or effects answers the questions "How did that happen?" and "What happened as a result?" Tell students that writers often signal cause-and-effect relationships by using clue words and phrases such as *because, as a result, this led to…, from this…,* and *therefore.*

### Reading Strategy

#### Understanding Text Structures (Strategy 2)

To help students identify several cause-and-effect relationships described in the last half of the text (pages 145–147), use Strategy 2 in Content-Area Reading Strategies. Offer students a Cause-and-Effect Organizer (Graphic Organizer 2), and work with them to identify and map at least one cause-and-effect relationship. [There are three.] Start by identifying a cause, and have students look for one or more effects. For example, tell students that one cause is Leonardo's habit of observing natural events, such as the movement of water. Guide stu-

dents to look for cause-and-effect clue words, which should lead them to see the following effects:

- Leonardo started asking questions.
- He set up an experiment.
- He invented tools for measurement.
- He recorded the results.

# DURING READING

## Using the Side-Margin Feature
- Church Chants and Love Songs

Ask students to discuss how different their favorite music would be today if Renaissance musicians had not begun using harmony. If possible, bring in recordings of medieval or any pre-Renaissance-age music as well as Renaissance-age music for students to hear. Invite students to share their reactions to the music.

## Reading Informational Material

▶ **Teaching Tip**

*Recording Details* While the reading selection is expository, it is also highly descriptive. Students may remember the content better if they make a list of the sensory-oriented details in the text. Have students draw a two-column chart with the names of the five senses in the left-hand column. Then, ask them to fill in the other column with details that relate to each sense.

### Viewing the Art
- *Mona Lisa*

Refer students to the reproduction of Leonardo's *Mona Lisa* on page 143. Take a moment to explain that this soft blending of colors and tones, known as sfumato, makes the woman in the painting appear three-dimensional. Before Leonardo, painters often outlined their figures, which made them appear flat. Leonardo gave the *Mona Lisa* an illusion of depth—a concept new to painting.

### Differentiating Instruction
- Learners Having Difficulty

Help students see the organization of the selection by creating a Cloze Concept Map. Draw a rectangle labeled "Leonardo's notebooks." Place two rectangles under it labeled "anatomy" and "scientific method." Draw at least six rectangles below these two. Fill two with appropriate details. Connect lower and upper rectangles appropriately. Distribute the organizer to students and ask them to work in pairs to fill in the rectangles.

# AFTER READING

## ✔ Reading Check

The following are sample answers to questions on student text page 147.

1. Leonardo da Vinci was more creative when he was alone.

2. He was left-handed and preferred to write backward.

3. He dissected human and animal bodies and made careful drawings of what he observed.

4. The steps were observing, asking questions, making a hypothesis, and setting up an experiment to test the hypothesis.

5. Leonardo correctly believed that the rocks on the mountains once lay at the bottom of the sea. Others thought that the great biblical flood had floated the fossils up onto the mountains.

### Reteaching
If students have trouble identifying cause-and-effect relationships in the reading selection, you might reverse your teaching strategy. Consider offering students one or more effects and asking them to trace backward to the cause. Again, use the Cause-and-Effect Chart (Graphic Organizer 2), but this time fill in one of the "effect" boxes with an effect such as "asking questions." Guide students to go backwards through the paragraph to find the cause.

### Connecting to Language Arts
▪ Writing
**Historical Character Journal** By now students have a good sense of the kinds of notes Leonardo kept in his notebooks. Have students research Leonardo's time and place, as well as his daily life.

Ask students to create a journal entry and record a day in the life of Leonardo da Vinci. Have them jot down notes that reflect Leonardo's thoughts and ideas as well as his actions. Tell students that their journal entries should also include at least one drawing.

### Connecting Across the Curriculum: Social Studies
*Leonardo's World* Suggest that students explore the world of fifteenth-century Italy by researching some aspect of Renaissance life, such as the city-states of Italy, the fashions of the times, the weaponry of the armies, the music, the art, the medicine, the role of women, the trade routes, or the power of the Church. Have students create one of the following:

- ▪ a Renaissance art gallery with informative labels
- ▪ an illustrated Web site that explains some aspect of Renaissance life

### Further Resources
**Museums**
The Louvre Museum, the Metropolitan Museum of Art, and the Museo Scienza. All maintain Web sites in English.

## Assessment

Turn to page 139 for a multiple-choice test on the selection.

*Test Answers*
1. b  2. a  3. c  4. b  5. d
6. d  7. c  8. d  9. a  10. c

# Michelangelo

from *Italian Renaissance (Living History Series)*
edited by JOHN D. CLARE
*(student text page 148)*

**Reading Level:** Average

## Special Considerations

The artists of the Renaissance often depicted the human body in its nude form. The editors of the Pupil's Edition have taken care to provide illustrations that avoid full nudity; however, if you plan to have students do outside research on the art of Michelangelo, such as his statue *David,* you may wish to prepare students for the reproductions of the artwork first, in order to avoid offending students or their parents.

## Text Summary

This excerpt from the book *Italian Renaissance (Living History Series)* highlights moments in the long, productive life of sculptor, painter, poet, and architect Michelangelo, who is well known for his painting of the ceiling of the Sistine Chapel in Rome. The writer provides anecdotes that illustrate the artist's famously independent and often temperamental character.

# BEFORE READING

## Make the Connection

Ask students to brainstorm words, phrases, or ideas that they associate with artists. Jot their responses on the chalkboard or on an overhead transparency. Then, as a class, work to place the responses in categories, such as creative, unconventional, antisocial. As students read about Michelangelo, have them list under the appropriate description specific examples of things Michelangelo did or said.

## Build Background

▪ Motivate

If possible, bring in reproductions of several of Michelangelo's works of art, and invite students to respond to them. Ask students what they notice about the artworks and what they like or dislike about them. Challenge students to speculate about the kind of person who could create such works and the time in history in which that artist lived.

## Vocabulary Development

The following words are underscored and defined in the student text.

**stereotype:** a rigid, too-simple notion held by many people about a person or group.
**apprentice:** someone studying and working with a master to learn an art or skill.
**discarding:** throwing away; getting rid of.
**depiction:** portrayal; image.
**temperamental:** moody; excitable; unpredictable.
Before assigning the reading, you may want to introduce students to any words that could cause pronunciation or definition problems.

---

## *Vocabulary Tip*

**Making Word Associations** Consider the following strategy as you introduce the vocabulary words for this selection. First, read aloud the vocabulary words. Then, write them on the chalkboard, leaving space around each word. Next, ask students to offer ideas, words, or phrases that come to mind when they think of each word. Before students look at the definitions in their books, guide them to roots, affixes, or similar elements to form their own definitions. After students see the definitions in the book, ask them to evaluate their first impressions and to discuss what led to their definitions.

---

CONTENT-AREA VOCABULARY

Although the following words are important to an understanding of the text selection, some of them may be unfamiliar to students. Put the words on the chalkboard or on an overhead transparency, pronounce each word, and ask students to define the words if they can. Ask students what the words have in common. [All of the words relate to art.]

**classical\*:** in the artistic style of the ancient Greeks and Romans.

**italic script:** a typeface used by printers in which the letters are slanted to the right.

**plaster\*:** a pastelike mixture made of sand, water, and other materials and spread on walls or ceilings and dried as a hard surface.

**Mannerism:** an artistic school in which human and natural figures were idealized to the point of being distorted and manipulated for stylistic effect.

\*Although students may be familiar with other meanings of these words, the words as used in the selection have specific meanings that pertain to the content area.

## Reading Informational Material

### Reading Skill
#### Identifying Supporting Details
Explain to students that the main idea of any piece of writing must be supported by details. Supporting details may take the form of examples, anecdotes, facts, or sensory descriptions.

### Reading Strategy
#### Constructing Concept Maps (Strategy 4)
To help students identify supporting details as they read, use Strategy 4 in Content-Area Reading Strategies. You may want to substitute a Cluster Diagram (Graphic Organizer 3). After students have read the first three paragraphs of the selection, they should state the main idea in the top box of the diagram. ["Michelangelo was a typical genius—brilliant, rude, independent, and emotionally off-balance."] Guide students to place each adjective in its own box. After they have read the selection, ask them to create and fill in additional boxes with details from the selection that illustrate each characteristic.

## DURING READING

### Using the Side-Margin Feature
#### Art, Money, and Medicis
Ask students to think of people who are extremely wealthy, successful, and larger-than-life. [Students might mention basketball legend Michael Jordan, television talk show host Oprah Winfrey, or software billionaire Bill Gates.] Tell students they may do research on their chosen celebrity to find details about his or her life. Then, ask students to compare these modern celebrities to Lorenzo de'Medici. Offer students a Venn Diagram (Graphic Organizer 11) to identify the similarities and differences between the modern and Renaissance "stars."

▶ **Teaching Tip**
*Creating Subheads*   Point out that the selection contains only one subhead. Invite students to generate and list two more subheads on self-adhesive notes. Then, ask students to place the notes at appropriate places in the text. Challenge students to write subheads that are accurate, informative, and eye-catching. Allow time for students to compare subheads.

### Viewing the Art
■ **Sistine Chapel and Statue of Moses**
Have students look at the illustrations of Michelangelo's painting of the prophet Isaiah on the Sistine Chapel (page 150) and his statue of Moses (page 152). Both were completed by Michelangelo around the same time in his life (1512 and 1515, respectively). Ask students to record the similarities and differences between the two works of art on a Venn Diagram (Graphic Organizer 11). Finally, ask students what both artworks reveal about Michelangelo's style. [Students may mention that the subject matter in both cases is Biblical. They may suggest that while the Sistine Chapel is painted and Moses is a statue, both are detailed and powerful. Both media can evoke strong responses in the viewer and depict the emotions of the subjects.]

### Differentiating Instruction
■ **Learners Having Difficulty**
Students may have difficulty understanding artistic terms such as *perspective* and *Mannerism*. They may also resist reading about works of art that they have not seen. Ask the art teacher at your school for illustrations that demonstrate the meanings of the terms as well as for reproductions of some of the artworks mentioned in the selection. Use the illustrations to support discussion of the unfamiliar vocabulary and to maintain students' interest in the selection as they read.

# AFTER READING

##  Reading Check

The following are sample answers to questions on student text page 152.

1. Michelangelo was brilliant but moody, rude, messy, and arrogant.

2. He was apprenticed to the painter Ghirlandaio.

3. He felt that rules should be ignored if they got in the way of the effect he was trying to produce.

4. Michelangelo also excelled in architecture and poetry.

5. Michelangelo said he was a sculptor, not a painter. He refused to work with assistants and painted the entire ceiling himself.

## Reteaching

If students still have trouble identifying supporting details, you may wish to create a Cloze Concept Map, discussed in Strategy 4. Insert some of the information from the selection into the diagram. For example, you might write two of the four characteristics and one detail from the selection in the appropriate boxes in the diagram. This information should guide students to additional details.

## Connecting to Language Arts

### ▪ Writing

*Art Review* The writer of the selection describes the circumstances in which some of Michelangelo's artworks were created. Have students write a short review of one piece of art by Michelangelo. Students may instead compare artworks that the artist completed at two different points in his long career. In their reviews, students should identify and discuss at least three points about the artwork or artworks. [Students might consider size, color, detail, message, and emotions evoked.] Invite students to post their reviews with a picture of the art piece. If possible, post the reviews with scanned-in art on your school's Web page.

## Connecting Across the Curriculum: Math

*Formulas for Perspective* Have students research and explain at least one area of mathematics that Michelangelo used (or ignored) in his paintings, sculptures, or architectural designs. For example, geometry is key to painting perspective or designing a dome. Students may wish to consult a math teacher or art teacher for help. After students have completed their research, they might share their information by completing one of the following assignments:

- demonstrating how perspective is measured by drawing an example on the chalkboard or overhead transparency
- solving a relevant mathematical equation on the chalkboard and explaining how it ties into art or design
- building an architectural model

## Further Resources
### Web Sites

Michelangelo.COM, Inc. See the *Michelangelo Buonarroti* site. Be aware that some images show full nudity.

Wayne State University. See its site *Michelangelo: Sistine Chapel Ceiling*.

### Books

*Michelangelo Buonarroti* by Richard Tames (Heinemann Library, 2001).

*Michelangelo and the Creation of the Sistine Chapel* by Robin Richmond (Crescent Books, 1995).

*Michelangelo (Masters of Art)* by Gabriella Di Cagno, translated by Simon Knight (Peter Bedrick Books, 2000).

## Assessment

Turn to page 140 for a multiple-choice test on the selection.

**Test Answers**

1. d   2. a   3. b   4. c   5. d
6. d   7. a   8. b   9. a   10. c

# from Martin Luther and the Reformation

*Rats, Bulls, and Flying Machines: A History of the Renaissance and Reformation*

by DEBORAH MAZZOTTA PRUM
(*student text page 153*)

**Reading Level:** Average

## Special Considerations

The reading selection focuses on the figure of Martin Luther and his role in history; however, at the center of the Reformation is Luther's criticism of the Roman Catholic Church. Because both faiths still have many followers today, try to keep discussions of the church's corruption and the innovations of the Protestants in a historical context. Guide students away from choosing sides or making judgments.

## Text Summary

The excerpt from *Rats, Bulls, and Flying Machines: A History of the Renaissance and Reformation* describes the life, religious beliefs, and courage of Martin Luther, who, in 1517, challenged the authority of the Roman Catholic Church in the name of reform. The excerpt explains that Martin Luther is responsible for the Protestant Reformation, a religious movement that emphasized the ability of the individual worshiper to read the Bible and worship God without the intervention or guidance of a Catholic priest.

# BEFORE READING

## Make the Connection

Ask students what they know about the Roman Catholic and Protestant faiths. [The Roman Catholic Church has a pope and saints, and only male priests may deliver sacraments. Protestant sects do not have an overall figurehead, and many do recognize saints. Most Protestant sects allow women to become ministers. Both churches are Christian, and both have particular rites, liturgies, and prayers.] Draw a Venn Diagram, and ask students to identify similarities and differences between the two religions. To broaden students' perspective, you may wish to demonstrate a Venn Diagram comparing a non-Christian religion to the Catholic or Protestant faiths.

## Build Background
■ More About the Topic

Although the selection is careful to point out that today Catholics and Protestants in the United States can live and work together with ease, you may wish to point out that in Northern Ireland the relationship between Catholics and Protestants is troubled. Since the 1600s, Protestant English have been present in Ireland, a predominantly Catholic country, and claimed it for England. In the 1920s, Ireland was divided, and Northern Ireland remained a part of Great Britain. In the 1960s, Northern Irish Catholics demanded, but did not receive, their civil rights. As a result, over the last three decades, Catholics and Protestants have resorted to violence in the name of independence (for the Irish Catholics) or for loyalty to England (for the English Protestants). Despite peace talks and agreements in the last decade, the disagreement between the two groups has not been resolved.

## Vocabulary Development

The following words are underscored and defined in the student text.

**confess:** tell a fault or crime.

**condemn:** to penalize for wrongdoing; judge harshly.

**corruption:** dishonest or evil behavior.

**conscience:** thoughts and feelings urging one to do what is right.

**defied:** openly opposed or resisted; fought against.

Before assigning the reading, you may want to introduce students to any words that could cause pronunciation or definition problems.

*Vocabulary Tip*

**Using Affixes** Many of the unfamiliar vocabulary words in the selection have common affixes. Before introducing the new vocabulary, take a few minutes to discuss the meanings of some common prefixes and suffixes, such as *con–, –ed, de–, –ion,* and *in–*. Challenge students to guess at the meanings of the unfamiliar words by understanding the meanings of the affixes. Then, send them to a dictionary to check, confirm, or revise their guesses.

### CONTENT-AREA VOCABULARY

Although the following words are important to an understanding of the text selection, some of them may be unfamiliar to students. Invite students to brainstorm the connection between the words. [All words as defined here have religious connections.]

**monastery:** the building that houses monks or people who have withdrawn to practice their faith.
**cardinal\*:** a high position within in the leadership of the Roman Catholic Church.
**indulgences\*:** official pardons by the Roman Catholic Church that spare the forgiven people from suffering after death.

\*Although students may be familiar with other meanings of these words, the words as used in the selection have specific meanings that pertain to the content area.

### Reading Informational Material

#### Reading Skill
Identifying Text Structure: Sequence
Remind students that they should always preview, or glance through, a text before reading it. Tell students, as they preview this reading selection, to look for signal and transition words that suggest sequence or chronological order. Elicit from them examples of sequence clue words, such as *when, then, next, later, soon after, now, finally,* and *after.*

▶ **Teaching Tip**
   *Summary* The reading selection is long and covers several key developments in history. It will help students if you stop after every page or two and ask them to summarize what they have read so far. Remind students that a summary is only a few sentences long and should contain only important ideas

and key details. You may wish to have students give oral summaries, although students will also benefit from writing their summaries in reading notebooks.

#### Reading Strategy
Understanding Text (Strategy 2)
To help students understand that the reading selection uses the text structure of sequence or chronological order, use Strategy 2 in Content-Area Reading Strategies. Provide students with a Sequence or Chronological Order Chart (Graphic Organizer 10) to help them map the course of events described in the text. Suggest that students write the signal or transition words on the lines that connect the boxes in the diagram.

## DURING READING

### Correcting Misconceptions
Almost ninety percent of people who practice religion in the U.S. are Christian. Judaism, the next largest group, is practiced by only two percent of Americans. In the world, however, the numbers are different. In 2001, about 2 billion people practiced Christianity; however, the next most practiced faith was Islam, with 1.3 billion practitioners.

### Differentiating Instruction
■ English-Language Learners
Students who are not from a Christian or European background may struggle with the ideas and language in the selection. Prepare students for the reading by helping them create a three-column chart of key vocabulary words. Label one column "Church," the next "History," and the third "Other." Then, list or have students compile lists of words from the selection. Students should define the words or read the definitions you provide and place the words in appropriate columns.

## AFTER READING

### ✔ Reading Check

The following are sample answers to questions on student text page 160.

**1.** Some people believed that the church had lost touch with the old ways or traditions and that its leaders were corrupt and not spiritual enough.

2. After being struck by lightning, Luther vowed he would give his life to God.

3. The purpose of the theses was to argue against corrupt practices in the Roman Catholic Church, such as selling indulgences. People responded by protesting against the church, causing tremendous change in Europe.

4. The printing press helped spread Luther's ideas and made the Bible available to anyone who could read it.

5. A "papal bull" is an edict or order issued by the pope. Luther responded by burning it.

## Reteaching

If students struggle with the concept of identifying chronological order, try engaging them in an oral round-robin storytelling session. Ask each student to offer one sentence that develops a story. You might start off with "On my way to school today, I saw a white elephant and then..." (If students avoid transition words or rely too much on *and*, suggest another transition word.) After all students have contributed to the story, draw attention to their use of words such as *then* and *next*. Draw the connection between their own use of clue or transition words and that of the author. Afterwards you may wish to have students tell the story of Martin Luther in the same way.

## Connecting to Language Arts

■ Writing

*Newspaper Article* The reading selection was written almost five hundred years after the events it describes. Invite students to write a short newspaper article of at least one event in Luther's life as if they had witnessed it themselves. The article should answer the *5W–How?* questions and include sensory details that re-create the scene. Students should research life in Wittenberg during Luther's time in order to provide accurate details. Have students publish their accounts in a class or school newspaper or on the school Web site.

## Connecting Across the Curriculum: Music

*Heavenly Voices* With the Reformation came the establishment of new churches, and in those churches, new music was sung. Ask students to research some of the music of the Catholic and Protestant traditions. They may compare music of the same period or explore how music changed over a span of years. They may also look at music from different areas of the world where Protestantism is practiced. Students may present their findings by completing one of the following assignments:

- playing recordings for the class and explaining some key points (or key differences, if they are comparing styles of music)
- performing the music themselves, alone or with a group
- creating a Renaissance songbook of lyrics arranged on illustrated pages
- designing a chart showing the typically used Renaissance musical instruments with a paragraph describing their sound, and their modern use, if any

## Further Resources
### Online

KDG Wittenberg is a Web site that chronicles Luther's life, accomplishments, friends, and even the city and church where he made his stand. Translated into English and illustrated with period art, this is a well-rounded site for students. *The Reformation Guide* is a site for more advanced students and includes biographies of other well-known Reformation leaders.

### Book

*By Faith Alone,* by Martin Luther, edited by James Galvin (World Pub., 1998).

## Assessment

Turn to page 141 for a multiple-choice test on the selection.

*Test Answers*

1. a   2. c   3. b   4. a   5. b
6. a   7. c   8. d   9. d   10. d

# from Galileo Galilei: Inventor, Astronomer, and Rebel

by MICHAEL WHITE
*(student text page 161)*

**Reading Level:** Advanced

## Special Considerations

In this selection, the Roman Catholic Church is presented as an institution that did not tolerate new or challenging ideas. Try to keep discussions of the church and the Inquisition in a historical context. Be sure to point out that the Roman Catholic Church eventually did accept Galileo's revolutionary ideas and that, in 1992, 350 years after Galileo's death, Pope John Paul II publicly acknowledged the church's error in condemning the scientist.

## Text Summary

The selection begins by focusing on scientist Galileo Galilei's arrest in 1633 by leaders of the Roman Catholic Church on the charges of having supported the idea that the earth was not the center of the universe. It then covers different points in time to explain why Galileo's ideas caused so much trouble. The selection also explores the influence of the Catholic Church, the scientific writings of Aristotle, and the work of the astronomer Copernicus.

# BEFORE READING

## Make the Connection

Ask students to talk about what they know about the planets and the sun. [There are nine planets, and they revolve around the sun, which is the center of the solar system.] Then, have students discuss where and when they first learned these ideas. Finally, ask students to talk about whether these ideas made sense to them the first time they heard them. Did they accept these ideas or did they disagree with them? [Students may remember that it seemed illogical that the sun was stationary and the earth in motion because the earth does not appear to move.]

## Build Background

▪ Building Prerequisite Skills

Explain to students that for this selection they will be practicing the skill of previewing. Tell students that previewing requires them to glance through new reading materials and draw conclusions based on what they see. Students should realize that, in previewing, there are no right or wrong answers. Students should look at illustrations and their captions and at subheadings, underlined words, footnotes, and pull-out quotations to generate ideas and questions about the reading. Explain that previewing can help make their reading more focused and productive.

## Vocabulary Development

The following words are underscored and defined in the student text.

**deviated:** moved away from; strayed from.

**censored:** examined for forbidden ideas, which are then taken out.

**implication:** a suggestion; act of implying or hinting at a connection.

**misconceptions:** mistaken ideas.

**scorned:** disliked; made fun of; treated with contempt.

Before assigning the reading, you may want to introduce students to any words that could cause pronunciation or definition problems.

┌─ *Vocabulary Tip* ─

**Using Context Clues** The level of difficulty of some of the vocabulary in the selection is high. You may wish to help students by using the vocabulary words to make some general remarks about the selection. The remarks will allow students to hear how the words sound and will give them a chance to use context to guess at the words' meanings. Sample statements:

"Many people who have underlined revolutionary ideas are rejected by their community."

"A notion that is very different from traditional ideas may be difficult to accept."

"Throughout history, some churches or governments have censored new ideas."

## CONTENT-AREA VOCABULARY

Although the following words are important to an understanding of the text selection, some of them may be unfamiliar to students. Present the list of words and definitions to students, and invite students to think about the connection between the words. Encourage them to discuss other meanings of the words.

**proposal\***: a suggested plan.

**argument\***: reasons offered to explain something.

**conclusion\***: the last step in the process of reasoning or of understanding something.

**heretical**: characteristic of a belief that goes against established ideas.

**philosophy\***: a system or way of acting or thinking.

**celestial**: of or in outer space or the sky.

**notion**: belief or idea.

**revolutionary\***: characteristic of something that causes or may cause great and sudden change.

**theory**: an idea that has some evidence to support it.

\*Although students may be familiar with other meanings of these words, the words as used in the selection have a specific meanings that pertain to the content area.

## Reading Informational Material

### Reading Skill
Previewing

Tell students that previewing allows them to establish a purpose for reading, to identify important ideas, and to connect the new ideas to what they already know.

▶ **Teaching Tip**
*Identifying Purpose* Before students preview the text, offer them the following questions to help them identify the text's most important ideas and their purpose for reading:
Important Ideas:
- Is there anything in the subheadings, illustrations, captions, or quotations that can help me understand the "big ideas"?
- What are the key vocabulary words I should understand?

Purpose:
- What am I going to do with this information when I finish reading?
- How does this text fit in with other selections in this chapter?

### Reading Strategy
Previewing the Text (Strategy 1)

To help students preview the selection in order to define their purpose for reading, identify important ideas, and connect the text to what they already know, use Strategy 1 in Content-Area Reading Strategies. You may want to provide students with a KWL Chart (Graphic Organizer 6) to help them with the third part—connecting to what they already know. Have students fill out the first two columns before reading and the third column after reading.

# DURING READING

## Correcting Misconceptions

Students should realize that even today there is no one accepted, foolproof way to study a scientific problem. Scientists still rely on a combination of careful observation and reasoning to work out the answers to tough scientific problems. Even today scientists often disagree about the results of scientific studies and their implications. What is different from Galileo's day, however, is that modern scientists rarely have to defend their ideas before an institution such as the church.

▶ **Teaching Tip**
*Discovering Narrative* The selection is from a book-length biography of Galileo Galilei, but it does not follow a straightforward sequential narrative. The narrative starts in 1633 but jumps around in time and place in order to provide background on Galileo, Aristotle, Copernicus, and the Catholic Church. Offer students a Cluster Diagram (Graphic Organizer 3) with these topics in the large circles. Invite students to draw and fill in additional circles with information they learn about the topics as they read the selection.

## Differentiating Instruction
■ **Learners Having Difficulty**

Because the text does not tell the events of Galileo's ordeal in sequential order, students may benefit from creating a time line. Help students get started by putting a time line on the chalkboard or on an overhead transparency and marking "1633" above and "Galileo arrested" below a hatch mark near the center of the time line. Explain to students that the selection will give them the information that should go before and after 1633.

Students who do not speak a Romance or Latin-based language as their first language may struggle with the vocabulary in this selection. You may wish to offer students a list of Latin roots and suffixes and their definitions. Have groups of students use the list to figure out the meanings of unfamiliar words.

# AFTER READING

## Reading Check

The following are sample answers to questions on student text page 165.

1. Copernicus was the first scientist to understand that the planets revolve around the sun, not the earth.

2. The Catholic Church and the teachings of Aristotle were the two main forces that affected learning in seventeenth-century Europe.

3. The Inquisition was a group of Church leaders who made sure that what people wrote and said agreed with traditional Catholic teaching.

4. The earth was the center of the universe, according to authorities of Galileo's time. Galileo believed that the earth circled the sun instead of being fixed in space.

5. The author suggests that scientific advancement could have been delayed for hundreds of years.

## Reteaching

If students still struggle with the concept of previewing, ask them to think about how they react to and make use of the movie trailers, or previews, that they see at the movies or in television commercials for upcoming films. Ask students to think of a preview they have seen recently and to talk about what they learned from it. Students should be able to point out that a preview lets them know the movie's title, stars, and genre (comedy, thriller, and so on), as well as a rough idea of the plot. Guide students to see that the illustrations, captions, highlighted vocabulary, headnotes, and pull-out quotations in this selection serve the same purpose as a movie trailer.

## Connecting to Language Arts
■ Writing

*Time Capsule* Tell students to imagine that Galileo understood at the end of his life that his work would be recognized some day and that it would help scientists hundreds of years later. Then, ask them to imagine that before he died the scientist assembled a time capsule of objects, books, and mementos. Invite students to find, make, or draw objects, such as books and laboratory equipment, and create laboratory notes or journal entries that Galileo might have included in such a capsule. Finally, ask students to write a brief letter by Galileo that lists and explains the objects in the time capsule.

## Connecting Across the Curriculum: Science

*Galileo's Gravity Experiment* Ask students to review the side-margin feature "Prove It!" on page 163. Then, challenge students to re-create the experiment using ordinary objects. Students may consult with the science teacher at your school for help in understanding the principles of gravity as well as for help in designing the experiment. Students should document in a lab report the process of researching and performing the experiment. They should demonstrate the experiment at least twice for the class.

## Further Resources
### Online Resources
■ Rice University's Web site, the Galileo Project is interactive. It includes facts and images about his family and the science and scientists of the time.
### Book
■ *Galileo's Daughter: A Historical Memoir of Science, Faith, and Love* by Dava Sobel (Walker & Co., 1999).

## Assessment

Turn to page 142 for a multiple-choice test on the selection.

*Test Answers*
1. c   2. b   3. d   4. c   5. b
6. d   7. c   8. b   9. b   10. a

# *from* Making Archaeology a Science

*from Dig This! How Archaeologists Uncover Our Past*

by MICHAEL AVI-YONAH
*(student text page 166)*

CONTENT-AREA CONNECTIONS

SCIENCE •———
ART •———
HISTORY •———

**Reading Level:** Average

## Text Summary

The selection, which is an excerpt from a longer book, discusses two time periods in the development of archaeology—the early sixteenth century and the mid-eighteenth century. It explains that, in the beginning, the field of archaeology was pursued by book collectors, lovers of ancient languages, and artists. Two hundred years later, archaeologists adopted a more scientific approach. The author shows that the shift of archaeology from art to science and hobby to profession changed its focus from the appreciation of art forms to the study of past cultures.

## BEFORE READING

### Make the Connection

Ask students to brainstorm for words, phrases, or images that come to mind when they hear the word *archaeology*. [Students may cite movies, such as *Raiders of the Lost Ark,* that romanticize the role of the archaeologist. Or, they may mention aspects of archaeology, such as digs.] Have students talk about what makes or does not make archaeology an appealing career. [Students may think that archaeology is appealing because archaeologists get to go to exotic places.]

### Build Background
■ Motivate

Display photographs of artifacts found in famous archaeological excavations, such as the treasures of King Tutankhamen. Explain that such artifacts are available for us because of the work of archaeologists who understand the need to preserve them. Lead a short discussion about what makes King Tut's mask so valuable: its gold or its age and history?

### Vocabulary Development

The following words are underscored and defined in the student text.

**authentic:** real; genuine.

**sites:** places; locations.

**artifacts:** items made by human beings that are studied for their historical value.

**excavations:** areas where artifacts or buildings are being uncovered.

**conserve:** keep safe from damage.

---

### *Vocabulary Tip*

**Predicting Meanings** Invite students to use word association as a way to predict the meanings of unfamiliar words. For example, write the word *sites* on the chalkboard, and ask students to call out words, ideas, or phrases that they associate with the word. For example, students might say the word reminds them of the word *sights,* which makes them think of seeing or specifically seeing places while on vacation. Guide students to predict the meanings of words before checking definitions in the glossary or dictionary. As a class, pay attention to words whose associations do not point to the correct meaning.

---

### CONTENT-AREA VOCABULARY

Although the following words are important to an understanding of the text selection, some of them may be unfamiliar to students. Present the list of words and the definitions to your students. Invite students to think about the connection between the words. Encourage them to discuss other meanings of the words.

**remains\*:** traces of an event or place from the past.

**ruins\*:** physical objects, such as buildings and walls, left after a city or civilization has fallen or been destroyed.

**amateurs:** untrained experts who pursue a particular interest, such as sports or science, because they enjoy it.

**expeditions\*:** journeys or trips taken for the purpose of exploring or discovering something.

**dismantling:** the taking apart of something.

*Although students may be familiar with other meanings of these words, the words as used in the selection have specific meanings that pertain to the content area.

## Reading Informational Material

### Reading Skill

**Identifying Text Structure: Comparison and Contrast**

Explain to students that when a text uses comparison-and-contrast patterns, it highlights similarities and differences between two things. In this case, the text focuses on the differences between the early years of archaeology and its later practice.

▶ **Teaching Tip**

*Using Context Clues* Explain that often a writer will include clue words or phrases that indicate comparison and contrast. *However, unlike,* and *on the other hand* are a few examples. Point out to students that, in this selection, the comparison and contrast is usually implied. In separate sections, the writer discusses the two periods of archaeology and their differences but does not compare them directly. Students should look for clue words and phrases that indicate time passing, such as *at this stage* or *later.*

### Reading Strategy

**Using Graphic Organizers (Strategy 3)**

To help students identify the differences and similarities between the practice of archaeology in the sixteenth and eighteenth centuries, use Strategy 3 in Content-Area Reading Strategies. A Venn Diagram, (Graphic Organizer 11), will help students record the similarities and differences.

## DURING READING

### Correcting Misconceptions

Students may be interested to know that modern archaeology requires more planning and managing than excavating. An archaeologist may spend years looking for physical clues to a site, raising large amounts of money, finding people to work, getting permission from foreign officials, and coordinating a dig. Once artifacts are found, they must be carefully mapped, photographed, removed, identified, studied, cataloged, and stored.

### Using the Side-Margin Feature
■ Where Time Stopped

Explain to students that Pompeii is one of the rare sites that contains so many well-preserved objects. Most sites suffer much more destruction. Lead students in a discussion in which they imagine what archaeologists in the year 3002 might find if they were to excavate the students' hometowns, cities, or neighborhoods. What objects or buildings do students think are most likely to survive? What conclusions will people of the next millennium make based on these findings?

▶ **Teaching Tip**

*Discovering Sequence* To help students focus on the sequential order of events in the reading selection, draw a time line on the chalkboard or an overhead transparency. Work with students to fill in key dates and events as they read. Students should pay attention to the events the writer describes, beginning in 1506. Other events, such as the eruption of the volcano at Pompeii, may be added to the time line with the information placed in brackets to distinguish it from the narrative flow of the text.

### Viewing the Art
■ Statue of Laocoön

Encourage students to study the picture of the statue of Laocoön on page 167. Then, show them a picture of a Baroque or Renaissance painting or sculpture, such as those on pages 143 or 152. You might want to work with an art teacher to establish a list of criteria for evaluating art, and then ask students to use the list to make comparisons of the artworks. A Venn Diagram (Graphic Organizer 11) may help students record their findings.

### Differentiating Instruction
■ Advanced

Students may be interested in knowing the story behind the statue of Laocoön. Challenge students to read Greek mythology or consult art books to find out who Laocoön was and why he is depicted in the statue. (Be aware that the full statue of Laocoön is a well-known work of Roman art, but the figure is nude.) Ask students to present an oral report to share their information with the class.

# AFTER READING

##  Reading Check

The following are sample answers to questions on student text page 170.

1. Investigators found a statue of Laocoön and his sons being killed by sea serpents. The Roman historian Pliny had written about its location.

2. The Baroque style is based on the sculpture. Baroque art is vivid and full of action, flowing shapes, and ornamentation. It emphasizes depth and space and contrasts light with shadow.

3. The first archaeologists were amateurs who were guided to old ruins by ancient texts. They searched mostly in Rome.

4. They formed societies to study early remains, hired artists to draw and paint likenesses of ancient ruins, and organized expeditions to Greece, Lebanon, and Syria.

5. Archaeologists now work to conserve and restore findings at the locations themselves.

### Reteaching

If students still have trouble identifying implied comparison-and-contrast text patterns, offer them the following fill-in-the-blank sentences:

"_____ involves
_____, but
_____ involves
_____. Still, both
_____ and
_____ involve
_____."

Practice with students by filling in the first and third blanks of the first sentence with simple examples, such as "hiking" and "bicycling." You can help students further by filling in the first and third blanks with "Archaeology in the 1500s" and "Archaeology in the 1700s." Students should then read the text selection to find information that will complete the sentences.

### Connecting to Language Arts

▪ Writing

***Descriptive Letter*** The writer explains that archaeologists in the 1700s were often Europeans who traveled to faraway places such as Greece and the Middle East in order to search for buried artwork. They wrote about their findings in letters to family and friends back home. Invite students to imagine that they are archaeologists in an exotic place excavating the find of the century. Students should write a letter to those at home describing their imagined archaeological adventures. Their letters should contain at least one drawing of their "find" as well as a complete description of what they found, where they found it, and what they think its use was.

### Connecting Across the Curriculum: Science

***Archaeology Today*** Modern archaeology has been changed by developments in technology. Have students research the role of technology in archaeology today. Suggest that they look at how computers have changed the way archaeologists work to find a site, excavate a site, identify artifacts, or preserve the artifacts. After students have completed their research, they may complete one of the following assignments:

▪ a how-to report or demonstration of the use of technology to find an archaeological site

▪ a chart showing modern excavation tools

### Further Resources
#### Online Sources
The Archaeological Institute of America's site features article abstracts and news.
*World Atlas of Archaeology on the Web* is an extensive listing of archaeological resources.
#### Books
*100 Greatest Archaeological Discoveries* by Jacqueline Dineen (Grolier Educational, 1997).
*Lessons from the Past: An Introductory Reader in Archaeology* Compiled by Kenneth L. Feder (Mayfield Publishing Company, 1999).

### Assessment

Turn to page 143 for a multiple-choice test on the selection.

***Test Answers***

**1.** b   **2.** c   **3.** b   **4.** c   **5.** a
**6.** a   **7.** b   **8.** d   **9.** d   **10.** c

# *from* Isaac Newton: Discovering Laws That Govern the Universe

by MICHAEL WHITE
*(student text page 171)*

**Reading Level:** Advanced

## Text Summary

The reading selection, which is an excerpt from a longer book, focuses primarily on the tremendous scientific breakthroughs made by Isaac Newton. Especially during the year 1666, Newton posed and solved questions about gravity, light, motion, and mathematics. His ideas would change forever the way scientists understand the physical world. The author makes clear that Newton's work was the basis for many fields of modern science.

## BEFORE READING

### Make the Connection

Bring a rubber ball to class and let it roll off a table in front of the class. After students watch the ball fall and bounce on the floor, ask them to talk about what they saw. Challenge students to think about what they already know about concepts such as gravity and motion. Have them write their thoughts in a brief journal entry.

### Build Background
■ More About the Topic

In 1666, Isaac Newton fled London during an outbreak of bubonic plague. The disease was caused by bacteria transmitted by flea bites. Fleas that had bitten infected rats in turn passed the disease to humans, who then suffered from raging fevers, swollen lymph nodes, and great pain before dying. The plague hit London regularly in the course of forty years, killing 75,000 people. The Great Fire, which destroyed most of London in 1666, seemed to give the city and its people a fresh start by freeing them from the threat of plague and allowing them to rebuild in grand fashion.

### Vocabulary Development

The following words are underscored and defined in the student text.

**properties:** characteristics.
**theory:** an idea that is not obvious but can be proven to be a law or principle.
**principles:** basic truths or laws.
**phenomena:** events or conditions that can be seen or experienced and described scientifically.
**revolutionize:** make a complete change in.

---

### *Vocabulary Tip*

**Using Suffixes** Before you introduce the Content-Area Vocabulary words, take a moment to talk about the suffix *–ics.* Explain that the suffix has several meanings, but here it means "science or study of." After reviewing the new vocabulary, challenge students to think of other words that use the *–ics* suffix and to decide if the meaning of the suffix is the same. [*mathematics, aerobics, dynamics*]

---

### CONTENT-AREA VOCABULARY

Although the following words are important to an understanding of the text selection, some of them may be unfamiliar to students. You may want to present this list of words and the definitions to your students. Invite students to think about the connection between the words. Encourage them to discuss other meanings of the words.

**mechanics*:** the study of the way objects move in relation to one another.
**orbits:** the paths in which one celestial body moves around another, such as a planet circling a star.
**physics:** the science of the way matter (objects) and energy interact.
**optics:** the study of the movement and properties of light and vision.

* Although students may be familiar with other meanings of this word, the word as used in the selection has a specific meaning that pertains to the content area.

## Reading Informational Material

### Reading Skill

#### Identifying Main Idea

Explain to students that the main idea is the central thought that is developed in a reading selection. Students can learn to pinpoint the main idea of a reading passage by noticing what ideas are stressed repeatedly by the writer.

▶ **Teaching Tip**

*Previewing* Challenge students to preview the reading selection and to make predictions about its main idea. Ask students to skim the selection, noticing the subheadings and illustrations, as well as the overall tone of the writer's language. Then, have students jot down their predictions and list at least one detail to support each. Remind students that their predictions do not have to be correct. Tell students to keep their predictions handy so that they can confirm or correct them later as they read the selection.

### Reading Strategy

#### Constructing Concept Maps (Strategy 4)

To help your students identify the main idea of the reading selection, use Strategy 4 in Content-Area Reading Strategies. Have students create a Concept Map, or provide them with a Cluster Diagram (Graphic Organizer 3) that will allow them to organize key details and identify the idea that connects them. Have students label four of the boxes in the diagram with the selection's subheadings. Remind students to look for words in the selection that indicate what the writer thinks about Newton and his work and to include examples in their diagrams. Have students share their ideas with the class, and ask the class as a whole to agree on a good statement of the main idea.

## DURING READING

### Using the Side-Margin Feature

▪ **The Great Experimenter**

After students read the feature, ask them what they know about eye safety. Students might mention that staring at the sun can cause blindness or that poking oneself in the eye is dangerous. Ask students for their reactions to Newton's willingness to risk his eyesight in order to answer scientific questions.

▶ **Teaching Tip**

*Identifying Main Idea* Help students identify the main idea in the reading passage by drawing their attention to the way the author sums up each section on Newton's life or studies. After reading each summary, ask students to restate its main idea in their own words.

### Viewing the Art

▪ **Sir Isaac**

The portrait of Sir Isaac Newton on page 172 was painted by Godfrey Kneller, one of England's foremost portrait painters. Kneller, however, was born in Germany. He came to England after spending time in Italy and studying with Rembrandt in Amsterdam. An introduction to George I, another German, resulted in Kneller's being named to the office of principal painter and, eventually, knighthood. His portraits contributed heavily to the development of English portrait painting. Invite students to examine the portrait for similarities to Baroque and Renaissance styles.

### Differentiating Instruction

▪ **English-Language Learners**

Students may have difficulty with the scientific vocabulary in the selection. Because it will not be possible to provide students with illustrations of these scientific concepts, you may have to consult an expert. Invite the science teacher at your school to talk to students in general terms about concepts such as gravity, motion, light, and calculus. Encourage students to take notes using terms from their original languages.

▪ **Learners Having Difficulty**

Students may struggle with the selection because it does not have an obvious text pattern. It may help students to focus on identifying the questions Newton asked and the general solutions he found. Students may work in pairs and read aloud, stopping after each paragraph or two. At that point, students should ask "What question did Newton ask here?" or "How did he answer that question?" By the time students reach the end of the selection, they should have a clearer picture of Newton's works.

# AFTER READING

## ✔ Reading Check

The following are sample answers to the questions on student text page 176.

1. Newton came up with the theory of gravity.

2. The year 1666 was called miraculous because Newton accomplished many amazing breakthroughs in mathematics and physics, including the development of calculus.

3. According to the author, the greatest development in the history of mathematics was calculus. It is used in computer programs and by economists today.

4. People thought that the universe was controlled by a powerful god and spirits.

5. Modern inventions made possible by Newton's theories of light include better telescopes, microscopes, eyeglasses, cameras, and inventions such as television and lasers.

## Reteaching

Students may have trouble identifying the main idea from the details and tone of the reading selection. Help students by offering them several possible main ideas. Below are some examples. (The second main idea is, of course, the correct one.)

- Newton was lucky to live in a time of great scientific exploration.
- Newton made scientific discoveries that changed the world forever.
- Newton's scientific errors set back scientific developments about a hundred years.

Then, ask students to read the selection in order to decide which statement is true. Students should be able to point to words and ideas in the text that support their choice.

## Connecting to Language Arts

- Writing

*Dramatic Monologue*   Newton's year of isolation in the English countryside inspired his greatest work. Ask students to put themselves in Newton's place and imagine what he might have thought and felt at this exciting time in his life. Challenge students to write a short dramatic monologue that captures Newton's personality and his thoughts and feelings in 1666. Students should do research from a variety of sources. (For example, Samuel Pepys's has diary entries about life in England in that year.)

## Connecting Across the Curriculum: Social Studies

*The Best and Worst of Times*   The year 1666 was a tremendous year not only for Newton but for England, particularly its capital city, London. Ask students to research what life was like in that city in the middle of the seventeenth century. They may wish to focus on the disasters of the plague and the fire, on the aftermath and city's rebuilding, on the arts, or on the changing politics of the time. After students complete their research, they should choose one of the following assignments:

- build a model of London after the fire
- write a ballad about London's troubles
- write and perform a possible conversation about the plague and fire among four noted people of that time
- reenact the beginning of the fire

## Further Resources

### Online Sources

The Isaac Newton Institute for Mathematical Sciences of Cambridge, England, hosts the Isaac Newton Resources Web page with a wide variety of reviewed links.

### Books

*Famous Experiments You Can Do* by Robert Gardner (Franklin Watts, 1990).

*Isaac Newton and the Scientific Revolution* by Gale E Christianson (Oxford University Press, 1996).

## Assessment

Turn to page 144 for a multiple-choice test on the selection.

*Test Answers*
1. b   2. d   3. b   4. b   5. d
6. c   7. a   8. d   9. b   10. a

The following criteria can help you evaluate each student's success in completing the activities prompted by the Cross-Curricular Activities feature in the student textbook.

**\*Note:** Activities marked with an asterisk allow the involvement of more than one student. For these activities you may wish first to evaluate each student on his or her individual contribution and then give groups an overall rating.

### Science/Art
#### Picture This
- The student draws a diagram on poster board of one of Galileo's scientific theories.
- The student explains how Galileo arrived at his theory, what observations and experiments he made, and how his conclusions differed from accepted views of the time.
- The diagram is neat and visually appealing, and the explanations are clear.

### Language Arts/Art
#### Top Ten Works by the Master
- The student creates a list of ten favorite artworks by Michelangelo.
- The student adds an illustration and a short description of each work.
- The student presents the list to the class, explaining clearly why he or she chose these particular works and rejected other specific works.

### *History/Drama
#### Martin Luther Speaks Out
- The student reenacts Luther posting his theses to the Wittenberg church doors. The student performs in a group with some students portraying students and professors questioning Luther's ideas.
- If used, props, costumes, music, sound effects, and other enhancements contribute to the overall effectiveness of the scene.
- As performed, the scene effectively conveys Luther's ideas, leaving the audience with a clear picture of the topic.

### History/Science/Art
#### When Did That Apple Hit Isaac's Head?
- The student creates a time line showing major scientific discoveries and inventions of the Scientific Revolution.
- The time line includes dates, the names and nationalities of the scientists or inventors, and a short description of the discoveries, inventions, or theories.
- The student illustrates the time line effectively with original drawings or photocopied pictures.

### *Language Arts/Science
#### Useful Gadgets
- The student conducts research on Leonardo da Vinci's inventions.
- Alone or with a partner, the student compiles a short fact book describing some of Leonardo's inventions.
- The student describes what the invention was designed to do, whether it really could have worked, whether it was actually built and widely used, and how it is similar to something made today.
- The student presents the fact book to the class and explains how each invention worked.

## CHAPTER 6

# Oceans of Exploration
## From Europe to the Americas 1400–1800

### Prince Henry the Navigator

from *Around the World in a Hundred Years:
From Henry the Navigator to Magellan*
by JEAN FRITZ
*(student text page 181)*

**CONTENT-AREA CONNECTIONS**

HISTORY ●
GEOGRAPHY ●

---

**Reading Level:** Average

**Text Summary**

Prince Henry (1394–1460), son of the Portuguese king, longed to find out more about the western coast of Africa in hope of discovering a new trading route to Asia. He developed knowledge of sailing, sparked Europeans' interest in discovering new lands, and financed numerous exploratory voyages that added to Europeans' knowledge of the African continent.

---

## BEFORE READING

### Make the Connection

Show students a map of your state on which you have covered up most of the area between two major cities. Ask students to imagine starting a journey whose route does not appear on a map. Ask how they would plan for such a trip. [Students may say that they could not judge how long such a trip would take, so they would have to take many supplies. They might say that they would have to be prepared to turn back because they might meet obstacles that they could not overcome.]

### Build Background

■ More About the Topic

Sea exploration was a dangerous, expensive undertaking. Prince Henry was head of the Order of Christ, a powerful military group, but also a strong political and financial force that provided funds for his voyages of discovery. At its peak the Order of Christ included 454 groups in Portugal, Africa, and the Indies. The order may even have had indirect

influence in New World exploration because Christopher Columbus, who married the daughter of one of Henry's favorite captains, spent time carefully examining his father-in-law's sailing records and charts—material that would have been collected for Henry and his seagoing order.

### Vocabulary Development

The following words are underscored and defined in the student text.

**obsessed:** fascinated.
**spoils:** things of value taken by force during a war.
**currents:** parts of a body of water that move more quickly than other parts.
**inferior:** of a lesser quality.
**arrogance:** state of feeling superior or overly proud. Before assigning the reading, you may want to introduce students to any words that could cause pronunciation or definition problems.

**CONTENT-AREA VOCABULARY**

Although the following words are important to an understanding of the text selection, some of them may be unfamiliar to students. Present this list of words and the definitions to students.

**conquer:** to defeat; to control.
**ransacking\*:** plundering; robbing.
**colonized\*:** settled; formed a colony.
**brazen:** daring.

\*Although students may be familiar with other meanings of these words, the words as used in the selection have a specific meaning that pertains to the content area.

## Vocabulary Tip

**Evaluating Connotations** The content-area vocabulary words all describe aggressive acts or attitudes. Before students read the selection, ask them to look at the content-area vocabulary and predict the types of actions that will be discussed in the selection. Discuss with students whether the vocabulary words have positive or negative connotations. Ask students to think of words with similar meanings and to explain the differences between these synonyms. [*Courageous* is a more positive term than *brazen; destroy* is a more negative term than *conquer.*]

## Reading Informational Materials

### Reading Skill
Developing Vocabulary Knowledge

Explain to students that we can use several strategies to help figure out unfamiliar words. We may use context clues to determine the meanings of unfamiliar words, or we may study the words' prefixes, suffixes, and roots.

### Reading Strategy
Developing Vocabulary Knowledge (Strategy 11)

To help students when they encounter unfamiliar words, use Strategy 11 in Content-Area Reading Strategies. Provide students with a Contextual Redefinition Chart (Graphic Organizer 4) to use with the Wordbusting, or CSSD, strategy.

▶ **Teaching Tip**

*Affixes and Roots* Provide students with a list of the selection's words containing prefixes, suffixes, and Greek and Latin roots. [for example, *unknown, impressed, astronomy, slowly, geographer, cartographer*] Have students brainstorm other words— either in the selection or from their own background knowledge—that use the same word parts. After students have suggested more words with the same word part, write a definition of the prefix, suffix, or root. When they have finished, have students check their definitions in a dictionary.

# DURING READING

## Correcting Misconceptions

Discuss with students how Prince Henry's reputation as an innovative explorer might be viewed very differently by a native of Africa. From the perspective of Africans in Morocco and on the continent's west coast, Henry's exploration was not carried out for the advancement of scientific or human knowledge, but rather out of greed or cruelty.

## Using the Side-Margin Features
▪ An Island of Rabbits *and* A Tree to Dye For

After students have read "An Island of Rabbits" and "A Tree to Dye For," talk with them about the idea of ecological balance. What conditions are required for a species to maintain the proper population size? [Students may say that plants and animals need the proper level of competition from predators. Without competition, the population of a species may increase to the point that some individuals starve from lack of resources. Too much competition will drive a species to extinction, upsetting a balance for another species of plant or animal.] Ask students to think of modern examples in which human beings have affected the balance of plants or animals in an area. [Students may mention fish populations that have been diminished or areas where newly introduced plant species have taken over the habitats.]

## Differentiating Instruction
▪ Learners Having Difficulty

Make maps of Europe and Africa available to students to refer to while reading the selection. Tell them that the selection mentions Morocco, the Canary Islands, Porto Santo, Cape Bojador, the Cape Verde Islands, and the Azores. Ask students to find the locations named and to describe the relation of these areas to Prince Henry's kingdom of Portugal.

# AFTER READING

## ✔ Reading Check

The following are sample answers to questions on student text page 189.

1. Prince Henry became curious about Africa after leading an expedition against a city in Morocco and hearing stories about the Green Sea of Darkness.

2. People thought that if they sailed too far down the west coast of Africa, the sea would boil, sailors would turn black, ships would catch fire, and people would choke on poisonous air.

3. Gil Eanes sailed out to sea before reaching Cape Bojador, passed the cape while at sea, and then sailed back to shore.

4. Prince Henry wore a prickly hair shirt next to his skin because he wanted to remember that Christians should not be too comfortable or too proud.

5. The Africans were of interest because Portugal was experiencing a labor shortage and some people thought that the Africans could be used as slaves.

## Reteaching

Discuss with students the different types of context clues found in the selection. A *definition/explanation clue* provides the exact meaning of the word within a sentence. A *restatement/synonym clue* restates an idea using other words, often using signal words such as *for example* or *especially*. A *contrast/antonym clue* gives the opposite meaning of an unfamiliar word, sometimes using signal words such as *despite* or *however*. Tell students that *inference/general context clues* are not as obvious as the other types of context clues discussed. A reader must infer an unfamiliar word's meaning from other details within a passage. What clues did they use to determine the meanings of words such as *navigable, lumbering,* and *confound*?

## Connecting to Language Arts

■ Writing

*Case Study* How did the country of Portugal become such a leader in world explorations? Ask stu-dents to find out more about Portugal at the time of Prince Henry and to write a summary of the issues the kingdom faced. The summary should consider Portugal's trading concerns, as well as the importance of sea travel to Portugal's economy.

■ Speaking and Listening

*So How Did You Enjoy the Trip?* Ask students to find out more about Prince Henry's ships and sailors. Then, have students stage imaginary interviews between Prince Henry and captains returning from exploratory voyages down the African coast. Students may work in groups to decide on the types of information Prince Henry would want to know about the trip and to find out more about the voyages of John Gonçalves, Tristan Vaz, Gil Eanes, or Antam Gonçalves. Have students perform their interviews for the class.

## Connecting Across the Curriculum: History

*Exploring African Cultures* Have students learn more about West Africa at the time Portuguese explorers became aware of it. Ask students to research one of the peoples—the Wolof, the Malinke, or the Soninke—who lived in West Africa and to write a fact sheet describing the art, religion, or government of the group. Each student should mark the people's homeland on a map of Africa and illustrate a fact sheet with photographs or illustrations of objects from that culture. Display the results of students' research.

## Further Resources

■ Online resources

The Associação Nacional de Cruzeiros, a Portuguese Web site devoted to sailing, provides information in English about the *barca,* the *caravela,* and the *nau,* as well as links to sites relating to Prince Henry and Portuguese kings.

## Assessment

Turn to page 145 for a multiple-choice test on the selection.

*Test Answers*

1. d  2. b  3. c  4. a  5. b
6. b  7. d  8. c  9. c  10. a

# The Mapmakers

from *If You Were There in 1492*

by BARBARA BRENNER
*(student text page 190)*

**Reading Level:** Average

## Text Summary

The art of mapmaking kept pace with explorers' need for up-to-date geographical records. As printing capabilities improved in the fifteenth century, more affordable maps could be produced on paper, rather than on expensive vellum. The year 1492 was important for both exploration and for mapmaking: In that year, a German craftsperson produced the first globe to be manufactured since ancient Greek times.

# BEFORE READING

## Make the Connection

Show the class an outdated map in which new highways do not exist or on which political boundaries have changed. Discuss with students the difficulty of getting from one place to another when names of roads do not appear on maps. Ask them to consider how explorers might have felt when they encountered lands that did not appear on their maps. [Students may say that an outdated map could be confusing, or even dangerous, since it might give misleading information about how long a trip would take.]

## Build Background

■ More About the Topic

Ptolemy, an astronomer who lived in second-century Alexandria, undertook the first study of cartography. He collected many maps in his book *Geographica,* but the text was lost until medieval times. In about 1210, a Byzantine monk discovered a copy of Ptolemy's manuscript, and the ancient text was preserved in a library in Byzantium. When the city fell to the Turks in 1453, Sultan Mohammed II asked a philosopher to create a world map based on Ptolemy's studies. The sultan, who wanted to preserve the ancient map, became the world's first map collector. He even had a copy of this world map woven into a carpet.

## Vocabulary Development

The following words are underscored and defined in the student text.

**misinformation:** false or wrong information.
**profession:** occupation involving special skills or advanced education.
**mold:** form which gives shape.
**sphere:** globe-shaped form; ball.
**miniature:** small.

Before assigning the reading, you may want to introduce students to any words that could cause pronunciation or definition problems.

┌─ *Vocabulary Tip* ─────────────

**Recognizing Word Parts**  The content-area vocabulary words all describe items or qualities that could be found on a medieval map. Tell students to find a familiar word or word part [*letter, imagine, maid*] within the new longer word and to use the meaning they know to help them speculate about the meaning of the new word.

└────────────────────────────

( **CONTENT-AREA VOCABULARY** )

Although the following words are important to an understanding of the text selection, some of them may be unfamiliar to students.

**lettering\*:** letters marked on a surface by writing or painting; letters inscribed.
**imaginary:** not real.
**mermaids:** legendary sea creatures with fish tails and women's heads and torsos.

\*Although students may be familiar with other meanings of these words, the words as used in the selection have a specific meaning that pertains to the content area.

## Reading Informational Material

### Reading Skill
**Summarizing**

Discuss with students the purpose of a summary: restating the main ideas of a piece of writing in only a few words. Tell students that being able to summarize a text can help them better understand and remember the meaning of what they read.

### Reading Strategy
**Understanding Text (Strategy 2)**

To help students summarize the selection, use Strategy 2 in Content-Area Reading Strategies. Provide students with a Cluster Diagram (Graphic Organizer 3) to help them organize main ideas and supporting details. Students can work in pairs to write brief summaries of the selection based on their diagrams.

▶ **Teaching Tip**

*Comparing Globes and Maps* Discuss with students why explorers would be interested in using a globe rather than a map. Have students compare representations of northern countries, such as Greenland and Iceland, on both a map and a globe. How could the images on a map be misleading? [Because a flat map distorts the round shape of the earth, northern countries appear much larger on a map than they actually are. A globe gives a more accurate representation of the earth.]

## DURING READING

### Using the Side-Margin Feature
▪ Juan de la Cosa

After students have read "Juan de la Cosa," discuss with them the degree to which mapmaking is a science, an art, or a political instrument. Have students discuss the ways in which a map could reveal information that might be politically sensitive for a country's leaders. [Students may say that maps could reveal that glaciers have melted, that rivers have grown smaller, or that shorelines have eroded.]

### Differentiating Instruction
▪ **Learners Having Difficulty**

Because modern maps are accurate, plentiful, and fairly cheap, some students may have difficulty understanding why they were so important in medieval times. Find an illustration of a medieval map and discuss its details with students. Ask students to think about what such materials and craftsmanship would cost today. In addition, have them think about what an accurate map could mean to a ruler who wanted to claim new lands for his or her country. [A good map could help explorers find previously unexplored territory and claim the new lands and riches for the ruler; a poor map might cause the ruler's explorers and their expensive ships and equipment to be lost.]

▪ **English-Language Learners**

The selection includes some unfamiliar words that are not critical to students' understanding of the text's main idea. Point out to English-language learners some words that are not vital to the story's main idea, such as *Majorca* and *gazelle*. Discuss with them how skipping words that are not key to the main idea can be a strategy for understanding a new text.

## AFTER READING

### ✔ Reading Check

The following are sample answers to questions on student text page 193.

1. Cartography is mapmaking.

2. If early mapmakers had no information about an area, they would fill it in with pictures of imaginary creatures and countries.

3. In 1492, maps were in demand because they had to be made for explorers, because kings and queens gave maps as gifts, and because more people could afford the less expensive maps available as a consequence of improved printing techniques.

4. Martin Behaim created a globe. Other maps of the time were flat, but Behaim's was a sphere.

5. Behaim misrepresented the size of the earth, making it appear 25 percent smaller than it actually is. His mistake might have made Christopher Columbus optimistic about the possibility of reaching the Indies.

## Reteaching

To help students summarize the selection, have them focus on the text by looking for its most important words. Have students review the text and write down five or six words they think are important to understanding its meaning. [*mapmaker, exploration, geographical, printing, globe*] Students should then write a brief explanation of each choice, describing why they think it should be included in a summary. Have students discuss their choices in pairs, narrowing their lists down to one word. Then, have students use this word to write a sentence or two summarizing the selection. [most important word: *mapmakers*] [Cheaper printing processes and less expensive paper aided mapmakers in keeping up with the need to make accurate records of the geographical information coming from new-world exploration. Martin Behaim's new globe, based on the wrong information, unfortunately misled explorers.] You may want to have the entire class work together and vote on which words they think are most important. Be sure to have students explain the reasons for their answers, and emphasize that students' explanations are as important as the words they choose.

## Connecting to Language Arts
▪ Writing

*Résumés* Ask students to assume the identity of Abraham Zacuto or Martin Behaim, each a famous mapmaker. Have students write a short résumé of their chosen mapmaker. The résumés should include information about the mapmakers' training, special skills, accomplishments, and ambitions.

▪ Speaking and Listening

*Interviewing* Have volunteers portray an interview between Martin Behaim and city officials in Nuremberg, Germany. Why would this German city want to spend so much money on a globe? Have Martin tell them! Students portraying the Nuremberg officials can raise their doubts and concerns for the student portraying Behaim to address.

## Connecting Across the Curriculum: History

*Using Graphic Organizers* Have students research how the map of a particular area has changed over time. Have students pick a spot anywhere in the world and find an early representation of it on a map. Ask students to find a more contemporary but outdated map and a current one. Have them create a graphic organizer, such as a Venn Diagram (Graphic Organizer 11) or a Cluster Diagram (Graphic Organizer 3) showing how the maps have evolved. Students should include any change in the countries' names or political boundaries. Have students display their maps in chronological order and post them, with the organizers, on the class bulletin board.

## Further Resources
▪ Online resources

The School of Art and Design at San José State University has a Web site that offers illustrations of maps and drawings (including Martin Behaim's globe), as well as biographies of artists and scientists of the fifteenth and sixteenth centuries. The site also includes images of historical navigation equipment, including sextants, quadrants, astrolabes, and compasses.

### Assessment

Turn to page 146 for a multiple-choice test on the selection.

*Test Answers*

**1.** a **2.** d **3.** b **4.** a **5.** c
**6.** d **7.** c **8.** d **9.** b **10.** a

# from Ancient Healing

from *Science of the Early Americas*
by GERALDINE WOODS
*(student text page 194)*

**Reading Level:** Average

## Special Considerations

The text mentions the Aztec practice of human sacrifice. Discuss with students how these rituals, which seem cruel and barbarous to modern people, reflected strong religious beliefs.

## Text Summary

By the time the Europeans had arrived, the peoples of the New World had developed many sophisticated techniques for treating injuries and illness. Their approaches to healing involved the invention of tools, such as syringes, surgical knives, and tourniquets, as well as the use of herbal medicines to ease pain. Despite their knowledge of medicine, American Indians had little resistance to the deadly diseases introduced by Europeans.

# BEFORE READING

## Make the Connection

Ask students whether they are familiar with the practice of folk medicine, a type of health care in which people use traditional techniques and remedies, such as native plants and herbs. Tell students that their grandparents or great-grandparents may have frequently used elements of folk medicine when other medical treatments were not available. Point out to students that many alternative medicines today are similar to the types of cures that were used by our ancestors.

## Build Background

■ More About the Topic

The Aztec people employed a great number of medical workers to treat many specific types of ailments. A person called a *temixihuitiani,* a term that means "to give birth," assisted during childbirth. A *tetlacuicuilique* was a healing woman who drew out stones from the body. Aztec medicine included the worship of particular deities. Quetzalcoatl, called the Lord of Healing and Magical Herbs, was thought to have given knowledge of medicine to the Aztec people.

## Vocabulary Development

The following words are underscored and defined in the student text.

**functions:** works.

**internal:** inside.

**circulating:** moving or flowing in a circular course.

**domesticated:** tamed.

**resistance:** ability to fight off disease.

Before assigning the reading, you may want to introduce students to any words that could cause pronunciation or definition problems.

─ *Vocabulary Tip* ─

**Using Words with Multiple Meanings** The content-area vocabulary words describe medical conditions or treatments. Discuss with students how words can take on particular meanings when they are applied to special subjects, such as sports, medicine, or law. Have students think of other words that can have a special meaning when applied to a particular field. [*Stroke,* heart *attack,* and *cast* have special meanings when they are used in relation to medicine.]

◯ **CONTENT-AREA VOCABULARY**

Although the following words are important to an understanding of the text selection, some of them may be unfamiliar to students.

**dislocated\*:** referring to a condition in which a bone has been moved from its normal position in the joint.

**searing\*:** burning with a heated iron in order to stop bleeding.

**dressings\*:** medicine and bandages applied to a wound.

*Although students may be familiar with other meanings of these words, the words as used in the selection have a specific meaning that pertains to the content area.

Present this list of words and the definitions to students, and have them brainstorm connections between the words. [Each word can have a connection to a medical treatment.] Encourage students to discuss other meanings they know for these words.

## Reading Informational Material

### Reading Skill
#### Making Generalizations
Discuss with students how generalizations use specific information to form broad ideas or principles. To form generalizations, readers gather textual clues, combine this information with what they already know about a topic, and then infer an explanation about the situation discussed in the text.

### Reading Strategy
#### Constructing Concept Maps (Strategy 4)
To help students organize the selection's descriptions of different medical techniques and treatments, use Strategy 4 in Content-Area Reading Strategies. Provide students with a Cluster Diagram (Graphic Organizer 3) or have them create a concept map. Then, have students work with a partner to brainstorm generalizations based on the details in their organizers. Students can share and explain their generalizations in a class discussion.

### ▶ Teaching Tip
*Location, Location*  Discuss with students the fact that ancient peoples of the Americas were able to use only plants and materials available in their areas. For example, the rubber available to the Arawak would not have grown where Plains Indians lived. Point out the homelands of different American Indian peoples on a map, and discuss with students what types of resources might have been available in different regions. [Plains Indians would have had access to many native grasses; the bones and horns of bison also would have been an important resource. Jungle plants, such as rubber, could have been used by Mayan and Aztec peoples.]

# DURING READING

## Using the Side-Margin Feature
■ Mummies on the Mountain
After students have read the feature "Mummies on the Mountain" on page 196, discuss with them the Inca practice of human sacrifice, called *capacocha*. Tell students that these sacrifices were often a response to threatening events, such as eclipses, earthquakes, or the death of an emperor. Ask students to estimate the age of the child in the picture. Do students believe the child understood what was happening?

## Viewing the Art
■ Inferring from the Details
Refer students to the illustration of the mummified Incan child on page 196. Ask students to comment on aspects of the mummy's clothing. What do these details say about the event and the people involved? [Students may say that the child appears to be carefully groomed and richly dressed. Great attention to appearance could indicate that the child was honored as if he or she were royalty.]

## Differentiating Instruction
■ Learners Having Difficulty
The selection is organized by categories of health care, and it lists several different American Indian peoples within each section. Students who have difficulty following the references may be helped by organizing the selection's details according to the peoples being discussed. Draw and distribute to students a Cloze Concept Map to chart these details. You will want to provide students with a general heading such as *Ancient Healing* and then fill in names of the different peoples—*Aztec, Inca,* or *Maya.* Start students out by filling in some subheadings and details in the Cloze organizer. For example, under the subheading *Aztec,* you could include the details "removal of living heart," "observation of lungs and heart," "plaster casts," and "bone needles."

# AFTER READING

## ✔ Reading Check

The following are sample answers to questions on student text page 198.

1. Incas learned about the body's internal organs by removing them to mummify their dead. Aztecs learned about internal organs because they removed the human heart during ritual sacrifice.

2. Sweat lodges were small, round buildings heated to high temperatures. People stayed inside for several hours to sweat out impurities.

3. Tourniquets are strips of rope or cloth that are tied tightly around a part of the body to stop blood flow. American Indians used tourniquets to stop bleeding and to treat snakebites.

4. American Indians treated gum infection by cutting and draining the infected area and then searing the incision with heat. They pulled out decayed teeth with tools such as bone tweezers.

5. European diseases were deadly to American Indian populations because the American Indians had neither resistance to nor cures for these diseases. The diseases carried by Europeans originally spread to them from domesticated animals unknown to American Indians.

## Reteaching

Help students combine new information with their own knowledge to form generalizations. Have students create a five-column organizer and label the columns *Question, The Text Says, My Comment, My Inference,* and *My Generalization.* Then, provide students with a *Question* that requires an inference, for example, *How would American Indians have learned to make knives from volcanic glass?* In *The Text Says* column, have students write information from the text on the subject. [The selection says that people in Central and South America made obsidian knives. The text says these people lived near volcanoes.]

In the *My Comment* column, students should write their responses to this information. [Sample response: Only people living near ancient volcanoes would have seen this kind of glass.] In the *My*

*Inference* column, students should infer something not actually stated in the text. [The people who lived near volcanoes had access to a special resource. They must have noticed the sharp edges of broken rock and experimented with them.]

When students have completed the chart, have them use the *My Generalization* column to form an overall statement about the information presented in the selection. [Experimenting with the resources available in their particular areas, ancient peoples developed new tools and methods to cope with illness and injury.]

## Connecting to Language Arts
▪ Writing

*Healthful or Harmful?* Ask students to learn more about a medicinal plant or tool used by ancient peoples in North or South America. Have students write a short description, such as one that might be used as an entry in a medical encyclopedia. When students have completed their descriptions, combine the entries to form a class encyclopedia of ancient medicine.

## Connecting Across the Curriculum: Science

*Researching the Outdoor Pharmacy* Ask students to read more about the medicinal plants of the New World. Have students work in groups to find out which of these plants are still used today. Students can display their research results in a poster that illustrates the medicinal plant, the areas where it is found, and the types of medicines made from the plant. Display students' posters to illustrate the "outdoor pharmacy" available to ancient peoples.

## Further Resources
▪ Book

*American Indian Healing Arts: Herbs, Rituals, and Remedies for Every Season of Life* by E. Barrie Kavasch and Karen Baar.

## Assessment

Turn to page 147 for a multiple-choice test on the selection.

*Test Answers*
1. b   2. a   3. c   4. b   5. d
6. a   7. d   8. b   9. a   10. c

# A Strange, Funny-Looking Vegetable

from *The Amazing Potato: A Story in Which the Incas, Conquistadors, Marie Antoinette, Thomas Jefferson, Wars, Famines, Immigrants, and French Fries All Play a Part*

by MILTON MELTZER
(student text page 199)

**Reading Level:** Average

## Text Summary

The invading Spanish army came to Peru searching for the Incas' gold and silver. In addition to these precious metals, they found another treasure: the potato. The Spaniards learned that this unfamiliar vegetable was not only tasty, but also profitable. Today, the potato crop is worth much more than the gold and silver originally sought by the conquistadors.

# BEFORE READING

## Make the Connection

Have students think back over their meals for the past several days. Ask them to list the number of times and different ways in which they have eaten potatoes. Ask students to try to think of a substitute for potatoes in their diet—what food could replace them? Tell students that potatoes are the most important food for Peruvians, where ten percent of the calories in people's diets come from potatoes.

## Build Background

■ More About the Topic

Early Peruvian farmers used foot plows, called *tacllas*, to cultivate their potato fields. Their *tacllas* did not resemble European plows that were pulled behind horses. The Peruvian device was a five-foot-long stick with handles. Its tip was hardened by fire or covered in copper. Farmers used the sticks as levers to turn the heavy ground and prepare it for planting. These foot plows, now with steel tips, are still used by farmers in South America.

## Vocabulary Development

The following words are underscored and defined in the student text.

**irregular:** uneven; lopsided.

**staple:** most important or basic to the diet.

**vegetarian:** of a diet containing no meat.

**bartered:** traded without using money.

**speculators:** investors who take risks, hoping to make big profits.

Before assigning the reading, you may want to introduce students to any words that could cause pronunciation or definition problems.

## Vocabulary Tip

**Comparing Word Connotations** The content-area vocabulary words relate to the Spanish conquistadors. Before students read the selection, have them look at the vocabulary and predict what will be discussed in the selection. Discuss with students the words' connotations. Does *loot* have a positive or negative association? Ask students to think of words with similar meanings and to explain the differences between these synonyms. [*Ambitious* is more positive than *greedy*; *lugged* is more negative than *carried*.]

### CONTENT-AREA VOCABULARY

Although the following words are important to an understanding of the text selection, some of them may be unfamiliar to students.

**greedy:** wanting to have more than one needs or deserves.

**loot:** stolen goods.

**lugged:** carried or dragged.

Present this list of words and their definitions to your students, and have students brainstorm any possible connections between the words.

### Reading Skill

**Finding the Main Idea**

Tell students that the topic developed in an article or in a section of an article is called its main idea. The author's primary message is the one he or she most wants readers to understand. It may be stated directly or it may be implied from the details included.

### Reading Strategy

**Activating and Using Prior Knowledge (Strategy 8)**

To help students activate their knowledge of Peru and the origin of potatoes, use Strategy 8 in Content-Area Reading Strategies. Provide students with a KWL Chart (Graphic Organizer 6). You may help students build background by having them preview the illustrations in the selection or by providing them with a map that illustrates the Andes Mountains and the Inca empire.

▶ **Teaching Tip**

*Food for Thought* Discuss with students how cultures can be defined by their methods of feeding their people and the types of foods they eat. Have students identify some staple foods associated with both early and modern cultures. [Students may mention rice as a staple in Asian countries. Plains Indian peoples depended upon the bison for their survival, while American Indians in the northwest depended upon fish, such as salmon.]

## DURING READING

### Using the Side-Margin Feature

▪ **The Great Hunger**

After students have read "The Great Hunger," help them explore the conditions that contributed to the famine in Ireland. Discuss with students why the poor in Ireland would have depended upon potatoes. [The New World food was cheap and easy to grow.] Introduce students to the concept of a "monoculture," in which only one crop is grown and eaten. What are the dangers of depending upon only one food source? [People depending on a single food source are vulnerable to the effects of weather and disease on their crops; their limited diets also may be unhealthy.]

### Differentiating Instruction

▪ **Learners Having Difficulty**

Discuss with students the use of specific time order in this selection. Point out that the selection includes examples of two types of time order: chronological information about the Spanish conquest of the Incas and a sequential description of making *chuno*. Provide each student with a Sequence or Chronological Order Chart (Graphic Organizer 10) to help them list the order of these events.

▪ **English-Language Learners**

The Spaniards' introduction to a new, unusual, and unfamiliar food may seem very familiar to some English-language learners. Ask language learners to share experiences of being introduced to new types of foods or of introducing foods from their culture to friends and acquaintances.

## AFTER READING

### ✔ Reading Check

The following are sample answers to questions on student text page 202.

1.  The Spaniards were looking for gold, silver, and precious stones. They found maize (corn), beans, and potatoes.

2.  The Incas used potatoes for healing. They also depended on potatoes for food.

3.  The potato was especially important in the highlands of Peru because corn and many other vegetables could not grow there.

4.  The Incas preserved their potato crop by spreading the potatoes on the ground and letting the potatoes freeze. The next day, the Incas, using their bare feet, stamped out the potatoes' moisture. They repeated this procedure until all the moisture in the potatoes was removed. This process created potato flour, which could be stored for many years.

5.  The annual value of the potato crop has become three times greater than the value of all the gold and silver taken by the Spaniards. The

writer calls this observation a twist of history because the Spaniards killed for gold and silver but did not recognize the value of the vegetable that was worth much more.

## Reteaching

If students have difficulty stating the selection's main idea, have them write key words in a Cluster Diagram (see Graphic Organizer 3 and Strategy 3). Have students group clusters of related words and use one or two of the words to build sentences discussing the selection. For example, students may build clusters by jotting down details about the words *Spaniards, potatoes,* and *diet.* [For example: **Spaniards** *invaded Peru* searching for *silver and gold.*] Then students can add words from other clusters to the original sentence. [**Spaniards** found out about **potatoes** when they *invaded Peru* searching for *silver and gold.*] After students have built several sentences using the key words from their cluster diagrams, have them discuss how the sentences reflect the text's main idea.

## Connecting to Language Arts

### ▪ Writing

***Would You Like Fries with That?*** Have students write a recipe to give to a Spaniard who has never before seen a potato. Ask students to choose a simple recipe, such as mashed, fried, or baked potatoes, and write down the information needed by those unfamiliar with the dish. For example, how will they know when the potatoes are fully cooked? How many potatoes will be needed for each person? Have students write their instructions on large recipe note cards; you may want to collect the cards to create a class Potato Cookbook.

### ▪ Speaking and Listening

***Starring Mr. Potato Head™?*** The Spaniards have just figured out the importance of these funny-looking tubers. Have students work in groups to create a radio script in which the Spaniards get out the word on the importance of this vegetable. Students may want to show originality in their production by including a character part for each group member. Students can produce segments on the potato's appearance, its vitamin content, and the process of growing and harvesting, as well as menu options. Have students present their pro-

gram to the class or record their performance to hear at a later time.

## Connecting Across the Curriculum: History

***One Potato, Two Potato*** Ask students to find out the history of how the potato spread to a particular area. Have students choose an Old World country and learn about how potatoes were introduced there. How did people learn to grow, cook, and eat this new vegetable? Have students create fact sheets telling when it became part of that country's diet and describing how the potato was cultivated. In addition, ask students to find potato recipes that originated in these Old World countries.

## Further Resources

▪ Online resources

The Prince Edward Island Web site includes information about the history of the potato, potato cultivation, the consumption of potatoes during war, and potato "fun facts."

The Public Broadcasting System has a Web site to accompany its documentary *The Conquistadors.* It includes lesson plans and teaching guides in the feature section "Pizarro and the Incas."

### Assessment

Turn to page 148 for a multiple-choice test on the selection.

*Test Answers*

**1.** b  **2.** a  **3.** c  **4.** d  **5.** a
**6.** c  **7.** a  **8.** d  **9.** d  **10.** b

# "Let's Play Ball!"

from *Calliope*
by PETER KVIETOK
*(student text page 203)*

**Reading Level:** Average

## Special Considerations

The text refers to human sacrifices performed as religious rituals. Tell students that many ancient peoples once incorporated sacrifices into their worship. The Celts of Britain, for example, observed a holiday called Beltane during which a victim would be sacrificed to ensure that the summer harvest would be successful. Discuss with students why early peoples might have thought that a human sacrifice would ensure the health, prosperity, or safety of a community. [Worshipers may have thought they were making the gods happy by offering up one of their own and that the gods would then try to please the humans by sending good crops.]

## Text Summary

The Mayan people, who lived in ancient Central America, played a sacred game with a rubber ball. *Pok-ta-pok,* or "rubber-to-rubber," was played inside an elaborately decorated stone court. Teams who lost at *pok-ta-pok* could be sacrificed in religious ceremonies.

# BEFORE READING

## Make the Connection

Ask students how they learned the rules of a new game. Were the rules written, or were students taught the rules by a person who played the game? Discuss with students how games in a culture are passed down over time. [Students may say that many games are passed down by one person teaching another. They may observe that games change over time or as technology improves.]

## Build Background

▪ More About the Topic

The Great Ballcourt at Chichén Itzá, the largest of its type in the world, has remarkable acoustics. At each end of the Great Ballcourt is a raised temple area; a whisper at one temple can be heard at the other end, 500 feet away. The transmission of sound is so exceptional that conductor Leopold Stokowski tried to learn its secrets for an open-air theater he was designing. Stokowski spent four days at the site in 1931, but he, like many others, was not able to explain why sound is transferred so clearly in this Mayan ball court.

## Vocabulary Development

The following words are underscored and defined in the student text.

**participants:** players.
**stakes:** money or prizes to be won.
**ritual:** act done according to religious law.
**vertical:** upright; straight up or down.
**accounts:** descriptions or stories.

Before assigning the reading, you may want to introduce students to any words that could cause pronunciation or definition problems.

---

*Vocabulary Tip*

**Identifying Multiple Meanings** In the selection the vocabulary word *ritual* is used to describe a religious ceremony. However, students will also be familiar with many secular rituals. Discuss with students the types of rituals that they may witness in their school or community. [saluting a flag, reciting a creed for a club, introducing players at a sporting event]

---

**CONTENT-AREA VOCABULARY**

Although the following words are important to an understanding of the text selection, some of them may be unfamiliar to students. Present this list of words and the definitions to your students. Have students brainstorm the connections between the words. [All the words refer to the appearance of something.] Encourage students to discuss other meanings they know for these words.

**decorated:** adorned; made attractive.
**fancy:** showy; highly decorated.
**ornate:** gaudy; heavily or elaborately decorated.
**elaborate:** complex; full of details.

---
*Vocabulary Tip*
---

**Using Connotations** The content-area vocabulary words all indicate different degrees of attractiveness or complexity. Discuss with students the words' subtle differences in meaning. How would a *fancy* object compare to a *decorated* one? [An item could perhaps be *decorated* in an understated way without being *fancy*.] What connotations would be associated with *ornate* as compared to *elaborate*? [*Ornate* may imply a negative judgment, meaning that an item appears too busy or fussy. *Elaborate* is more likely to describe something that is difficult or complex.]

## Reading Informational Material

### Reading Skill
#### Monitoring Reading Comprehension
Discuss with students the importance of thinking about the act of reading while they are reading. As readers are aware that they need help figuring out a text, they can then find methods to help improve understanding.

### Reading Strategy
#### Taking Effective Notes (Strategy 10)
To help students mark areas in the text that may require re-reading or the use of other resources, use Strategy 10 in Content-Area Reading Strategies. To help students take notes using the Cornell, or divided-page, system, provide them with a Key Points and Details Chart (Graphic Organizer 5).

#### ▶ Teaching Tip
*Using Maps* Review with students the locations of major American Indian empires at the time of the Spanish arrival in the New World. Have students find on a map the areas occupied by the Mayas, Aztecs, and Incas. You may also want to discuss some of the notable cultural accomplishments of each empire, for example, the Mayas' sophisticated knowledge of mathematics and astronomy; the Aztecs' intensive systems of farming and irrigation; and the Incas' huge network of roads, tunnels, and bridges.

# DURING READING
## Using the Side-Margin Feature
■ You Need to Know
Archaeologists have looked at several types of evidence to find out which events might have contributed to the decline of the Mayan civilization. By examining bone samples, some scientists have determined that the Mayan people—even the culture's upper classes—suffered from malnutrition and anemia. Houses near hillsides have revealed signs of erosion—evidence that the hillsides were overfarmed. Some scientists theorize that the Mayan civilization gradually collapsed because of overpopulation, crop shortages, malnutrition, and disease. Others point to a major climate change or drought, rain-forest destruction, and tribal warfare as possible reasons for the Mayan decline.

## Differentiating Instruction
■ Learners Having Difficulty
Students may benefit from using graphic organizers to help visualize the *pok-ta-pok* game. Encourage them to sketch the ball court described on page 204, jotting down information about dimensions or the types of materials used in construction. Students may also want to use a Cluster Diagram (Graphic Organizer 3) to organize the description of rules of the Mayan ball game.

# AFTER READING

## ✔ Reading Check

The following are sample answers to questions on student text page 206.

1. The boys won the matches they played with the Lords of Death. One boy had his head bitten off by a giant bat, and both boys were burned and their bones thrown into the river. In the river they become handsome boys who can once again play ball.

**2.** Players on losing teams could have had their heads cut off in ritual sacrifices to the gods.

**3.** The ball was made of natural rubber from the sap of trees. It was about the size of a volleyball.

**4.** Without protective equipment, players could have been killed by the heavy, fast-moving ball. The equipment also helped them hit the ball harder. Also, players sometimes had to dive on the hard floor to return a low ball.

**5.** Players moved the ball around the field by hitting it with any part of their body except their hands or feet.

## Reteaching

Have students monitor their comprehension by reading aloud sections of the text with a partner. Tell students to stop at regular intervals to make a comment, ask a question, or connect one idea in the text to another. [Comment: This game must have been very exciting to watch. Question: Why would anyone play a game that was so dangerous? Connection: The description of the ball court makes it sound like a modern football stadium.] Have students create a three-column chart with the headings *Comment, Question,* or *Connection.* Ask them to put a check mark in the proper column for each comment, question, or connection. Tell students that if they are unable to make one of these types of observations about the text, then they need to re-read the passage. When students have finished their readings, they should discuss their observations with their partners. Students may find that their partners can answer questions that were raised earlier. Ask students to pay special attention to passages that seemed difficult or complicated on their first reading. Do these passages make more sense after discussing them with a partner?

## Connecting to Language Arts
▪ Writing

*Plea for Clemency* Students who find the Mayan practices harsh may wish to write a plea to the committee of Mayan elders asking for clemency for the losing team. Students should consider what could be offered to the gods instead of human sacrifice. What advantage could the saving of these lives bring to the community and its members?

▪ Speaking and Listening

*Halftime Interview* Have students learn more about the rules and rituals of *pok-ta-pok.* Then, have a student acting as a sports journalist interview a group of volunteers during an imaginary "halftime" program. The journalist will want to learn more about the rules, equipment, and rituals associated with the game, as well as how *pok-ta-pok* has become so popular. Have volunteer players perform their sports interview for the rest of the class.

## Connecting Across the Curriculum: Physical Education/History

*My Sport's Better Than Your Sport* Many cultures are closely associated with one particular sport. For example, sumo wrestling is popular in Japan, soccer is the favorite sport in Brazil, and chariot racing was enjoyed in ancient Rome. Have students research a sport popular in ancient or modern times and compare its cultural importance to that of *pok-ta-pok.* Ask students to look at the kinds of people who played and watched the sport, and to determine why the activity was important to the people of that culture. Have students prepare thumbnail sketches of the two sports and summarize major similarities and differences.

## Further Resources
▪ Online resource

The Texas Humanities Resource Center has a Web site, based on a traveling exhibition (*Mexico: Splendors of Thirty Centuries*) arranged by the Metropolitan Museum of Art in New York City. It provides images of Mayan and Aztec art and architecture, including Mayan ball courts.

### Assessment

Turn to page 149 for a multiple-choice test on the selection.

*Test Answers*

**1.** d   **2.** b   **3.** d   **4.** a   **5.** c
**6.** b   **7.** a   **8.** c   **9.** c   **10.** a

# All That Glitters

from *Read*

*(student text page 207)*

**Reading Level:** Average

## Text Summary

Since before the time of the ancient Egyptians, people have admired the beauty of gold. This precious metal lured explorers to the New World and continues to create "gold rushes" whenever a new source is discovered. The possibility of finding gold and "striking it rich" continues to inspire people's imaginations, just as the word *gold* continues to highlight important concepts in our language.

## BEFORE READING

### Make the Connection

Ask students to imagine that they are visiting our planet from another galaxy. How would they know that the metal called gold is important to people on earth? What clues would they observe in our appearance and language? [Students might say that visitors would notice that gold is expensive, that people seem to want it very much, and that the word *gold* is often used to describe something special.]

### Build Background

■ More About the Topic

Because of the newly-invented daguerreotype (a device that printed photographs on metal), the California gold rush was one of the first major historical events to be recorded with a camera. More than 100,000 miners went to California in the first year of the gold rush, and many of them sent photographs home to their families, ensuring a visual record of the search for gold. One other small but significant artifact has been preserved, as well. The quarter-ounce nugget said to have been found at a sawmill in 1848—the piece of gold that started the California gold rush—is displayed at the University of California at Berkeley.

## Vocabulary Development

The following words are underscored and defined in the student text.

**lavished:** given very generous amounts of (something).

**exquisite:** perfect or extremely beautiful.

**quest:** search, especially a search for something important.

**extravagant:** more than necessary.

**notorious:** widely known as having a bad reputation.

Before assigning the reading, you may want to introduce students to any words that could cause pronunciation or definition problems.

┌─ *Vocabulary Tip* ──────────────

**Evaluating Multiple Meanings** All the content-area vocabulary words have particular meanings that relate to gold. Have students discuss how the selection's context helps them understand these special meanings. [Students may say that *hammered* and *sheets* were clues that "gold leaf" is a thin layer of metal. They may also say that they imagined a literal leaf made of gold, which would have to be very thin.]

**CONTENT-AREA VOCABULARY**

Although the following words are important to an understanding of the text selection, some of them may be unfamiliar to students. Present the list to students, and have them predict what the selection will discuss. [gold, searching for gold, finding gold]

**gold leaf\*:** thin sheet of gold used for gilding, or covering an object with a layer of gold.

**nuggets\*:** small, solid lumps.

**gold rush\*:** sudden rush of people to an area where gold has been discovered.

**lode\*:** an abundant deposit of ore.

*Although students may be familiar with other meanings of these words, the words as used in the selection have a specific meaning that pertains to the content area.

## Reading Informational Material

### Reading Skill

Identifying Text Structures: Causes and Effects

Discuss with students the relationship between causes and effects. Explain that *causes* create an action, and that *effects* are the results of these actions. If both causes and effects are not clearly explained in a text, readers must make inferences by using their own knowledge.

### Reading Strategy

Anticipating Information (Strategy 9)

To help students find relationships between causes and effects within the selection, use Strategy 9 in Content-Area Reading Strategies. Students may want to use the Anticipation Guide (Graphic Organizer 1) to organize their thoughts. Statements might include *The search for gold has always led to important discoveries, Civilizations have always benefited from the presence of gold,* or *People value gold largely because of its beauty.*

▶ **Teaching Tip**

*Creating Time Lines* Students may follow the selection's chronology more easily if they create a time line on which to jot down important events. Emphasize to students that the selection is not strictly chronological and that a time line can help them follow the history of gold.

## DURING READING

### Using the Side-Margin Feature

■ Sidelight

After students have read the excerpt from "Eldorado," have them discuss the various meanings of the word *shadow* in the poem. [In the first stanza, *shadow* refers to the type of weather or weather conditions. In the second stanza, a shadow is a feeling of doubt or disappointment. The "pilgrim shadow" in the third stanza and the "shade" in the fourth verse are the ghost of a "pilgrim," or one who has gone before and is now dead.] What is the shadow's message to the gallant knight?

What has been the result of the knight's quest? [The shadow urges the knight ever forward, just as people's greed might urge them to search for gold. The knight has spent his strength searching for gold, but he has learned nothing from his quest.]

## AFTER READING

### ✔ Reading Check

The following are sample answers to questions on student text page 212.

1. El Dorado was a legendary city where gold was plentiful. Explorers wanted the gold in El Dorado.

2. Alchemists tried to turn common metals into gold. Their studies developed into the science of chemistry.

3. Spain became wealthy by taking millions of ounces of gold from native peoples of Central and South America.

4. Gold nuggets were discovered at Sutter's Mill, and the discovery began the California gold rush.

5. The SS *Central America* was carrying more than twenty tons of gold when it sank off the coast of South Carolina.

### Reteaching

If students are still having difficulty recognizing cause and effect, offer them the following formula:

*Who or what* (moving force) *did* _____, *which caused* (cause of conflict) _____.

First, have students offer statements based on the material they have read, and record the statements on the chalkboard or on an overhead transparency. Sample statements:

■ Europeans looked for gold in Central and South America.
■ Explorers destroyed Indian civilizations.
■ Gold was found in California.
■ A gold rush drew many people to California.

Have students put their information into the formula statement.

- [(*Who or what*) European explorers (*did*) looked for gold (*which caused*) explorers to destroy wealthy Indian civilizations in Central and South America to get their gold.]

Then, have students use the material to develop a sentence beginning with *because* and followed by the cause statement. [(*Because*) European explorers went looking for gold, they destroyed Indian civilizations in order to get their gold.]

You may want to repeat this process using the following example: [(*Who or what*) People (*did*) found gold nuggets at Sutter's Mill (*which caused*) a gold rush drawing many people to California. [(*Because*) gold was discovered at Sutter's Mill, many people rushed to California.]

## Connecting to Language Arts
### ▪ Writing
***Creating a Children's Book*** Ask students to write a children's picture book that highlights some aspect of the history of gold. The book could show how gold has been used by different cultures through the ages; it could also note places that have been rich sources of the metal or tell the story of a gold miner. Students can use illustrations, such as maps, their own drawings, or pictures of golden objects. When students have completed their books, they may want to donate copies of them to a grade school.

### ▪ Speaking and Listening
***What Gold Has Meant to Me*** Ask volunteers to present a round-table discussion in which historical figures talk about how gold has affected their lives. The historical figures might include King Tutankhamen, a Spanish conquistador, an Inca villager, or Captain Kidd. Students can work in groups to create discussion questions for the characters and find out information to help the characters prepare their answers. Record the round-table discussion to share with the entire class.

## Connecting Across the Curriculum: Science/History
***Gold Strike!*** Have students find out more about a famous gold strike: California, the Klondike, Australia, or along the Orinoco River in Venezuela. Ask students to find out how the gold strike began, how much gold was found at the site, and how the discovery of gold changed the area. Students should write up the results of their findings in a case study that examines the benefits of the gold strike as well as the problems that came with striking it rich.

## Further Resources
### ▪ Online resource
The Web site for Klondike Gold Rush National Historic Park documents the gold rush of 1897–1898. The Web site includes maps of the area and historical photographs. The park is located in both Alaska and Washington.

### ▪ Video
Have students learn more about the personal experiences of Klondike prospectors from the PBS program "Gold Fever." This documentary from *The American Experience* features the personal correspondence of prospectors, as well as stories told by their families, and period photographs.

### Assessment

Turn to page 150 for a multiple-choice test on the selection.

***Test Answers***

| | | | | |
|---|---|---|---|---|
| **1.** a | **2.** d | **3.** c | **4.** b | **5.** c |
| **6.** c | **7.** d | **8.** a | **9.** b | **10.** d |

The following criteria can help you evaluate each student's success in completing the activities prompted by the Cross-Curricular Activities feature in the student textbook.

**\*Note:** Activities marked with an asterisk allow the involvement of more than one student. For these activities you may wish first to evaluate each student on his or her individual contribution and then give groups an overall rating.

## \*Geography/Art
### Where in the World Is It?

- Student groups conduct research to find maps drawn during the age of exploration (fifteenth to eighteenth centuries).
- Each group creates a montage of three or four maps of Africa or the Americas to show how the maps changed over time.
- Each group conducts research to find current maps of the same places.
- Groups write the date on each current map and list three ways all maps differ from one another.
- The montage is neat, visually appealing, and has clear explanations.

## Language Arts/Music
### The View from the Shore

- The student creates three short stories on the experience of a person in Africa who sees Portuguese ships sailing along the coast of Africa or meets sailors who come ashore.
- The student selects and records background music that effectively enhances the mood of the stories.
- The student puts the stories and music together on an audiotape and plays it for the class.
- The tape effectively evokes the historical period, leaving the audience with a vivid picture of an African storyteller's view of the events.

## \*History/Geography
### Striking It Rich

- The student designs a poster about the locations of at least two famous gold strikes.
- The poster may be a map alone or a map with text around it.
- The student indicates where and when the gold was discovered and how much gold came from the area. If possible, he or she could also note the depth of the mines, the richness of the lodes, and interesting prospecting techniques.
- The student places the posters in the classroom.

## Science/Art
### Look at This

- The student conducts research on one of the medical treatments or medicinal plants used by American Indians.
- The student draws a cartoon strip with at least four sections or scenes: discovery of the treatment or plant, how it was used or how it worked, final results, and its modern use.
- The student posts the cartoon strip in the classroom.
- The writing is relatively free of errors in spelling, grammar, usage, and mechanics.

## Health/Art
### Extraordinary Tuber

- The student conducts research to find a recipe for a potato dish.
- The student prints the recipe in the center of a large sheet of poster board and surrounds it with information about the nutritional benefits of the potato.
- The student illustrates the poster with other potato recipes or with scenes from the recipe's country of origin.

## Selection Test

*from* The Roads to the Spiceries
*from Roman Roads*
by VICTOR W. VON HAGEN

### COMPREHENSION QUESTIONS

Circle the letter of the best answer to each of the following items. *(50 points)*

1. The Emperor Trajan could focus on road building because
   a. the people of Hither Asia were excellent workers
   b. the Roman Empire needed more soldiers
   c. the Roman Empire was at peace
   d. the Roman legions kept the peace

2. The city of Petra was
   a. located a great distance from the Via Traiana
   b. carved from limestone
   c. redesigned in the Nabatean style
   d. independent of the Roman Empire

3. Transporting goods over land routes often depended on the
   a. horse          c. oxen
   b. dog            d. camel

4. Slaves in the ancient world
   a. could be found only in Rome
   b. might have sold themselves into slavery
   c. were never from countries defeated by the Romans
   d. always paid their debts

5. Luxury items in Roman markets
   a. came primarily from Egypt
   b. were too heavy to carry by camel
   c. included bananas and sugar cane
   d. were light and easy to transport

### VOCABULARY

Using your knowledge of the underlined word, circle the letter of the word or phrase that best completes each statement. *(50 points)*

6. An unruly tribesman would be inclined to
   a. work well with others
   b. follow directions
   c. break rules
   d. wait patiently

7. The hewn buildings in Petra were
   a. constructed from brick
   b. shaped by an ax
   c. forged from steel
   d. shaped from poured concrete

8. A sheen refers to a pearl's
   a. costly price          c. smooth texture
   b. shiny appearance      d. dull color

9. A Roman soldier might feel invulnerable when he was
   a. well protected by armor
   b. in the line of enemy fire
   c. recovering from an injury
   d. building the Via Traiana

10. When people in India and along the Nile cultivated cotton, they
    a. harvested it from the desert
    b. wove it into cloth
    c. grew it as a crop
    d. gathered it from the field

## Selection Test

### Hadrian's Wall
from *Walls: Defenses Throughout History*
BY JAMES CROSS GIBLIN

## COMPREHENSION QUESTIONS

Circle the letter of the best answer to each of the following items. *(50 points)*

1. Hadrian's Wall was built to protect
   a. only one city
   b. the Emperor Hadrian
   c. two specific castles
   d. Rome's northernmost colony

2. The milecastles in Hadrian's Wall
   a. often were located next to a village
   b. housed about 50 soldiers
   c. were built about four miles apart
   d. contained stables for horses

3. Soldiers fortified Hadrian's wall with
   a. deep V-shaped ditches on both sides
   b. speaking tubes
   c. a second wall on its north side
   d. a small ditch on its south side

4. During the 250 years that Hadrian's Wall was defended, its enemies never
   a. captured its watchtowers
   b. damaged its stonework
   c. captured or held large sections of the wall
   d. sent raiding parties to attack it

5. Soldiers who had guarded Hadrian's Wall were transferred from Britain to fight
   a. the Scots
   b. the Goths and the Persians
   c. the Saxons
   d. tribes in the south of England

## VOCABULARY

Using your knowledge of the underlined word, circle the letter of the word or phrase that best completes each statement. *(50 points)*

6. A subdued country is
   a. successful          c. conquered
   b. rich                d. hungry

7. Laborers recruited to build Hadrian's Wall were
   a. dismissed from their job
   b. hired to work on the project
   c. trained to be soldiers
   d. imprisoned in forts

8. The intervals between milecastles were
   a. spaces
   b. forts
   c. soldiers' quarters
   d. horse stables

9. Soldiers who guarded a sector of Hadrian's Wall were responsible for
   a. only the Wall's milecastles
   b. the entire fortification
   c. a section of the wall
   d. taking care of the cavalry

10. When northern tribes formed an alliance with the Scots, they
    a. created a financial partnership
    b. forced them out of their territory
    c. rebelled against the Scots' authority
    d. united with them for a common purpose

## Selection Test

### A Persecuted Faith Becomes a World Religion
from *Calliope*
by S.E. TOTH

### COMPREHENSION QUESTIONS

Circle the letter of the best answer to each of the following items. *(50 points)*

1. The Emperor Diocletian launched a persecution of Christians to
   a. raise money to rebuild Rome
   b. support the policies of the Emperor Nero
   c. punish Christians for the burning of Rome
   d. restore belief in the Roman Empire and its gods

2. The Christians' catacombs
   a. are off limits to visitors today
   b. are decorated with paintings
   c. were not used for worship
   d. can be found only in Rome

3. Constantine waged war against other Roman rulers
   a. to show his dislike of Maxentius
   b. to win the support of his army in Gaul
   c. to expand his control of the Roman Empire
   d. to get control of Spain and North Africa

4. The Edict of Milan
   a. freed Christians from persecution
   b. was issued only by Licinius
   c. did not affect the Western Empire
   d. applied only to Christians

5. The Hagia Sophia
   a. was built by the Emperor Constantine
   b. remains the center of the Eastern Orthodox Church today
   c. was replaced by the Magale Ekklesia.
   d. burned and was rebuilt by the Emperor Justinian

### VOCABULARY

Using your knowledge of the underlined word, circle the letter of the word or phrase that best completes each statement. *(50 points)*

6. When Nero ordered a persecution, he allowed Christians to be
   a. rewarded
   b. praised
   c. tormented
   d. promoted

7. An idea that is tolerated would be
   a. allowed        c. abused
   b. celebrated     d. ignored

8. The rigor of early Christianity indicates that the religion
   a. had been heavily persecuted
   b. had strict standards
   c. was loosely defined
   d. was very similar to other faiths

9. Christians' fervor was a sign of their
   a. mild fear      c. calmness
   b. bravery        d. intense emotion

10. Ornate Christian churches would have
    a. elaborate decorations
    b. simple designs
    c. poor craftsmanship
    d. large meeting rooms

## Selection Test

**The Fall and the Legacy**
from *Ancient Rome*
by CHRISTOPHER FAGG

## COMPREHENSION QUESTIONS

Circle the letter of the best answer to each of the following items. *(50 points)*

1. Diocletian's system of dividing the empire
   a. sped up the decline of the empire
   b. lasted until the reign of Constantine
   c. made sure that a new Caesar would take over every 50 years
   d. prevented rivalries from arising

2. The Visigoths and Vandals
   a. demanded to join the empire
   b. threatened Rome's eastern territory
   c. raided along coasts in the west
   d. defeated the Huns

3. The Visigoth leader Alaric
   a. ignored Rome because he wanted Gaul
   b. protected Rome from the Huns

   c. killed the emperor Romulus Augustulus
   d. led his army to sack and burn Rome

4. One of the strongest reminders of the Roman Empire was
   a. the disappearance of Latin
   b. Christianity
   c. Roman ruins
   d. books about King Arthur

5. Constantine was named emperor after
   a. he moved the capital to Constantinople
   b. he defeated his co-rulers
   c. he made Christianity the official religion
   d. the crafting of the Nicene Creed

## VOCABULARY

Using your knowledge of the underlined word, circle the letter of the word or phrase that best completes each statement. *(50 points)*

6. The <u>rivals</u> for Rome's leadership
   a. competed for power
   b. made sure of a smooth transition
   c. cooperated in ruling the empire
   d. shared the responsibility of governing

7. Constantine's <u>treacherous</u> co-rulers
   a. equally divided the empire
   b. faithfully supported the divided system
   c. were disloyal to him
   d. could be trusted to rule fairly

8. When the Visigoth Alaric <u>seized</u> provinces, he
   a. shared them with other groups
   b. lost them after a long battle

   c. gave them a democratic government
   d. took them by force

9. The <u>deposed</u> leader Romulus Augustulus
   a. was re-elected for another term
   b. was removed from power
   c. ruled together with an Ostrogoth leader
   d. voluntarily retired from office

10. Those who wanted to <u>convert</u> barbarians hoped to
    a. protect them from change
    b. record their customs
    c. educate them
    d. change their religion

## Selection Test

**from Travel Through the Empire**
from *The Arabs in the Golden Age*
by MOKHTAR MOKTEFI

### COMPREHENSION QUESTIONS

Circle the letter of the best answer to each of the following items. *(50 points)*

1. A camel caravan's journey
   a. moved 220 pounds of goods
   b. carried merchandise on enclosed couches
   c. usually consisted of five thousand camels
   d. could last for several months

2. Trade among merchants was
   a. aided by the Crusades
   b. expanded when problems arose in China
   c. always safe in the Arab world
   d. protected from local revolts

3. In the tenth century, Arabs did not travel to
   a. South Africa
   b. southern France
   c. Spain
   d. eastern Europe

4. Arab ships
   a. avoided monsoon winds
   b. traveled on both rivers and seas
   c. easily avoided Indian pirates
   d. did not transport passengers

5. The bathhouses in caravansaries
   a. were attached to mosques
   b. were used only for religious ceremonies
   c. could be found in private homes
   d. used only cold water

### VOCABULARY

Using your knowledge of the underlined word, circle the letter of the word or phrase that best completes each statement. *(50 points)*

6. When the Arabs encountered difficult terrain, they found
   a. land with harsh natural features
   b. guides with no sense of direction
   c. strong winds
   d. slow, heavy sailboats

7. To navigate a caravan is to
   a. supply its food and water
   b. care for its camels
   c. protect its merchandise
   d. direct its course

8. Something that is an indispensable part of a caravan
   a. can be substituted for a more expensive product
   b. is always on time
   c. cannot be left out
   d. is required for finding directions

9. A person in a convoy is
   a. using unsafe transportation
   b. boarding a boat
   c. traveling in a group
   d. vacationing alone

10. A communal item is
    a. used only one time
    b. shared by a group
    c. discarded after use
    d. restricted for special occasions

## Selection Test

**Cordoba—Jewel of the World**
from *Calliope*
by DIANA CHILDRESS

### COMPREHENSION QUESTIONS

Circle the letter of the best answer to each of the following items. *(50 points)*

**1.** The Great Mosque of Cordoba
   **a.** was built entirely of white stones
   **b.** was enlarged as the city's Muslim community grew
   **c.** was designed to conceal its supporting columns
   **d.** contained all the city's gold

**2.** Commerce in Cordoba
   **a.** was isolated from the Mediterranean Sea
   **b.** included both trade and manufacturing
   **c.** depended heavily on the tanning industry
   **d.** did well only around the Great Mosque

**3.** The rulers of Cordoba
   **a.** created beautiful palaces and gardens
   **b.** were less wealthy than Baghdad's leaders
   **c.** shared their riches with Baghdad
   **d.** lived modestly

**4.** Cordoba's system of education
   **a.** was always expensive
   **b.** excluded women
   **c.** attracted international scholars
   **d.** was limited to Muslim scholars

**5.** Europeans were brought into closer contact with Muslim technology and learning by
   **a.** Christian scholars
   **b.** by conservative religious leaders
   **c.** the efforts of the caliph of Spain
   **d.** the crusades and reconquest of Spain

### VOCABULARY

Using your knowledge of the underlined word, circle the letter of the word or phrase that best completes each statement. *(50 points)*

**6.** A metropolis such as Cordoba would
   **a.** be a rural community
   **b.** consistently grow smaller
   **c.** have a large population
   **d.** locate most of its people in outlying areas

**7.** The artisans of Cordoba were
   **a.** known for studying in the Great Mosque
   **b.** skilled in a trade or type of art
   **c.** known for their limited craftsmanship
   **d.** required to take reading tests

**8.** Mosaics are artworks that are
   **a.** made of small pieces of stone or glass
   **b.** considered to be very old
   **c.** found only in prayer niches
   **d.** carved from marble or jasper

**9.** The Muslim trade in textiles
   **a.** involved fine cotton cloth
   **b.** later was made illegal
   **c.** refers to goods made of leather
   **d.** developed around delicately worked metals

**10.** A conservative Muslim leader would
   **a.** develop alternative prayers and rituals
   **b.** resist adding new prayers
   **c.** introduce modern rituals
   **d.** encourage adopting new customs

## Selection Test

*from* **The Magic of Mathematics**
from *Science in Early Islamic Culture*
by GEORGE BESHORE

### COMPREHENSION QUESTIONS

Circle the letter of the best answer to each of the following items. *(50 points)*

**1.** Numerals from India were
   **a.** first described by Al-Khwarizmi
   **b.** praised by a great Moslem mathematician
   **c.** invented by Severus Sebokht
   **d.** not accepted by the Western world

**2.** The scholar Al-Khwarizmi
   **a.** took his name from a body of water
   **b.** gave his name to the process of algebra
   **c.** improved the process of algebra
   **d.** taught the use of decimals to the Greeks and Egyptians

**3.** The process of trigonometry
   **a.** is used when part of an equation remains unknown
   **b.** is based on the use of decimals.
   **c.** comes from Arabic for "restitution"
   **d.** is about angles and triangles

**4.** The publication of Ptolemy's maps shows how
   **a.** wrong information can be widely spread
   **b.** the circumference of the earth was determined
   **c.** Eratosthenes' and Posidonius' work was compared
   **d.** geographers got accurate measurements

**5.** Moslem scientists gathered information from
   **a.** mathematicians in Baghdad
   **b.** the ruler Al-Ma'mum
   **c.** interviews with older scientists
   **d.** many old manuscripts

### VOCABULARY

Using your knowledge of the underlined word, circle the letter of the word or phrase that best completes each statement. *(50 points)*

**6.** A number written as a decimal can
   **a.** have a written denominator
   **b.** give the same information as a fraction
   **c.** have no numerator
   **d.** include no decimal point

**7.** A mathematician's calculations
   **a.** are the processes of figuring with numbers
   **b.** can be discovered only through algebra
   **c.** were first arrived at by Ptolemy
   **d.** must include a decimal point

**8.** A ratio of a triangle
   **a.** adds the triangle's sides using fractions.
   **b.** compares the lengths of a triangle's sides
   **c.** determines that the figure is a right triangle
   **d.** is the basis of algebra

**9.** To compute a problem, you would
   **a.** use arithmetic to figure an answer
   **b.** ask for more information
   **c.** do research
   **d.** suggest an idea

**10.** A mathematician's procedures are the
   **a.** instruments used to determine an angle
   **b.** publications used to spread knowledge
   **c.** methods used to solve a problem
   **d.** types of numbers selected for an equation

**Selection Test**

## The Coming of Islam
from *The Royal Kingdoms of Ghana, Mali, and Songhay: Life in Medieval Africa*
by PATRICIA AND FREDRICK MCKISSACK

## COMPREHENSION QUESTIONS

Circle the letter of the best answer to each of the following items. *(50 points)*

1. Muhammad wrote the Koran
   a. immediately after his revelation
   b. over the course of twenty-two years
   c. with the help of other prophets
   d. after leaving Mecca

2. Muslims believe that because Allah controls human destiny
   a. Muhammad is God's prophet
   b. all people are related
   c. prayer is necessary
   d. human beings cannot escape their fate

3. The countries of North Africa
   a. refused to speak Arabic
   b. held off a Muslim invasion
   c. became a united Arabian stronghold
   d. conducted a holy war against the Muslims

4. Before the arrival of Islam missionaries, the Ghanians
   a. had no written language
   b. did not believe in a god
   c. wrote in many languages
   d. had already rejected Islamic merchants and traders

5. The King of old Ghana and his subjects
   a. quickly converted to the Islamic religion
   b. asked the *ulama* for religious instruction
   c. remained faithful to their traditional religions
   d. initially objected to Muslim institutions within their country

## VOCABULARY

Using your knowledge of the underlined word, circle the letter of the word or phrase that best completes each statement. *(50 points)*

6. A person who has a revelation
   a. submits to the will of others
   b. starts a new religion
   c. understands something not known before
   d. gathers clues for others to interpret

7. A sacred writing would be described as
   a. ancient         c. expensive
   b. common          d. holy

8. An event that is one's destiny
   a. is sure to happen
   b. should always be avoided
   c. can probably be controlled
   d. can always be delayed

9. The obligations of Islam are believers'
   a. chants, or *shahada*
   b. pilgrimages
   c. prayers
   d. duties

10. To testify to his or her faith, a person makes a
    a. denial
    b. declaration
    c. compromise
    d. journey

## Selection Test

**from Mali: Empire of the Mandingoes**
from *A Glorious Age in Africa:*
*The Story of Three Great African Empires*
by DANIEL CHU AND ELLIOT SKINNER

### COMPREHENSION QUESTIONS

Circle the letter of the best answer to each of the following items. *(50 points)*

1. Mali's ruler Mansa Wali
   a. was the father of Sundiata
   b. oversaw a pagan empire
   c. was a better leader than his own father
   d. began a royal tradition of being very religious

2. During Mansa Musa's reign,
   a. Mali became an Islamic country
   b. Mali lacked a strong ruler
   c. Mali grew strong and rich
   d. Local chiefs shot arrows at their subjects

3. Mansa Musa's pilgrimage was
   a. similar to those made by other rulers
   b. unusual because of its show of wealth
   c. taken at a bad time
   d. a private display of religious feelings

4. From the list of travelers included in Mansa Musa's caravan, we can conclude that
   a. the local chiefs sometimes caused trouble in the Malian empire
   b. there were no children in the caravan
   c. no government business took place in the ruler's absence
   d. the Malian ruler traveled only with his servants

5. The sultan of Cairo
   a. made the Malian visitors welcome
   b. was afraid of Mansa Musa
   c. sold supplies to the Malian caravan
   d. loaned money to Mansa Musa

### VOCABULARY

Using your knowledge of the underlined word, circle the letter of the word or phrase that best completes each statement. *(50 points)*

6. Mansa Musa's <u>pilgrimage</u> took him to a
   a. new territory     c. holy place
   b. vacation site     d. trading center

7. When countries reach an agreement through <u>diplomacy</u>, they
   a. negotiate a decision
   b. are forced to find a new leader
   c. must call in a neutral party to make a decision
   d. decide to vote on it

8. <u>Commerce</u> in Mali might have included all of the following **except**
   a. weaving cotton
   b. giving away goods to Egypt
   c. grinding grain for bread
   d. melting gold for coins

9. Mansa Musa's <u>descendants</u> included
   a. Sundiata
   b. "the Red King"
   c. his children
   d. his grandfather

10. An <u>elaborate</u> ceremony might be described as
    a. sincere
    b. simple
    c. short
    d. detailed

## Selection Test

### Talking Drums and Talking Gongs
from *Faces*
by ENID SCHILDKROUT

### COMPREHENSION QUESTIONS

Circle the letter of the best answer to each of the following items. *(50 points)*

1. Europeans discovered talking drums when
   a. Africans took instruments to Europe
   b. their own bush telegraphs failed
   c. villagers always expected their arrival
   d. they researched African music

2. An hourglass-shaped drum
   a. uses two resonators
   b. has only one membrane, or skin
   c. has thongs to change its tone
   d. is called a *ntumpane*

3. The makers of talking drums
   a. often create special drums for themselves
   b. create drums according to religious rituals
   c. give special gifts to the chief
   d. are the most gifted drummers

4. To produce two tones, wooden gongs are
   a. slit in the center
   b. decorated with animals at each end
   c. called husband and wife drums
   d. carved to be two different thicknesses

5. Many African languages
   a. use tone to determine meaning
   b. cannot be expressed through talking drums
   c. use tone only for emphasis
   d. cannot be expressed in written form

### VOCABULARY

Using your knowledge of the underlined word, circle the letter of the word or phrase that best completes each statement. *(50 points)*

6. Languages use <u>emphasis</u> to show
   a. volume
   b. stress
   c. rhythm
   d. politeness

7. The <u>variables</u> of a project are things that
   a. can be changed
   b. can be deleted
   c. must be included
   d. should be repaired

8. To <u>convey</u> a message is to
   a. communicate its meaning
   b. hide a secret
   c. understand a code
   d. misread a note

9. A drummer's <u>repertoire</u> includes subjects that he or she
   a. has recently learned
   b. has taught to younger drummers
   c. often uses
   d. finds difficult

10. A village would <u>commemorate</u> a great victory by
    a. apologizing for it
    b. forgetting about it
    c. analyzing it
    d. honoring it

## Selection Test

**Land of Discovery**
from *Scholastic Update*
by PHIL SUDO AND JEAN CHOI

### COMPREHENSION QUESTIONS

Circle the letter of the best answer to each of the following items. *(50 points)*

1. Understanding the importance of nutrition, early Chinese doctors cured many diseases through
   **a.** acupuncture
   **b.** diet
   **c.** surgery
   **d.** aspirin

2. Karate, judo, and tae kwon do are
   **a.** skills that require little training
   **b.** not yet popular in the United States or Asia
   **c.** exercises to build muscles
   **d.** Japanese and Korean adaptations of martial arts

3. The crossbow was
   **a.** feared because it could pierce armor
   **b.** developed after land mines
   **c.** China's first explosive device
   **d.** more destructive than gunpowder

4. With the principle of *shu*, Confucius
   **a.** states an important idea about God
   **b.** declares the importance of human beings
   **c.** sets out rules for prayer
   **d.** describes a principle of give and take

5. The unity of yin and yang
   **a.** can be found only in special objects
   **b.** pulls together two very positive forces
   **c.** makes up *tao*, the ultimate way of the universe
   **d.** proves that opposites cannot be combined

### VOCABULARY

Using your knowledge of the underlined word, circle the letter of the word or phrase that best completes each statement. *(50 points)*

6. Chinese who <u>adhere</u> to traditional beliefs in medicine might
   **a.** continue to use folk medicines
   **b.** change their medical treatments often
   **c.** prefer aspirin to herbs
   **d.** find an alternative to acupuncture

7. Because of a <u>surge</u> of Chinese immigration to the United States,
   **a.** fewer Chinese now live in the United States
   **b.** the number of Chinese in the United States sharply increased
   **c.** U.S. interest in natural medicines has decreased
   **d.** the number of Chinese in the United States has remained the same

8. A <u>legitimate</u> type of medicine is one that is
   **a.** unproven
   **b.** used only by Western doctors
   **c.** reasonable
   **d.** used mostly by new immigrants

9. A program with <u>rigorous</u> training would have
   **a.** casual participants
   **b.** relaxed standards
   **c.** voluntary rules
   **d.** strict requirements

10. A philosophy that <u>pervades</u> a society
    **a.** would be challenged by most people
    **b.** is not generally accepted
    **c.** has spread throughout the society
    **d.** has been rejected by society

## Selection Test

### The Biggest Wall of All
from *National Geographic World*
by MARGARET McKELWAY

## COMPREHENSION QUESTIONS

Circle the letter of the best answer to each of the following items. *(50 points)*

1. The Great Wall was begun
   a. at the same time that China was formed
   b. as soon as nomadic warriors threatened settlers
   c. after Qin Shi Huangdi's reign ended
   d. with the help of nomadic tribes

2. The brick-and-stone construction of the Great Wall today
   a. dates from the wall's beginnings
   b. occurred when local fortifications were first connected
   c. quickly wore away
   d. began in the 1300s

3. The Great Wall's length is
   a. estimated at about 2,500 miles
   b. much greater than the distance across the United States
   c. about 1,000 miles
   d. exactly 2,500 miles

4. The territory covered by the Great Wall
   a. is smooth and flat
   b. is entirely within a desert
   c. varies greatly
   d. does not pass through mountains

5. The defense provided by the Great Wall proved to be
   a. a failure
   b. always successful
   c. useful only against particular invaders
   d. usually effective

## VOCABULARY

Using your knowledge of the underlined word, circle the letter of the word or phrase that best completes each statement. *(50 points)*

6. A warrior's <u>loot</u> is always
   a. heavy          c. golden
   b. stolen         d. expensive

7. <u>Invaders</u> entered China
   a. by invitation
   b. to learn more about the country
   c. by force
   d. for peaceful visits

8. A person <u>plagued</u> by an event would be
   a. entertained
   b. rested
   c. interested
   d. troubled

9. A <u>continuous</u> barrier would
   a. have many gaps
   b. be solid and unbroken
   c. be especially tall
   d. have defensive towers

10. River <u>gorges</u> are always
    a. wide
    b. shallow
    c. deep
    d. flat

## Selection Test

*from* The Search for Genghis Khan
from *Current Events*

### COMPREHENSION QUESTIONS

Circle the letter of the best answer to each of the following items. *(50 points)*

**1.** Genghis Khan's funeral procession
  **a.** transported his body to a remote location
  **b.** took place in his capital, Karakorum
  **c.** carried the dead leader until it reached a yurt
  **d.** consisted entirely of mounted soldiers

**2.** Genghis Khan's tomb
  **a.** was found by a Japanese team
  **b.** was found by Maury Kravitz's team
  **c.** has been the subject of an intensive search
  **d.** is located near the leader's birthplace

**3.** The defeat of the Tatar people was probably
  **a.** the result of their inferior military training
  **b.** Genghis Khan's revenge for his father's death

  **c.** helped by the harsh Mongolian winters
  **d.** completed with the help of the Chinese

**4.** The Mongol leader thought China's Prince of Wei was
  **a.** an important person
  **b.** a competent ruler
  **c.** better than China's previous emperor
  **d.** not worthy of respect

**5.** Chinese armies
  **a.** prepared successful strategies to defeat Mongol warriors
  **b.** were well prepared for Genghis Khan's army
  **c.** were often defeated by Genghis Khan's intelligent battle plans
  **d.** learned how to counter the Mongols' "suicide corps"

### VOCABULARY

Using your knowledge of the underlined word, circle the letter of the word or phrase that best completes each statement. *(50 points)*

**6.** A resounding noise might be
  **a.** hard to hear
  **b.** very loud

**7.** The Mongol army's plunder might consist of
  **a.** goods from China
  **b.** Mongol weapons

**8.** If you encountered an old friend, the experience would be
  **a.** unexpected
  **b.** a tragedy

**9.** A person's reputation is known to
  **a.** a few close friends
  **b.** the public

**10.** When someone is renounced, he or she is
  **a.** blessed
  **b.** disowned

**11.** A delegation of people speaks
  **a.** only to each other
  **b.** for others

**12.** An eminent leader always possesses
  **a.** a high standing
  **b.** a temper

**13.** When fending off attacks, an army is
  **a.** resisting
  **b.** retreating

**14.** A special tactic would most likely be used in a
  **a.** military battle
  **b.** medical procedure

**15.** Genghis Khan's realm was his
  **a.** lost lands
  **b.** kingdom

Name _____ Class _____ Date _____

## Selection Test

### The Paper Revolution
from *Faces: The Magazine About People*
by JOHN S. MAJOR

## COMPREHENSION QUESTIONS

Circle the letter of the best answer to each of the following items. *(50 points)*

1. Papyrus was not a suitable writing material because it was
   a. too heavy
   b. too expensive
   c. easy to break
   d. awkward to carry

2. Recent evidence indicates that papermaking was invented
   a. by Ts'ai Lun
   b. around A.D. 100
   c. around 150 B.C. or earlier
   d. in Baghdad

3. The custom of folding letters into fancy shapes developed in
   a. Japan          c. Babylon
   b. China          d. Spain

4. Layers of paper treated with lacquer were used to create
   a. raincoats
   b. origami
   c. armor
   d. lanterns

5. Paper made with linen or cotton rags
   a. is very strong
   b. was developed to replace paper made from wood pulp
   c. is very cheap
   d. was first made on giant machines

## VOCABULARY

Using your knowledge of the underlined word, circle the letter of the word or phrase that best completes each statement. *(50 points)*

6. A perishable item must be protected from
   a. breaking
   b. melting
   c. spilling
   d. spoiling

7. An imperial officer works in the service of
   a. a democracy
   b. an empire
   c. a city official
   d. an international organization

8. A plant's fibers are suggestive of
   a. blocks
   b. threads
   c. wheels
   d. roots

9. A luxurious item would probably not be purchased by
   a. a person of refined tastes
   b. a successful business owner
   c. a person on a tight budget
   d. a professional athlete

10. To spur someone on is to
    a. threaten him or her with harm
    b. assist him or her financially
    c. worry him or her needlessly
    d. encourage him or her to action

## Selection Test

### from Prince Taishi Shōtoku Japan, A.D. 574–622

from *Heroes: Great Men Through the Ages*
by REBECCA HAZELL

## COMPREHENSION QUESTIONS

Circle the letter of the best answer to each of the following items. *(50 points)*

**1.** Prince Taishi Shōtoku was an effective leader because he
   **a.** was worshiped
   **b.** began ruling when he was a teenager
   **c.** fought with rival clans
   **d.** wanted to help his country

**2.** Confucius's teachings emphasized
   **a.** personal responsibility
   **b.** shared responsibility
   **c.** that power should go to people of special background
   **d.** that power should be inherited and kept within families

**3.** Some of Prince Shōtoku's achievements have been lost, including
   **a.** his written history of Japan
   **b.** the temples near Nara
   **c.** the introduction of Buddhism
   **d.** Japanese gagaku dance

**4.** During Prince Shōtoku's reign,
   **a.** a war broke out between Japan and China
   **b.** the Japanese nobility revolted
   **c.** the Shinto religion was banned
   **d.** Japan became more peaceful and prosperous

**5.** Culture and arts introduced from China include the
   **a.** tea ceremony
   **b.** Buddhist religion
   **c.** Shinto religion
   **d.** art of paper folding

## VOCABULARY

Using your knowledge of the underlined word, circle the letter of the word or phrase that best completes each statement. *(50 points)*

**6.** People in a <u>rustic</u> country would likely be most informed about
   **a.** agriculture      **c.** literature
   **b.** the arts          **d.** political science

**7.** <u>Rival</u> clans would view one another as
   **a.** co-workers      **c.** friends
   **b.** competitors     **d.** assistants

**8.** Only an <u>influential</u> group could make changes simply by
   **a.** studying
   **b.** hard work

   **c.** exerting power over others
   **d.** writing persuasive letters to leaders

**9.** A nation's <u>prosperity</u> might be indicated by its
   **a.** ambitious nobles
   **b.** unsophisticated government
   **c.** continued problems with rival clans
   **d.** healthy and robust citizens

**10.** Japan <u>adapted</u> Chinese ideas by
   **a.** preserving them exactly as they were
   **b.** dramatically changing them
   **c.** adjusting them as necessary
   **d.** completely rejecting them

## Selection Test

### from Murasaki Shikibu
from *Outrageous Women of the Middle Ages*
by VICKI LEÓN

## COMPREHENSION QUESTIONS

Circle the letter of the best answer to each of the following items. *(50 points)*

1. Japan's ancient capital of Kyoto was known for its
   a. commerce
   b. spring flowers
   c. religious ceremonies
   d. transportation

2. The Murasaki family took comfort from
   a. having a great deal of money
   b. their ties to a powerful clan
   c. their daughter's intellectual pursuits
   d. their influence with the Fujiwara clan

3. Murasaki Shikibu's diary reveals
   a. an outsider's view of Japanese society
   b. negative and positive self-evaluations
   c. mostly unimportant gossip
   d. little about her character

4. Murasaki Shikibu began writing a novel
   a. after her husband's death
   b. when she moved to a distant province
   c. as she began teaching the Empress Akiko
   d. to impress the emperor of Japan

5. Lady Murasaki's work for the empress meant that she
   a. could openly study Chinese
   b. had to teach routine assignments
   c. had a quiet and reserved life
   d. participated in lively outings

## VOCABULARY

Using your knowledge of the underlined words, circle the letter of the word or phrase that best completes each statement. *(50 points)*

6. The food served at a modest meal would probably be
   a. festive and extravagant
   b. scarce and not adequate
   c. rare and expensive
   d. ordinary and plain

7. A conceited person would likely be mostly concerned about
   a. focusing on himself or herself
   b. shifting attention to others
   c. listening to others
   d. sharing the spotlight

8. An era known for its elegance would be marked by its
   a. knowledge        c. power
   b. dishonesty       d. refinement

9. A novel considered to have low prestige would
   a. definitely be a boring read
   b. have many fans
   c. not have an impressive reputation
   d. be read repeatedly

10. One could prompt a classmate when he or she
    a. was not on time
    b. forgot an answer
    c. asked a question
    d. needed a library book

Name _____ Class _____ Date _____

## Selection Test

### COMPREHENSION QUESTIONS

Circle the letter of the best answer to each of the following items. *(50 points)*

**1.** Viking discoveries were helped by
   **a.** detailed maps    **c.** expensive ships
   **b.** careful planning    **d.** bad weather

**2.** In Bjarni Herjolfsson's time, trade between Norway and Iceland was probably
   **a.** unusual    **c.** prohibited
   **b.** common    **d.** interrupted

**3.** The first Viking leader to see North America
   **a.** described its beauty
   **b.** created a map to the site
   **c.** found the area unappealing
   **d.** collected samples of native plants

**4.** Thorvald Eriksson was one of the first Europeans to
   **a.** discover Greenland
   **b.** sight North America
   **c.** walk on the North American continent
   **d.** fight with North American inhabitants

**5.** Most experts believe that Vinland was located on
   **a.** Newfoundland
   **b.** Rhode Island
   **c.** Maine
   **d.** North Carolina

### VOCABULARY

Using your knowledge of the underlined word, circle the letter of the word or phrase that best completes each statement. *(50 points)*

**6.** To dispose of goods, Vikings might
   **a.** carve them    **c.** sell them
   **b.** buy them    **d.** store them

**7.** A resource that is exploited is
   **a.** given to charity    **c.** sold at a loss
   **b.** used successfully    **d.** saved for the future

**8.** A person making a sojourn might be
   **a.** resting after a trip
   **b.** cooking for a party
   **c.** planning a celebration
   **d.** visiting distant relatives

**9.** A person's ancestry would include
   **a.** livestock    **c.** money
   **b.** people    **d.** clothing

**10.** An idea that has receded is
   **a.** difficult to recall
   **b.** completely forgotten
   **c.** fully recorded
   **d.** well remembered

## Selection Test

### from Plague
from *Invisible Enemies: Stories of Infectious Diseases*
by JEANETTE FARRELL

## COMPREHENSION QUESTIONS
Circle the letter of the best answer to each of the following items. *(50 points)*

**1.** In the city of Siena,
  **a.** the plague did not affect Agnolo di Tura's family.
  **b.** victims were quickly buried in ditches.
  **c.** victims were treated through effective medical practices.
  **d.** the plague spared most children.

**2.** Many people who were threatened with plague in the Middle Ages responded by
  **a.** helping bury their neighbors.
  **b.** actively performing research.
  **c.** robbing the sick.
  **d.** ridding cities of rats.

**3.** The Mongol empire of Genghis Khan
  **a.** bound together large areas of Asia and Russia.
  **b.** prevented free trade across national boundaries.
  **c.** divided Central Asia into numerous kingdoms.
  **d.** allowed few trade routes.

**4.** People likely to contract the plague first might have lived
  **a.** in cold regions.  **c.** near lakes and rivers.
  **b.** in small towns.  **d.** near trading centers.

**5.** The pneumonic plague damages its victims'
  **a.** feet.  **c.** lungs.
  **b.** lymph nodes.  **d.** stomachs.

## VOCABULARY
Using your knowledge of the underlined word, circle the letter of the word or phrase that best completes each statement. *(50 points)*

**6.** A stench affects a person's sense of
  **a.** smell  **b.** sight

**7.** Calamities that affect a city might include a
  **a.** gentle rain  **b.** raging fire

**8.** People stupefied by the plague were
  **a.** stunned by its effects
  **b.** immune to its symptoms

**9.** A town in chaos would be notable for its
  **a.** confusion  **b.** leadership

**10.** An appeased person has been
  **a.** imprisoned  **b.** calmed

**11.** A ship that has been quarantined
  **a.** would be isolated from shore
  **b.** could send its crew ashore for supplies

**12.** During an epidemic,
  **a.** people's health improves
  **b.** disease spreads quickly

**13.** A substance disperses when it
  **a.** becomes invisible
  **b.** spreads apart widely

**14.** A person affected by a toxin would feel
  **a.** strong.  **b.** sick

**15.** An inexplicable tragedy would have
  **a.** no easy explanation
  **b.** a hero or heroine

## Selection Test

### Brother Sun . . . Sister Moon

from *Brother Sun, Sister Moon:*
*The Life and Stories of St. Francis*
by MARGARET MAYO

## COMPREHENSION QUESTIONS

Circle the letter of the best answer to each of the following items. *(50 points)*

1. St. Francis believes that praise should be
   a. awarded mostly to humans
   b. saved for special occasions
   c. given especially to the poor
   d. given entirely to God

2. The weather and elements should be praised, Francis implies, mostly because
   a. they are beautiful  c. they give us joy
   b. God made them   d. they are useful

3. The elements that can be both calm and stormy are
   a. Brothers Fire and Air
   b. Brothers Wind and Air
   c. Sister Moon and the Stars
   d. Sister Water and Brother Fire

4. The element that is considered joyful is
   a. Brother Fire       c. Sister Water
   b. Sister Earth       d. Brother Air

5. The Earth probably is compared to a mother because both
   a. are patient        c. provide food
   b. are strong         d. provide advice

## VOCABULARY

Using your knowledge of the underlined word, circle the letter of the word or phrase that best completes each statement. *(50 points)*

6. To nourish a plant, one would
   a. cut back its leaves
   b. move it to another spot
   c. photograph its flowers
   d. give it food and water

7. A person with the quality of humility would
   a. share resources with others
   b. take care of the sick
   c. not show pride at winning an event
   d. boast of his or her accomplishments

Name _____ Class _____ Date _____

## Selection Test

### Anna Comnena
from *Outrageous Women of the Middle Ages*
by VICKI LEÓN

## COMPREHENSION QUESTIONS

Circle the letter of the best answer to each of the following items. *(50 points)*

**1.** Anna Comnena's writing provides the perspective of a person who
   **a.** went on a crusade with other pilgrims
   **b.** watched the crusaders
   **c.** fought off crusaders
   **d.** ruled Constantinople during the Crusades

**2.** The first crusaders to arrive in Constantinople were
   **a.** peasants from France and Germany
   **b.** returning from Syria
   **c.** led by the Pope
   **d.** nobles from Hungary

**3.** Crusaders in Constantinople
   **a.** shared their supplies with city residents
   **b.** observed all city regulations
   **c.** were supplied with food, water, and transportation
   **d.** thanked the Byzantine emperor for his help

**4.** The Orphanage at Constantinople
   **a.** treated only paying patients
   **b.** was housed in a small facility
   **c.** was off-limits to Anna Comnena
   **d.** treated Christians returning from Jerusalem

**5.** Anna Comnena wrote *The Alexiad*
   **a.** after being banished from court
   **b.** while married to Nicephorus Bryennius
   **c.** during her engagement to Constantine Ducas
   **d.** before becoming heir to the throne

## VOCABULARY

Using your knowledge of the underlined word, circle the letter of the word or phrase that best completes each statement. *(50 points)*

**6.** A person performing <u>penance</u> would
   **a.** celebrate a holiday
   **b.** apologize for an action
   **c.** rebel against a leader
   **d.** observe an anniversary

**7.** The actions of a <u>fanatic</u> could best be described as
   **a.** extreme          **c.** enthusiastic
   **b.** quiet            **d.** moderate

**8.** A <u>destitute</u> person most needs
   **a.** an education     **c.** money for travel
   **b.** a larger house   **d.** food and clothing

**9.** Anna's <u>formidable</u> writing talents earned historians'
   **a.** envy             **c.** pity
   **b.** respect          **d.** disgust

**10.** Actions taken at a <u>momentous</u> event are considered
   **a.** interesting      **c.** important
   **b.** educational      **d.** amusing

## Selection Test

**The Children's Crusade**

from *Renaissance*
by CRISTINA PELAYO

## COMPREHENSION QUESTIONS

Circle the letter of the best answer to each of the following items. *(50 points)*

1. As Nicholas marched to Italy, his band of children
   a. received approval from the Pope
   b. became smaller
   c. steadily increased
   d. sent a message to the French king

2. Children who followed the French shepherd Stephen
   a. crossed the Alps
   b. reached Venice
   c. stopped in western Germany
   d. arrived at the port of Marseilles

3. The children who eventually reached southeast France
   a. arrived in the Holy Land safely
   b. may have later died in a storm
   c. were reported to be heroic in battle
   d. eventually all returned safely to their homes

4. Adults' reactions to the Children's Crusades indicate that
   a. older people feared that the children would not be safe
   b. more soldiers were required in Jerusalem
   c. the church approved of all such religious undertakings
   d. the children received more support in France than in Germany

5. The Children's Crusades illustrate that
   a. young peoples campaigns were better organized than adult crusades
   b. the Church strongly approved of their venture
   c. Jerusalem could not have been saved without children's help
   d. youth had strong religious beliefs in the Middle Ages

## VOCABULARY

Using your knowledge of the underlined word, circle the letter of the word or phrase that best completes each statement. *(50 points)*

6. A person approaching a task with underline zeal would
   a. avoid it
   b. postpone it
   c. show enthusiasm
   d. show fear

7. To redeem Jerusalem from the Saracens, the children would have to
   a. offer prayers of forgiveness
   b. take the city back from its invaders
   c. invite the Saracens to the Holy Land
   d. share the city with the Muslim people

8. People who deplored the Children's Crusade
   a. disapproved of it
   b. encouraged the children to plan more carefully
   c. stopped the children from leaving
   d. changed its travel routes

9. An impressionable person might
   a. be easily convinced by a bad argument
   b. refuse to hear ideas about a topic
   c. courageously stand up for his or her beliefs
   d. be unmoved by a persuasive speech

10. Which of the following groups might be described as a horde?
    a. a couple having dinner
    b. a class of students sitting in their desks
    c. a row of soldiers standing at attention
    d. a crowd of people walking in the park

## Selection Test

### The Sword of the Samurai
from *Calliope*
by CAROLYN GARD

## COMPREHENSION QUESTIONS

Circle the letter of the best answer to each of the following items. *(50 points)*

**1.** A samurai's sword could reveal a warrior's
   **a.** place of birth
   **b.** financial standing
   **c.** hobbies and interests
   **d.** social standing

**2.** A swordsmith approached his work with
   **a.** haste          **c.** caution
   **b.** respect        **d.** indifference

**3.** Some people say that swords made by great swordsmiths never had to be
   **a.** sharpened      **c.** polished
   **b.** cleaned        **d.** tempered

**4.** Which part of the swordmaking process took place quickly?
   **a.** polishing
   **b.** folding and beating
   **c.** sharpening
   **d.** tempering

**5.** The contest between Muramasa and Masamune illustrates that
   **a.** the sharpest swords are always the best
   **b.** swords are judged by only one type of standard
   **c.** the best swords can aid their owners with special powers
   **d.** swordmakers could not control their weapons' standards

## VOCABULARY

Using your knowledge of the underlined word, circle the letter of the word or phrase that best completes the statement. *(50 points)*

**6.** A warrior displaying <u>obedience</u> would
   **a.** question a leader's authority
   **b.** form his or her own army
   **c.** follow a leader's orders
   **d.** develop a new weapon

**7.** A person with the quality of <u>virtue</u> is likely to be
   **a.** respected      **c.** scorned
   **b.** suspected      **d.** feared

**8.** A swordsmith held in high <u>esteem</u> is likely to be
   **a.** trained        **c.** avoided
   **b.** criticized     **d.** praised

**9.** After having <u>fasted</u>, person will probably feel
   **a.** tired          **c.** bored
   **b.** hungry         **d.** refreshed

**10.** A instrument that has been <u>purified</u> is especially
   **a.** old            **c.** clean
   **b.** expensive      **d.** modern

## Selection Test

Getting Dressed

from *Armor*

by CHARLOTTE AND DAVID YUE

### COMPREHENSION QUESTIONS

Circle the letter of the best answer to each of the following items. *(50 points)*

1. When wearing a suit of armor, one would notice that it was generally
   a. easy to put on by oneself
   b. heavy and hot when worn
   c. constructed of only a few pieces
   d. not worn on horseback

2. An arming doublet and woolen hose were used
   a. to keep a knight adequately warm
   b. only for decoration
   c. to make wearing armor more comfortable
   d. so a knight could be easily identified

3. A knight began getting dressed by covering his
   a. head
   b. legs
   c. feet
   d. hands

4. The last pieces of armor that a knight put on were his
   a. helmet and gauntlets
   b. taces and tassets
   c. brayette and gorget
   d. greaves and cuisses

5. A knight who learned to move easily in his suit of armor had probably
   a. made the armor very light
   b. used no metal in his armor
   c. trained his squire well
   d. practiced wearing armor for many years

### VOCABULARY

Using your knowledge of the underlined word, circle the letter of the word or phrase that best completes each statement. *(50 points)*

6. A vulnerable knight is likely to
   a. wear the best armor
   b. be hurt on the battlefield
   c. move easily in his armor
   d. mount his horse quickly and easily

7. People who wield tools probably use them
   a. carelessly
   b. hesitantly
   c. dangerously
   d. skillfully

8. An agile person would most likely be notable for his or her
   a. cleverness
   b. gracefulness
   c. wealth
   d. generosity

9. A knight hoisted onto his horse has
   a. mounted the horse by himself
   b. recently fallen in battle
   c. been lifted by others
   d. had to remove the horse's saddle

10. An object impairing a knight's vision would likely
    a. fall in front of his eyes
    b. improve his ability to sight things at a distance
    c. affect only his ability to read
    d. have the same impact on his hearing

# Selection Test

### *from* The "Little Ice Age"
from *The Ice Ages*
by ROY A. GALLANT

## COMPREHENSION QUESTIONS

Circle the letter of the best answer to each of the following items *(50 points)*

1. If the growing season is shortened by a few weeks,
   a. precipitation may increase
   b. glaciers may advance
   c. crops may not mature
   d. poultry may not survive the cold

2. In Belgium during the summer of 1739,
   a. crops were harvested as usual
   b. wheat was ruined by rainy weather
   c. a late frost allowed an adequate fruit harvest
   d. food was imported from other areas

3. After the winter of 1709, people in France found that
   a. stables had adequately protected their livestock
   b. their spring crops were plentiful
   c. their supply of poultry had increased
   d. cold weather had killed many of their trees

4. The Little Ice Age was hardest on people living in
   a. Iceland          c. South America
   b. Africa           d. the Alps

5. The glaciers in the Chamonix Valley
   a. destroyed all of the area's villages
   b. crushed the inhabitants under ice
   c. buried all of the homes under rubble
   d. affected the area's agriculture

## VOCABULARY

Using your knowledge of the underlined words, circle the letter of the word or phrase that best completes each statement. *(50 points)*

6. A glacier is made mostly of
   a. water          c. loose rock
   b. ice            d. melting snow

7. A pile of rubble would primarily include
   a. small trees    c. rocks and debris
   b. grain          d. ice and frozen precipitation

8. A crop that has been sown has been
   a. harvested      c. planted
   b. destroyed      d. frozen

9. Poor people rioted when food was in short supply, creating a
   a. public disturbance
   b. peaceful debate
   c. change in agricultural practices
   d. new type of discussion

10. A severe winter could be best described as
    a. rainy          c. moderate
    b. short          d. intense

## Selection Test

*from* Leonardo da Vinci
by DIANE STANLEY

### COMPREHENSION QUESTIONS

Circle the letter of the best answer to each of the following items. *(50 points)*

1. Leonardo da Vinci's notebooks include all of the following **except**
   a. a grocery list
   b. a recipe for apple pie
   c. observations of nature
   d. weapons design

2. Leonardo was first interested in studying human anatomy because he was
   a. an artist
   b. a scientist
   c. ill
   d. curious

3. Leonardo learned about human anatomy
   a. by reading medical books
   b. by studying his own body
   c. by examining dead bodies
   d. by consulting doctors

4. The scientific method is based on
   a. memories
   b. observation
   c. the Bible
   d. science textbooks

5. Leonardo spent much of his time studying
   a. the Bible
   b. music
   c. popular theory
   d. nature

### VOCABULARY

Using your knowledge of the underlined word, circle the letter of the word or phrase that best completes each statement. *(50 points)*

6. After closely studying a situation in nature, Leonardo and other scientists would develop a hypothesis, or _____, about what they saw.
   a. a final conclusion
   b. a guess
   c. an experiment
   d. a possible explanation

7. How would a grotesque face in Leonardo's notebook look?
   a. beautiful      c. ugly
   b. rugged        d. bearded

8. When Leonardo dissected a body, he
   a. explained it
   b. buried it
   c. put it together
   d. cut it apart

9. A decision that is the opposite of moral is
   a. wrong      c. smart
   b. slow        d. right

10. When a body decomposes, it
    a. turns pale      c. rots
    b. shrinks         d. expands

## Selection Test

### Michelangelo
from *Italian Renaissance*
*(Living History Series)*
edited by JOHN D. CLARE

## COMPREHENSION QUESTIONS

Circle the letter of the best answer to each of the following items. *(50 points)*

**1.** All of the following words describe Michelangelo's character **except**
- **a.** rude
- **b.** stubborn
- **c.** moody
- **d.** passive

**2.** Early on, Michelangelo proved his artistic skills by
- **a.** impressing an art dealer
- **b.** selling art to the Medicis
- **c.** punching an assistant
- **d.** carving animals in the snow

**3.** Michelangelo sometimes ignored the rules of art because
- **a.** he did not understand them
- **b.** he wanted to create a certain effect
- **c.** he sculpted only Biblical characters
- **d.** he was a sculptor, not a painter

**4.** The first scene Michelangelo painted on the ceiling of the Sistine chapel
- **a.** faded
- **b.** was a great success
- **c.** was ruined
- **d.** caught on fire

**5.** Michelangelo was also known for his talent as a(n)
- **a.** boxer
- **b.** inventor
- **c.** singer
- **d.** architect

## VOCABULARY

Using your knowledge of the underlined word, circle the letter of the word or phrase that best completes each statement. *(50 points)*

**6.** A person who believes in a <u>stereotype</u>
- **a.** is open-minded
- **b.** enjoys listening to music
- **c.** is well liked
- **d.** has narrow ideas

**7.** What did Michelangelo do as an <u>apprentice</u>?
- **a.** study
- **b.** teach
- **c.** argue
- **d.** print books

**8.** When you are <u>discarding</u> old clothes, what do you do with them?
- **a.** buy them
- **b.** throw them out
- **c.** chop them up
- **d.** fold them neatly

**9.** A <u>depiction</u> is the same thing as a
- **a.** picture
- **b.** mirror
- **c.** reflection
- **d.** shadow

**10.** When Michelangelo was <u>temperamental</u>, he was
- **a.** predictable
- **b.** generous
- **c.** moody
- **d.** pleasing

Name _____  Class _____  Date _____

## Selection Test

*from* **Martin Luther and the Reformation**

from *Rats, Bulls, and Flying Machines: A History of the Renaissance and Reformation*
by DEBORAH MAZZOTTA PRUM

### COMPREHENSION QUESTIONS

Circle the letter of the best answer to each of the following items. *(50 points)*

1. Martin Luther first thought of God as
   a. a stern judge
   b. a loving father
   c. an indifferent being
   d. a pure spirit

2. Luther believed that God would forgive people if they
   a. bought indulgences
   b. confessed their sins to priests
   c. had faith
   d. followed Luther's own ideas

3. Luther's beliefs about indulgences threatened the Roman Catholic Church because indulgences
   a. were against the law
   b. revealed the corruption of the clergy
   c. had pagan roots
   d. were new

4. The printing press was essential to the success of Luther's reform efforts because without it
   a. few people would have read his essays
   b. few people could have known how to read
   c. he could not have published his theses
   d. the Bible would not have been translated

5. Why did Luther eventually wish that his work could be forgotten?
   a. so people would forget the Reformation
   b. so people would read only the Bible
   c. because Martin Luther realized his mistake
   d. because Martin Luther was afraid of being killed

### VOCABULARY

Using your knowledge of the underlined word, circle the letter of the word or phrase that best completes each statement. *(50 points)*

6. When you confess that you have made a mistake, you
   a. tell
   b. keep quiet
   c. refuse to tell
   d. regret

7. When Martin Luther thought God would condemn him, he thought that God would
   a. tease him
   b. thank him
   c. punish him
   d. forgive him

8. Signs of corruption include all of the following except
   a. greed
   b. cruelty
   c. dishonesty
   d. pain

9. Which of the following is the best definition for Martin Luther's conscience?
   a. his determination
   b. his desire to reform
   c. his ability to think
   d. his thoughts and feelings about right and wrong

10. When Martin Luther defied the church, he
   a. joined it
   b. praised it
   c. hated it
   d. fought against it

## Selection Test

*from* Galileo Galilei: Inventor, Astronomer, and Rebel
by MICHAEL WHITE

### COMPREHENSION QUESTIONS

Circle the letter of the best answer to each of the following items. *(50 points)*

1. Copernicus's ideas about the movement of the earth around the sun were revolutionary because they
   a. disagreed with the church's teachings
   b. were heretical
   c. said the earth was not the center of the universe
   d. disagreed with Galileo's ideas

2. When Pope Urban asked Galileo to write about the nature of the universe, the Pope expected Galileo to
   a. create new ideas
   b. disagree with Copernicus
   c. disagree with the Church's teaching
   d. investigate further through experiments

3. The Roman Catholic Church established the Inquisition because
   a. not enough people were becoming nuns or clerics
   b. the church had an overwhelming influence on people

   c. the church disagreed with Copernicus
   d. people were teaching ideas that were not literally from the Bible

4. The purpose of the Order of the Jesuits was to
   a. solve scientific problems
   b. make new discoveries
   c. make all new discoveries agree with the Church's teaching
   d. make Aristotle's ideas agree with the teachings of the Church

5. It is clear from the reading selection that Aristotle's ideas survived for more than a thousand years because they
   a. were right
   b. were adopted by the church
   c. were wrong
   d. put God at the center of the universe

### VOCABULARY

Using your knowledge of the underlined word, circle the letter of the word or phrase that best completes each statement. *(50 points)*

6. When Galileo's ideas deviated from those accepted by the Church, they
   a. were wrong
   b. reinforced Church teachings
   c. expressed Church teachings
   d. strayed from Church teachings

7. Books the church censored had to be
   a. shared          c. revised
   b. taught          d. read

8. An implication is a
   a. determination   c. connection
   b. suggestion      d. rejection

9. If you have misconceptions, then you have
   a. good ideas
   b. mistaken ideas
   c. terrible ideas
   d. challenging ideas

10. When the ideas of Copernicus were scorned by the Roman Catholic Church, they were
    a. treated with contempt
    b. supported
    c. argued with
    d. changed

Name _____ Class _____ Date _____

## Selection Test

### *from* Making Archaeology a Science
from *Dig This! How Archaeologists Uncover Our Past*
by MICHAEL AVI-YONAH

## COMPREHENSION QUESTIONS

Circle the letter of the best answer to each of the following items. *(50 points)*

1. What was significant about the discovery of the statue of Laocoön?
   a. The statue was unbroken under the soil
   b. An ancient history book described where to find it
   c. It was a Greek statue
   d. It was a Roman statue

2. The earliest archaeologists were all of the following **except**
   a. amateurs
   b. collectors
   c. scientists
   d. enthusiasts

3. Which of the following helped archaeology shift from a hobby to a profession?
   a. the discovery of the statue of Laocoön
   b. the publication of archaeology books
   c. the formation of French expeditions
   d. the discovery of the ruins of Rome

4. The discovery of the ruins of Pompeii and Herculaneum offered new opportunities for archaeologists to
   a. solve scientific problems
   b. create new art forms
   c. understand an ancient culture
   d. fill museums with artworks

5. It is clear from the reading selection that the writer believes that
   a. eighteenth-century studies improved archaeology
   b. sixteenth-century books improved archaeology
   c. scientists are better than artists
   d. books were an archaeologist's best resource

## VOCABULARY

Using your knowledge of the underlined word, circle the letter of the word or phrase that best completes each statement. *(50 points)*

6. The fact that the statue of Laocoön was authentic means that it was
   a. the original statue
   b. fake
   c. old
   d. broken

7. Archaeological sites are
   a. natural
   b. places
   c. museums
   d. views

8. All ancient artifacts were
   a. made of wood or stone
   b. buried in dirt
   c. destroyed by volcanoes
   d. made by humans

9. An excavation is a place to
   a. bury something
   b. draw artifacts
   c. quarry stone
   d. find artifacts

10. When archaeologists conserve an ancient piece of art, they
    a. bury it again
    b. describe it
    c. keep it safe
    d. sell it

## Selection Test

*from* Isaac Newton: Discovering
Laws That Govern the Universe
by MICHAEL WHITE

## COMPREHENSION QUESTIONS

Circle the letter of the best answer to each of the following items. *(50 points)*

1. The apple that fell on Newton's head was significant because it inspired his theory of
   a. optics
   b. gravity
   c. orbits
   d. movement

2. According to the author, Newton's development of calculus has helped us develop
   a. electric cars
   b. current economic problems
   c. television
   d. modern space travel

3. Today, whole areas of science are called Newtonian because Newton
   a. invented them
   b. provided the basic principles for them
   c. changed them
   d. named them

4. The people who owe Newton a great deal are those who
   a. inherited his patents
   b. wear eyeglasses
   c. inherited his money
   d. sued him and won

5. All of the following words describe Newton's work **except**
   a. accurate
   b. revolutionary
   c. miraculous
   d. predictable

## VOCABULARY

Using your knowledge of the underlined word, circle the letter of the word or phrase that best completes each statement. *(50 points)*

6. If we talk about the <u>properties</u> of an object, we mean its
   a. land
   b. things
   c. characteristics
   d. visibility

7. Newton's <u>theory</u> about gravity was
   a. a proven idea
   b. a new law
   c. a possibility
   d. a solution

8. The <u>principles</u> of the movement of the universe are
   a. causes
   b. challenges
   c. mistakes
   d. laws

9. Before you can truly understand a <u>phenomenon</u>, you must
   a. read about it
   b. experience it
   c. wash
   d. cut it apart

10. To <u>revolutionize</u> science is to
    a. change it
    b. describe it
    c. preserve it
    d. prove it

Name _____ Class _____ Date _____

## Selection Test

### Prince Henry the Navigator
from *Around the World in a Hundred Years:
From Henry the Navigator to Magellan*
by JEAN FRITZ

### COMPREHENSION QUESTIONS

Circle the letter of the best answer to each of the following items. *(50 points)*

1. In Prince Henry's time, maps of Africa were incomplete because
   a. mapmakers were improperly trained
   b. African natives had consistently fought off Portuguese explorers
   c. Europeans were not interested in maps of other continents
   d. Europeans had not yet investigated the African continent

2. When the Portuguese attacked Ceuta, they found that
   a. Morocco was too strong to defeat
   b. the city was filled with goods from India and Asia
   c. Muslim traders were ready to reveal their trade routes
   d. trade could continue there as usual

3. Muslim traders were not familiar with sailing
   a. the east coast of Africa
   b. the Red Sea
   c. the west coast of Africa
   d. the Mediterranean Sea

4. Henry hoped that Porto Santo might be useful as a
   a. way station
   b. breeding ground for rabbits
   c. site to study African cultures
   d. navigation school taught by Bartholomew Perestrelo

5. The *barca* sailed by Portuguese sailors
   a. had triangular sails
   b. was a Mediterranean trade ship
   c. could turn into the wind
   d. was small and easy to manage

### VOCABULARY

Using your knowledge of the underlined word, circle the letter of the word or phrase that best completes each statement. *(50 points)*

6. A person obsessed with sailing might
   a. be afraid of water
   b. show a lot of interest in ships
   c. travel to the seashore very rarely
   d. be bored by discussions of trading ships

7. A city's spoils are valuables that are
   a. sold at auction
   b. traded with enemy soldiers
   c. safely hidden from danger
   d. taken during a war

8. In a body of water, currents move
   a. only close to the shore
   b. only in a dangerous fashion
   c. more quickly than the surrounding water
   d. always from cooler water to warmer water

9. A customer probably would reject an inferior product because it is
   a. too expensive
   b. outdated and no longer stylish
   c. of a poor quality
   d. overly decorated

10. A person's arrogance indicates too much
    a. pride
    b. sincerity
    c. humility
    d. poverty

**Selection Test**

## The Mapmakers
from *If You Were There in 1492*
by BARBARA BRENNER

## COMPREHENSION QUESTIONS

Circle the letter of the best answer to each of the following items. *(50 points)*

**1.** Medieval maps were
  **a.** frequently inaccurate
  **b.** always made on the correct scale
  **c.** careful to include only factual information
  **d.** seldom updated

**2.** The majority of mapmakers in Majorca were
  **a.** Christian      **c.** Buddhist
  **b.** Muslim        **d.** Jewish

**3.** Globes were once produced by
  **a.** mapmakers in Majorca
  **b.** people of ancient Greece
  **c.** kings and queens
  **d.** many craftspeople in Nuremberg

**4.** Who did the Nuremberg city council hire to make their globe?
  **a.** a person who loved maps
  **b.** a person trained in mapmaking
  **c.** an artist
  **d.** an explorer

**5.** Martin Behaim's globe depicted
  **a.** land between Europe and the Indies.
  **b.** the Earth's size correctly
  **c.** more than a hundred miniature figures
  **d.** a very long voyage between Europe and the Indies

## VOCABULARY

Using your knowledge of the underlined word, circle the letter of the word or phrase that best completes each statement. *(50 points)*

**6.** A decision based on <u>misinformation</u> would most likely
  **a.** be the most accurate
  **b.** be timely
  **c.** include important data
  **d.** include errors

**7.** A person learning a <u>profession</u> must
  **a.** buy property
  **b.** receive little education
  **c.** learn a special skill
  **d.** invest money in a business

**8.** A <u>mold</u> can give a substance
  **a.** pride       **c.** value
  **b.** a disease    **d.** a shape

**9.** An object shaped like a <u>sphere</u> is a
  **a.** brick
  **b.** globe
  **c.** pyramid
  **d.** column

**10.** A <u>miniature</u> reproduction of an item would be
  **a.** smaller than the original
  **b.** taller than the original
  **c.** less expensive than the original
  **d.** less heavy than the original

## Selection Test

**Ancient Healing**
from *Science of the Early Americas*
by GERALDINE WOODS

### COMPREHENSION QUESTIONS

Circle the letter of the best answer to each of the following items. *(50 points)*

**1.** Some American Indians treated the human body primarily by
**a.** burying them alive
**b.** encouraging a "sweating"
**c.** studying native texts
**d.** examining wild plants

**2.** Plains Indians treated dislocated shoulders by
**a.** using a pulley system
**b.** bathing limbs in hot water
**c.** applying plaster casts
**d.** amputating limbs

**3.** Early Central and South Americans who lived near volcanoes had access to
**a.** sweat lodges
**b.** medicinal plants
**c.** glass that could be used for knives
**d.** rocks that could be used for healing

**4.** The Aztecs would most likely tend a cut by
**a.** using a syringe made from hollow bones
**b.** stitching it together with a bone needle
**c.** using an obsidian knife
**d.** performing surgery with a tool made from rubber

**5.** The ancient Mayas' use of dental fillings was
**a.** a technique for removing tartar
**b.** performed after inadequate tooth polishing
**c.** used when balsam of Peru failed
**d.** for decorative purpose

### VOCABULARY

Using your knowledge of the underlined words, circle the letter of the word or phrase that best completes each statement. *(50 points)*

**6.** A machine functions when it
**a.** is performing a type of work
**b.** is being repaired
**c.** is displayed in a museum
**d.** is being assembled

**7.** An internal organ is located
**a.** between the organs of sight and hearing
**b.** within another organ
**c.** on the skin's surface
**d.** inside the body

**8.** News that is circulating in an office would
**a.** stay in one place
**b.** be passed along by office workers
**c.** be kept secret
**d.** be heard among only a few people

**9.** After being infected with an illness, a person would
**a.** become sick
**b.** recover quickly
**c.** gain strength
**d.** be immune to other diseases

**10.** People's resistance to a disease would
**a.** pass the illness along to other people
**b.** make medicine work more effectively
**c.** help them fight off illness
**d.** make them more ill than some other people

( *Selection Test* )

### A Strange, Funny-Looking Vegetable
from *The Amazing Potato: A Story in Which the Incas, Conquistadors, Marie Antoinette, Thomas Jefferson, Wars, Famines, Immigrants, and French Fries All Play a Part*
by MILTON MELTZER

## COMPREHENSION QUESTIONS

Circle the letter of the best answer to each of the following items. *(50 points)*

**1.** The Incas' potatoes
 **a.** were well known to arriving Spaniards
 **b.** grew in many sizes and colors
 **c.** were difficult to store
 **d.** grew in smooth round or oval shapes

**2.** The Spaniards came to Peru primarily to
 **a.** search for riches
 **b.** learn about the Incas' technology
 **c.** collect plant and animal samples
 **d.** study Inca culture

**3.** The Incan people must have
 **a.** wanted their potatoes to look the same
 **b.** tried to avoid potatoes that were hard or red
 **c.** enjoyed different varieties of potatoes
 **d.** prized potatoes that were round and white

**4.** High in Peru's mountains,
 **a.** farmers grew more maize than potatoes
 **b.** fish was an important part of the Inca diet
 **c.** diets consisted mainly of guinea pigs and ducks
 **d.** people depended upon potatoes as a food source

**5.** *Chuno* must have been especially important because it
 **a.** could be stored over long periods
 **b.** was very tasty
 **c.** was not available in the highlands
 **d.** had to be kept from freezing

## VOCABULARY

Using your knowledge of the underlined word, circle the letter of the word or phrase that best completes each statement. *(50 points)*

**6.** An item with an irregular shape would
 **a.** be perfectly round
 **b.** have straight sides
 **c.** be bumpy or uneven
 **d.** have regular angles

**7.** A staple food is one that is
 **a.** an important part of a diet
 **b.** served only on holidays
 **c.** very expensive
 **d.** generally unhealthy

**8.** A vegetarian diet would include a great deal of
 **a.** fish and chicken
 **b.** red meats
 **c.** hamburgers and hot dogs
 **d.** nuts and grains

**9.** A bartered item
 **a.** is an important part of a nation's economy
 **b.** has been recently sold
 **c.** may not be returned to the store
 **d.** has been traded for another product

**10.** Speculators from Spain
 **a.** became interested in potato cultivation
 **b.** sold potatoes at great profits
 **c.** invested money in improving Peru's agriculture
 **d.** studied the minerals found in Peru's mountains

## Selection Test

"Let's Play Ball!"

from *Calliope*

by PETER KVIETOK

### COMPREHENSION QUESTIONS

Circle the letter of the best answer to each of the following items. *(50 points)*

**1.** The Lords of Death challenged two boys to a ball game because
a. the gods had perfected new gear
b. the gods enjoyed the game
c. the boys had reputations as fine players
d. the boys' running had disturbed the gods

**2.** The *Popol Vuh* must be
a. a book explaining the rules of *pok-ta-pok*
b. an important source of Mayan myths
c. a guidebook for ancient medicines
d. a modern explanation of Mayan customs

**3.** The Mayas combined sports with their practice of
a. education
b. music
c. government
d. religion

**4.** Mayan ballplayers were not allowed to touch the rubber ball with their
a. feet
b. thighs
c. heads
d. wrists

**5.** The ancient game of *pok-ta-pok*
a. is no longer played
b. does not require protective gear
c. is still played in Mexico
d. today requires elaborate rituals

### VOCABULARY

Using your knowledge of the underlined word, circle the letter of the word or phrase that best completes each statement. *(50 points)*

**6.** The participants of a game are those who
a. keep score
b. play the game
c. watch the action
d. create the equipment

**7.** A game played for high stakes might
a. feature a large prize
b. include many players
c. have little action
d. offer little excitement

**8.** A ritual act would be performed
a. as a business practice
b. by a musical entertainer
c. according to religious law
d. by people with little training

**9.** Which of the following objects is primarily vertical?
a. a carpet
b. a tablecloth
c. a flagpole
d. a roof

**10.** Which of the following items would be the best example of European accounts of the Mayan?
a. descriptions of the *pok-ta-pok* game
b. drawings of Mayan culture
c. totals of the Mayan wealth
d. drawings of ball courts

**Selection Test**

**All That Glitters**

from *Read*

## COMPREHENSION QUESTIONS

Circle the letter of the best answer to each of the following items. *(50 points)*

**1.** Gold is an element that
  **a.** can be easily shaped
  **b.** is not found in nature
  **c.** is difficult to form into jewelry
  **d.** is less valuable than mercury and zinc

**2.** The first people to mine large quantities of gold were in
  **a.** El Dorado
  **b.** Portugal
  **c.** Spain
  **d.** Egypt

**3.** Alchemists thought gold was a symbol of
  **a.** courage
  **b.** beauty
  **c.** perfection
  **d.** humility

**4.** In the nineteenth century, large quantities of gold were discovered in
  **a.** Australia and Italy
  **b.** California and Australia
  **c.** California and Venezuela
  **d.** Nova Scotia and Montana

**5.** The search for treasure lost hundreds of years ago
  **a.** is never successful
  **b.** is only done with high-pressure hoses
  **c.** can yield tons of gold
  **d.** can usually be done at little cost

## VOCABULARY

Using your knowledge of the underlined word, circle the letter of the word or phrase that best completes each statement. *(50 points)*

**6.** People who have <u>lavished</u> their time on a project have
  **a.** spent much money on it
  **b.** ignored it
  **c.** given it much attention
  **d.** completed it on schedule

**7.** An <u>exquisite</u> ornament would be described as
  **a.** solid
  **b.** moderately priced
  **c.** junk jewelry
  **d.** very beautiful

**8.** A person would set out on a <u>quest</u> in order to
  **a.** find something
  **b.** sell something
  **c.** eat something
  **d.** lose something

**9.** At an <u>extravagant</u> feast,
  **a.** guests will not have enough to eat
  **b.** there will be more than enough food
  **c.** food will be served in modest portions
  **d.** guests may eat only vegetables and fruits

**10.** Which of the following people would most likely be described as <u>notorious</u>?
  **a.** a singer
  **b.** a sports star
  **c.** a minister
  **d.** a criminal

## Content-Area Reading Strategies

for the
# Language Arts Classroom

by DR. JUDITH IRVIN
Florida State University

While teaching social studies in middle and high school, I worked primarily with students who struggled with reading and writing. In my desperate attempt to help them learn the content of history, geography, world cultures, economics, and so forth, I did what many good teachers did—I avoided the textbook. I engaged the students in inquiry, conducted simulations, showed videos, created maps and charts, and led lively discussions and debates. Oh, I trotted the textbook out occasionally to use the pictures, diagrams, and primary source material, but it was simply too difficult (or too much trouble) to ask students to read it.

When I did ask students to read, I used the only approach I knew—round-robin reading. This familiar classroom practice of having different students read paragraphs worked about as well as it did when I was in school. The students counted the paragraphs to see which one would be assigned to them and then agonized until their turns were over. No one really concentrated on what was being read. The strong readers were bored, and the struggling readers were embarrassed. I modified this approach by having students volunteer or call on the next reader. I even employed what is now called jump-in-reading, in which volunteers just start reading when another stops. These modifications created slightly more interest in the material, but they didn't stimulate any thought or motivation to learn. So, in desperation, I simply gave up using the textbooks.

### How I Learned to Teach Reading

Shortly after I shelved my textbooks, our principal made the announcement, "Every teacher is a teacher of reading." I learned that I was supposed to set aside my beloved history and geography to teach "finding the main idea" and "locating information" through skills worksheets. In my class, this generated even less enthusiasm than round-robin reading.

I became resentful. I nodded dutifully at in-service sessions and talked about how important it was that students read and write better. Then I shut my door and went back to my way of teaching social studies because I was annoyed at being asked not to teach what was important to me and to my students.

After a few more years, I began my Ph.D. studies in social studies education at Indiana University. During this time, I began taking courses in reading education. To my amazement, I discovered that I had been using very effective learning strategies through the social studies methods I had learned and applied in my classroom. But I fell short of helping students apply those concepts when reading their textbooks.

I finished my doctorate in reading education and wrote a dissertation that incorporated both social studies theory and reading theory. In all fairness to my former principal, the field of reading education was redefined during the period between his mandate and my doctoral studies and has continued to evolve over the past two decades.

## The Study of Reading

The research in reading falls into four categories:

- the text
- the context of learning
- the learner
- the learning strategies

These four factors can be conveniently separated for the purposes of discussion, but of course they are intricately linked and occur simultaneously. The figure below shows how these influencing factors interact with each other.

**The Text: Narrative to Expository** Good readers have expectations from text. When I curl up with a romance novel, I rarely bring a highlighter. Being residents of Florida, my husband and I read our homeowners' insurance policy very carefully after a hurricane. This is not the same way I read poetry or a menu. Good readers are flexible with a variety of text; poor readers read everything pretty much the same way.

Elementary students read primarily narrative text. Likewise, teachers teach children how to read a story by thinking about the setting or characters or by answering comprehension questions. Yet when elementary teachers embark on a social studies lesson, they generally jump straight to the content. They spend no time at all on how to read the textbook. When students enter middle school,

the demands for reading informational or expository text are much greater. Textbooks filled with new concepts replace stories. Charts and diagrams replace pictures. The vocabulary is more difficult and often essential in understanding the text.

Who in middle and high schools helps students read and write expository text? When I ask this question of a school faculty, the language arts teachers point to the social studies and science teachers because they are the ones with these types of textbooks. The social studies and science teachers point to language arts teachers because they "do" words. Even when students attend a reading class, what is usually taught is more narrative and on a lower reading level. What happens when students enter a social studies class and no one has helped them understand how to read the textbook?

Teachers often comment that students do not read anything outside of school. In reality, students read all kinds of text. They read e-mail, notes, magazines, TV listings, cereal boxes, video game instructions, T-shirts, movie posters, signs, song lyrics, and much more. We can connect to our students' real-world literacy by creating links from what they read outside of school to what we want them to read in school. We can connect song lyrics to poetry, movies to short stories, Internet

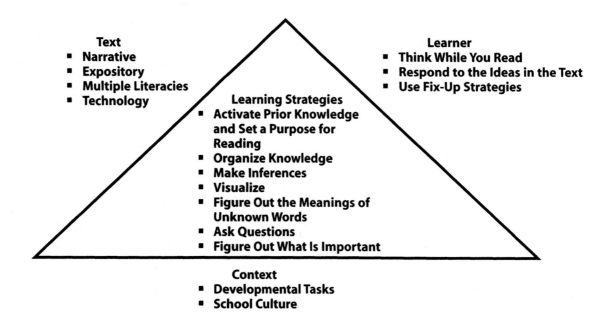

**Text**
- **Narrative**
- **Expository**
- **Multiple Literacies**
- **Technology**

**Learner**
- **Think While You Read**
- **Respond to the Ideas in the Text**
- **Use Fix-Up Strategies**

**Learning Strategies**
- **Activate Prior Knowledge and Set a Purpose for Reading**
- **Organize Knowledge**
- **Make Inferences**
- **Visualize**
- **Figure Out the Meanings of Unknown Words**
- **Ask Questions**
- **Figure Out What Is Important**

**Context**
- **Developmental Tasks**
- **School Culture**

sites about rock stars to biographies, video game instructions to expository text. Unless we recognize and provide links to the kinds of reading and writing that adolescents encounter in the "real world," they may never value what we are trying to teach them.

**The Context for Learning** Middle and high school students are immersed in life. The developmental tasks of becoming autonomous, forming a positive self-concept, learning social skills, progressing academically, and engaging in abstract thinking are all very important. To facilitate these developmental tasks, educators can create positive climates that reward effort as well as ability, provide a relevant curriculum, and motivate students to learn. We teachers have to ask ourselves, "What is worth knowing for adolescents in today's society?" and "How do we present this knowledge so that it makes sense to the lives and experiences of our students?"

**The Learner** Our students come to us knowing a lot of "stuff." This prior knowledge includes all that they have experienced, including their values, beliefs, and culture. You can think of this accumulated prior knowledge as a file cabinet. We all have multiple file folders, skinny or thick, on a variety of topics. For example, I have a big, thick file folder on soccer. My husband is a soccer coach; my daughter and son play soccer; and I played on a recreational team. On the other hand, I have a skinny file folder on football. I rarely attend a game and do not know much about the players.

Sometimes our job as teachers is to hand students a folder and have them label it and put things in it (building background information). Sometimes our job is to have students retrieve folders and read through them (activating prior knowledge). Sometimes our job is to help students organize their folders, placing labels on different parts so they can use this information in a new context (organizing knowledge). A good guiding principle is that students cannot learn anything new unless they are able to connect it to something they already know. To become strong

readers, students must engage with the text in various ways.

- **Think While You Read** Many students see reading as something to get through, rather than something to absorb, integrate, synthesize, and extend. Their eyes glance over the words, but they may not learn or remember the information because they have not thought about it.

- **Respond to the Ideas in the Text** When students are engaged in reading, they respond to the ideas in some way. They ask themselves questions, organize the ideas in a map, and connect the ideas with what they already know.

- **Use Fix-Up Strategies** Strong readers keep track of whether things make sense to them and do something to "fix up" their comprehension if things do not make sense. They might use the glossary, re-read, read ahead, think about the topic, or ask someone.

- **Activate Prior Knowledge and Set a Purpose for Reading** Before reading, good readers activate what they know about a topic by looking at the table of contents, glossary, titles, captions, section headings, and/or graphics. They make connections from the text to their experience and prior knowledge. They may skim the structure of the text for main ideas and think about what they will be expected to do with the reading.

- **Organize Knowledge** During and after reading, strong readers summarize the major ideas. They may skim the text and re-read portions to take notes or to create a concept map or an outline. This organization and reorganization of knowledge helps students understand, remember, and use the major concepts presented in the text.

- **Make Inferences** Strong readers make inferences throughout their reading. That is, they connect what is in their heads with what is on the page. If they see a building with an onion-shaped dome, they might infer that the setting is in Russia. Accurate inference making depends on the background knowledge of the reader.

- **Visualize** Proficient readers visualize the information presented in text. Nonproficient readers, on the other hand, do not seem to be able to create pictures in their minds. Having students sketch images or create concept maps, diagrams, charts, or other visual representations of the information helps them create these visual images.
- **Figure Out the Meanings of Unknown Words** As students read increasingly complex text, they encounter words they do not know. Previewing text for key vocabulary and using context and structural analysis can help students increase their understanding and their vocabularies.
- **Ask Questions** Before and during reading, strong readers ask themselves questions such as, "What do I know about this topic?" or "What is the meaning of a concept in bold print?" These questions indicate that students are thinking about the reading and connecting the ideas in the text to their prior knowledge.
- **Figure Out What Is Important** One of the most common question types on standardized tests is "finding the main idea." To comprehend text, readers must identify, remember, and summarize the major ideas presented in the text. Figuring out what is important in the text should be tied to the purpose for reading. Taking notes from text, constructing a concept map, or creating an outline all involve identifying what is important in the text.

You can talk to students about how effective and efficient learning takes place. If talking about effective reading behaviors becomes a natural part of classroom instruction, students can add these ideas to their repertoires and become stronger, more flexible, and more proficient readers.

## The Learning Strategies

Veteran teachers have heard the terms *skills* and *strategies* thrown around for many years. Skills must be automatically and consistently applied and require fairly low levels of thinking. Skills take practice. This fact became abundantly clear to me the first time I was in the car with my sixteen-year-old son, who had just gotten his driver's license. Making a left-hand turn in traffic takes a high level of driving skill and, initially, a lot of concentration. Checking both mirrors, gauging the distances of oncoming cars, and signaling the turn became automatic after practice. My son can now negotiate the same turn while carrying on a conversation and eating a candy bar.

While driving gets easier with practice, we all need a plan when navigating unfamiliar territory. We consult a map, ask for directions, and formulate a strategy for getting to our destination. A strategy is an overall plan requiring higher levels of reasoning. It is flexible in application and involves awareness and reflection.

Proficient reading takes both the execution of skills and a strategy for fulfilling the purpose for reading. With some practice, taking notes becomes a fairly automatic process of identifying important points and recording them in a way that can be used later. But it takes a strategy to put the pieces together to write a report. Before reading, strong readers use strategies to connect with what they know about the topic, while reading to maintain concentration and reflect on ideas in the text, and after reading to organize major points to fulfill the purpose for reading. The learning strategies in this book are designed to engage students in the behaviors of strong reading until these behaviors become part of the readers' repertoire.

## Helping Struggling Readers Become Strong Readers

Struggling readers can do the same thing as strong readers, but they need more help, more support, and more scaffolding. For example, my husband purchased a boat that sits very high in the water, which is wonderful when you are in the boat looking down. After snorkeling one day, I learned the downside of a high-riding boat. When it came time to get back in the boat, the platform and the one step were too high. I wanted two more steps—the scaffolding I needed to start climbing into the boat. Struggling readers have a similar dilemma. They often have difficulty getting started, and then they easily give up.

To avoid this, introduce each strategy with fairly simple reading so that students learn the steps of the strategy and do not have to face the additional challenge of difficult text. As you select an appropriate strategy, consider the students' prior knowledge about the topic, the type of text, and the purpose for reading. You will find that some strategies lend themselves better to the study of world cultures, and others to the study of history or economics. You will also find that you prefer some strategies over others. My purpose is to provide you with options to use in any teaching and learning context. It is my fervent hope that you find that these strategies enhance your instruction by engaging students more actively in learning.

Good Luck and Best Wishes,
Dr. Judith Irvin

### Read More About It

Irvin, J. L. *Reading and the Middle School Student: Strategies to Enhance Literacy* (2nd edition). Boston: Allyn and Bacon (1998).

Irvin, J. L., Buehl, D., and Klemp, R. *Reading and the High School Student: Strategies to Enhance Literacy.* Boston: Allyn and Bacon (2002).

Irvin, J. L., Lunstrum, J. P., Lynch-Brown, C., and Shepard, M. F. *Enhancing Social Studies Instruction through Reading and Writing Strategies.* Washington, D.C.: National Council for the Social Studies (1995).

# STRATEGY 1: PREVIEWING TEXT

When facing a textbook reading assignment, most students just plow in and try to finish it as quickly as possible. They may leaf through the chapter or passage to see how long it is, taking note of how many pages they can skip because of pictures or graphs. Proficient readers, on the other hand, take

a moment to consider the following things *before* they begin a textbook reading assignment:

> **P**urpose of the reading
> **I**mportant ideas
> **C**onnection to prior knowledge

This strategy of previewing text is therefore known as PIC. You can use the PIC strategy to help your students develop good reading habits by encouraging them to spend just a few moments organizing their thinking and setting their goals before beginning a reading assignment. In addition, this process leads students to speculate about the main idea of the passage before they start reading. After reading, they may change what they thought the main idea was or confirm that their prediction was correct.

### How Can the Strategy Help My Students?

The PIC strategy can get your students into the all-important habits of setting a purpose for their reading, identifying the most important ideas, and connecting with what they already know. Often when students read, they do not think about what is really important to remember. Previewing reading assignments helps students focus on the most important information and facilitates storing that information in long-term memory. If students take a few moments to go through the steps described below, they will better understand and remember the material they read.

### Getting Started

Here are the steps to the PIC strategy:

**Step 1: Purpose for Reading.** Make sure students know what they will be doing with the information after reading. (That is, what is the assignment or purpose for reading? What will they do with the information?) Have them peruse the structure of the assignment, noting special features such as summaries or guiding questions. Ask students to use the table of contents and glossary of the book to locate information. To establish a purpose for reading, students can ask the following questions.

- What am I going to do with this information when I finish reading?

- How does this text fit in with the material before or after it?

**Step 2: Important Ideas.** Students should flip through the assignment, noting any headings that indicate the major points in the reading. They should try to understand how this passage fits within the larger chapter, unit, or book. Students should also be familiar with any key vocabulary in boldface type or italics. These words are probably the most important concepts in the text. To identify important ideas, students can ask the following questions.

- Is there anything in the table of contents, index, or glossary that can help me understand the "big ideas"?
- What are the key vocabulary terms I should understand?

**Step 3: Connect to What You Know.** Students need to think about what they know about the topic before they start reading. Encourage them to wonder about the topic, asking themselves, "What would I like to find out?" Finally, students should identify questions they want answered about the topic. They can organize their ideas with a chart like the KWQ Chart below.

## Using the Strategy in Your Classroom
After students have read the text, they should go back to their KWQ charts to see if their questions were answered and to make sure they understand the key vocabulary. Feel free to vary the strategy as students become accustomed to previewing their assignments. You may wish to move from having students complete KWQ organizers to having them address just the purpose for reading,

important information about the topic, and connecting-to-prior-knowledge questions in a quick discussion or pre-reading assignment. You can also add an after-reading component by asking students to discuss, in small groups or as a class, the questions they still want answered. (**See Strategy 7, Graphic Organizers 6 and 7, and KWL and KWLS Charts.**) They may have some questions that were not answered in the text. These questions can be the basis of further research or projects.

## Extending the Strategy
Books use diagrams, charts, maps, and pictures to help the reader understand the content. As students become more familiar with previewing, you may wish to direct their attention to these graphic features, asking them in what ways these items will extend or support their learning.

The PIC strategy is simply a guide to help students preview the text before reading and focus on the most important points. It can be used in conjunction with other assignments or modified to serve as an aid for studying for a test or writing a report. For example, before students read you can ask them to sketch out a graphic organizer or a concept map (**See Strategies 3 and 4**) to fill in after they read. They can then use this organizer as a writing or study guide. (**See Graphic Organizer 3, Cluster Diagram.**)

## Some Final Thoughts
The purpose for previewing text is to get students to recognize the text's main idea, which could be a theme, something important to students, or the first sentence in a paragraph. However, helping

| ▶ What I *Know* About the Topic | ▶ What I *Wonder* About the Topic | ▶ Questions I Would Like to Have Answered |
|---|---|---|
| | | |

students identify the main idea of a text passage is often a difficult challenge. David Moore (1986) suggested that you engage students in stating what the text is about in one or two words and then add two or three other words to go with it. This usually comes closer to the author's intended main idea.

When students first use the PIC strategy, the process will seem very time-consuming. But as they become more familiar with the format and steps, they will move through the strategy more quickly. Feel free to modify the strategy to suit the needs of your students.

### Read More About It

Alvermann, D. E. "Graphic Organizers: Cueing Devices for Comprehending and Remembering Main Ideas." In *Teaching Main Idea Comprehension*, J. F. Baumann. Newark, DE: International Reading Association. 1986.

Avery, P. G., Baker, J., and Gross, S. H. "Mapping Learning at the Secondary Level." *The Clearing House* 70 (5) 1997: 279–85.

Heimlich, E., and Pittleman, S. D. *Semantic Mapping: Classroom Applications.* Newark, DE: International Reading Association. 1986.

Romance, N. R., and Vitale, M. R. "Concept Mapping as a Tool for Learning: Broadening the Framework for Student-Centered Instruction." *College Teaching* 47 (2) 1999: 74–79.

# STRATEGY 2: UNDERSTANDING TEXT

When you come home at the end of the day and flip through the mail, you probably don't read each item the same way. You would read a letter from a friend differently than you would read a notice from a lawyer you do not know. The items *look* different, use different vocabularies, and have different structures. Strong readers know how to adjust their reading depending on the text and their purpose for reading.

A textbook contains different forms of text. Students must interpret pictures, diagrams, figures, and charts. They read narrative accounts, diaries, and documents that support the major concepts. Then, there is the text itself. Expository or informational text is generally structured in one of the following five forms.

- cause and effect
- comparison and contrast
- description
- problem and solution
- sequence or chronological order

Particular content lends itself more or less to one structure or another. For example, while history is generally conveyed in a sequence or chronological order, geography may be best learned in a descriptive format. In addition, one or more forms may be used within a passage. The more that students can detect the structure of text, the better they can prepare themselves to think in a way that is consistent with that structure.

Signal or transition words usually indicate the structure of the text. Proficient readers intuitively notice the words that indicate the type of thinking required while reading. Signal words tell readers what is coming up. When you see *for example* or *for instance*, you know that examples will follow. On the next page is a chart with some of the most common signal or transition words.

An important reading strategy based on these words is called "Double S: *S*ignal Words That Indicate *S*tructure." This strategy is designed to help students recognize and use signal words to detect the structure of the text.

### How Can the Strategy Help My Students?

Good readers are flexible thinkers. Signal or transition words such as *different from, the same as,* or *compared with* indicate that the authors are presenting information that will compare and contrast at least two ideas. This comparison and contrast structure is read differently from one in which ideas are presented in sequence or chronological order. Signal or transition words indicate what the structure of text might be. When students notice these words in the text, especially before reading, they tend to get ready to think in a certain way. Struggling readers need to have these words pointed out to them and to be instructed on the function of these words while reading or writing. In time, they should be able to use signal words and move to more complex forms of text.

When students are learning to write expository text and must demonstrate that skill on a task such as producing a sample for a standardized test, these signal or transition words can help them express their points more clearly. As students recognize and use transition words and different text structures, they will (1) comprehend text more effectively, (2) produce more coherent expository writing, and (3) think more clearly and flexibly.

## Getting Started

Here are the steps in the Understanding Text strategy.

**Step 1: Survey the Text.** Have students flip through the text and list all the different types of items they will be reading, such as documents, charts, diagrams, maps, short stories, or expository text. Usually, the expository writing in

textbooks explains or informs the reader. But primary source material, such as a diary, may be read differently. The primary source probably supports one or more of the major points presented in the text.

**Step 2: Identify the Signal Words.** Have students list transition words in the text or allow students to attach self-adhesive notes to the text page to help them locate the transition words.

**Step 3: Identify the Structure of the Text.** Using their list of transition words, students, individually or in small groups, should identify the main structure of the text: cause and effect, comparison and contrast, description, problem and solution, sequence or chronological order. They should ask themselves, "What kind of thinking will be necessary to understand the information in the text?" and "How would I best display the information after reading?"

**Step 4: Predict the Main Idea of the Passage.** Using what they know about the signal words and the structure of the text, students should write a

## SIGNAL WORDS

| Cause and Effect | Comparison and Contrast | Description | Problem and Solution | Sequence or Chronological Order |
|---|---|---|---|---|
| because | different from | for instance | the problem is | not long after |
| since | same as | for example | the question is | next |
| consequently | similar to | such as | a solution is | then |
| this led to … so | as opposed to | to illustrate | one answer is | initially |
| if … then | instead of | in addition | | before |
| nevertheless | although | most importantly | | after |
| accordingly | however | another | | finally |
| because of | compared with | furthermore | | preceding |
| as a result of | as well as | first, second … | | following |
| in order to | either … or | | | on (date) |
| may be due to | but | | | over the years |
| for this reason | on the other hand | | | today |
| | unless | | | when |

sentence stating what they think the main idea of this passage will be.

**Step 5: Read the Text.**

**Step 6: Revisit the Main-Idea Prediction.** After reading, students should go back to their prediction of the main idea of the passage. They should then display the information on a graphic organizer appropriate to the text structure. (**Graphic Organizer 2, Cause and Effect; Graphic Organizer 11, Comparison and Contrast; Graphic Organizer 3, Description; Graphic Organizer 9, Problem and Solution; or Graphic Organizer 10, Sequence or Chronological Order.**) Then students may write a summary or in some other way organize what they have read.

## Using the Strategy in Your Classroom

We know that good readers use signal or transition words to help guide their understanding and their thinking. Struggling readers do not. So teachers can help struggling readers to recognize and use signal words through the Double S strategy. This does not mean asking students to memorize lists of words. Some teachers find it effective to write signal words on posters around the room or to give students a page to put in their notebooks. Students should also add their own signal words to such lists as they find them in the text. In time, they will use these words intuitively, and they will not need to go through the steps of identifying signal words before reading.

Discussing the structure of text is a little more difficult. The best way for students to "see" the structure is through graphic organizers (presented in Strategy 3). The more that students have these conversations about text, the more proficient they will become at recognizing and using text structure to guide their thinking.

For additional help in identifying and discussing text structures, refer to the Text Structure Reference Chart on pages 160–161. In addition to listing and defining the five main expository text structures discussed here, the chart lists the most common signal words associated with each text structure and provides a sampling of questions

that students can use to help them recognize the structures and further analyze them.

## Extending the Strategy

After students practice locating signal words and identifying text structure, you can link this strategy with Strategy 3: Using Graphic Organizers. The Double S strategy may also be linked to the PIC technique discussed in Strategy 1.

Traditionally, reading and writing have been taught separately. But practice with the Double S strategy also can help students write more effective expository pieces. Writing expository text is a major component of most state assessments.

## Some Final Thoughts

Unfortunately, not all texts are written in a format that has an identifiable structure. Similarly, there may be no signal words in the text. The text may also change structure within the passage. These more complex structures demand increasingly sophisticated reading ability. However, the Double S strategy can get students started on the road to becoming independent learners.

## Read More About It

Britton, B. K., Woodward, A., and Binkley, M., Eds. *Learning from Textbooks: Theory and Practice.* Hillsdale, NJ: Lawrence Erlbaum Associates. 1993.

Garner, R., and Alexander, P. A., Eds. *Beliefs About Text and Instruction with Text.* Hillsdale, NJ: Lawrence Erlbaum Associates. 1994.

Harvey, S. *Nonfiction Matters.* York, ME: Stenhouse Publishers. 1998.

McMackin, M. C. "Using Narrative Picture Books to Build Awareness of Expository Text Structure." *Reading Horizons* 39 (1) 1998: 7–20.

Quiocho, A. "The Quest to Comprehend Expository Text: Applied Classroom Research." *Journal of Adolescent and Adult Literacy* 40 (6) 1997: 450–54.

# TEXT STRUCTURE REFERENCE CHART

| ▶ Structure or Pattern | ▶ Signal Words | | ▶ Questions for Patterns |
|---|---|---|---|
| **Description, Simple Listing, Enumeration**<br><br>Information about a topic is presented through description, listing characteristics, features, and examples. | *to begin with*<br>*characteristics are*<br>*most important*<br>*the following*<br>*in many ways*<br>*for example*<br>*such as*<br>*to illustrate*<br>*furthermore* | *also*<br>*in fact*<br>*finally*<br>*as well*<br>*for instance*<br>*while*<br>*in addition*<br>*another* | What is the main topic?<br>What did the author say about (topic)?<br>How did the author present these ideas?<br>What ideas (or facts) are discussed?<br>Can you think of other ideas or facts about . . .? |
| **Sequence or Chronological**<br><br>Information is presented in sequence, usually in numerical or chronological order. | *first, second, third*<br>*next*<br>*then*<br>*finally*<br>*after*<br>*until*<br>*before*<br>*first/lst* | *on (date)*<br>*at (time)*<br>*not long after*<br>*now*<br>*as before*<br>*when*<br>*initially*<br>*lastly*<br>*preceding*<br>*following* | What was the first important idea discussed?<br>When did it occur?<br>What is the sequence of events?<br>Why did the author tell about this process in this order?<br>What would be included on a time line of the events?<br>What is the chronological order of the steps? |
| **Comparison and Contrast**<br><br>Information is presented by showing likenesses (comparison) and differences (contrast). | *different from*<br>*in contrast*<br>*alike*<br>*same as*<br>*on the other hand*<br>*however*<br>*but*<br>*as well as*<br>*not only . . . but*<br>*in a like manner*<br>*difference*<br>   *between*<br>*instead of*<br>*compared with* | *either . . . or*<br>*while*<br>*although*<br>*unless*<br>*similar to*<br>*yet*<br>*nevertheless*<br>*also*<br>*likewise*<br>*as opposed to*<br>*after all*<br>*and yet*<br>*as well as* | Why do you think the author wrote about this topic by showing likenesses and differences?<br>What is being compared here?<br>How were they alike? How were they different?<br>What do they have in common?<br>Can you think of other ways these (topics) are alike or different? |

| Structure or Pattern | Signal Words | | Questions for Patterns |
|---|---|---|---|
| **Cause and Effect**<br><br>Facts, events, or concepts (effects) come into being because of other facts, events, or concepts (causes). | *reasons why*<br>*if . . . then*<br>*as a result of*<br>*therefore*<br>*because (of)*<br>*thus*<br>*on account of*<br>*due to*<br>*may be due to*<br>*effects of* | *since*<br>*consequently*<br>*this led to*<br>*so that*<br>*nevertheless*<br>*accordingly*<br>*for this reason*<br>*then, so*<br>*in order to* | Can you tell me the cause of _____?<br>What was the effect of _____?<br>How should causes and effects be arranged on a chart?<br>Can you think of any other causes that might produce these effects?<br>Are there any other effects that can result from this cause?<br>Can you think of similar causes and effects? |
| **Problem and Solution or Question and Answer**<br>Information is stated as a problem and one or more solutions are presented. A question is asked and one or more answers are presented. | *a problem is*<br>*a dilemma is*<br>*a puzzle is*<br>  *solved*<br>*question . . .*<br>*answer*<br>*a solution*<br>*the best estimate*<br>*one may conclude* | *why*<br>*when*<br>*where*<br>*how*<br>*what*<br>*who*<br>*it could be that*<br>*how many* | What were the problems discussed here?<br>Are there solutions to this problem? What are they?<br>What caused the problem? How was it solved?<br>Can you think of any similar problems? How were they solved?<br>How would you solve this problem? |

# STRATEGY 3: USING GRAPHIC ORGANIZERS

Graphic organizers are made up of lines, arrows, boxes, and circles that show the relationships between and among ideas. They are sometimes called webs, semantic maps, graphic representations, or clusters. These graphic organizers can help students organize their thinking and their knowledge. While textbooks contain many types of text, the largest portion of text is expository or informational. Expository text has five major structures:

- cause and effect
- comparison and contrast
- description
- problem and solution
- sequence or chronological order

In this strategy, four types of text structure will be presented. Description will be presented in Strategy 4 because this type of text is best displayed with a concept map. The four types of text structure with accompanying graphic organizers are shown below and on the following pages.

**Cause and Effect:** Cause-and-effect patterns show the relationship between results and the ideas or events that made the results occur. (**See Graphic Organizer 2, Cause-and-Effect Chart.**)

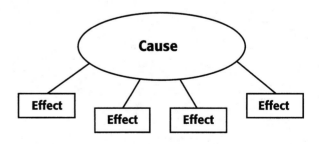

**Problem and Solution:** Problem-solution patterns identify at least one problem, offer one or more solutions to the problem, and explain or predict outcomes of the solutions. (**See Graphic Organizer 9, Problem and Solution Chart.**)

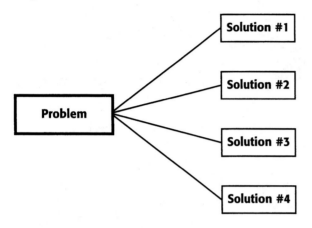

**Comparison and Contrast:** Comparison and contrast, or Venn, diagrams point out similarities and differences between two concepts or ideas. (**See Graphic Organizer 11, Venn Diagram.**)

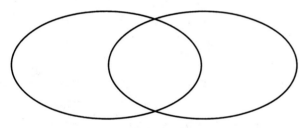

**Sequence or Chronological Order:** Sequence or chronological-order diagrams show events or ideas in the order in which they happened. (**See Graphic Organizer 10, Sequence or Chronological Order Chart.**)

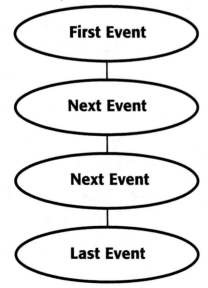

## How Can the Strategy Help My Students?

The way that ideas are presented in a textbook dictates the type of thinking that is necessary to understand and remember those ideas. Graphic organizers help students visualize the connections between and among ideas. They also help students organize knowledge so they can use it later to study for a test or write a report. The act of organizing information engages students in learning and helps them make connections to what they already know. In addition, discussing which graphic organizer might best display the information helps students "see" and use the structure of text to understand and remember more effectively.

## Getting Started

Any single piece of text can be displayed in more than one way, depending on the purpose for reading and the reader's prior knowledge of the topic. Below are the basic steps in one approach to using graphic organizers.

**Step 1:** Students preview the material to be read.

**Step 2:** Students hypothesize which of the four graphic organizers would be best to display the information and their understanding of the material. Their discussion should include the purpose for their reading, and they should note any signal or transition words that may indicate the type of thinking required for the reading and the best way to display the information. Be sure to tell students that the organizers can be modified to meet their needs. For example, the cause-and-effect graphic organizer has room for three effects, but the text may only state one or two.

**Step 3:** Students read the text silently, taking notes.

**Step 4:** Students work in cooperative groups to create a graphic representation of their understanding of the text.

**Step 5:** Students present the finished product to others in the class.

## Using the Strategy in Your Classroom

Previewing the text is essential for students to get an idea of the text's "layout." It helps students get ready to think and organize their ideas in a particular way. If students have not had any previous experience using graphic organizers, you may wish to introduce them to the students a little at a time. Here are some tips for helping students become more proficient users of graphic organizers.

- Begin the explanation of graphic organizers with simple text that has an obvious structure.
- Present one graphic organizer at a time.
- Then, move into having students compare and contrast representations.
- Help students use signal or transition words to determine the structure of a text. These are words such as *for instance, similar to, different from,* and *because* that indicate how ideas are related in a text.
- Then, have students use two, then three, then four types of organizers.

As students become more accustomed to discussing and using graphic organizers, they will be able to adapt them to both their purpose for reading and the type of text they are reading. Eventually, students should be able to generate graphic organizers on their own and use them in their note taking.

## Extending the Strategy

If students are using webbing in their reading or language arts class, be sure to help them make the connection that using graphic organizers is much the same process as creating webs. This would also be a good time to talk to students about the differences in narrative and expository text. Occasionally, pieces of narrative text are inserted in textbooks to elaborate on a point. Students can be shown the different functions of each type of text—graphic organizers are the perfect vehicle for achieving this goal.

Graphic organizers can also be used as a stimulus for writing expository essays. Students learning to compose essays in cause-and-effect, comparison-and-contrast, problem-and-solution, or sequence or chronological-order patterns should capture their ideas in a graphic organizer before they begin writing.

Previewing the text is essential in deciding which graphic organizer is most appropriate. Therefore, you may wish to connect this strategy with Strategies 1 and 2.

## Some Final Thoughts

Unfortunately, not all texts are neatly packaged into the tidy structures I have presented so far. Sometimes text does not follow a definite structure, and sometimes it changes from one structure to another in the same chapter. When this happens, it is wise to discuss the author's purpose for the text and help students construct their own way of organizing the ideas presented.

## Read More About It

Dye, G. A. "Graphic Organizers to the Rescue! Helping Students Link—and Remember—Information." *Teaching Exceptional Children,* 32 (3) 2000, 72–76.

Irwin-DeVitis, L., and Pease, D. "Using Graphic Organizers for Learning and Assessment in Middle Level Classrooms." *Middle School Journal* 26 (5) 1995: 57–64.

Robinson, D. H. "Graphic Organizers as Aids to Text Learning." *Reading Research and Instruction* 37 (2) 1998: 85–105.

# STRATEGY 4: CONSTRUCTING CONCEPT MAPS

As you saw in Strategy 3, graphic organizers can help students visualize and make sense of expository text. The type of graphic organizer we will focus on now is the concept map. A concept map, sometimes called a semantic map or a cluster diagram, allows students to zero in on the most important points of the text. The map is made up of lines, boxes, circles, and arrows. It can be as simple or as complex as students make it and as the text requires.

## How Can the Strategy Help My Students?

Struggling readers often get bogged down in the first three paragraphs of an expository text because they are having difficulty with comprehension. Consequently, they miss the most important points in the passage and never really figure out what the text is about. The concept map is designed to help students focus on and organize the most noteworthy points in the text so they can use them later for a discussion, a writing assignment, or a test. When students preview a reading passage and then work through a reading assignment, they can arrange and rearrange important concepts as needed.

## Getting Started

Previewing helps students see the structure of the passage. With a description-type structure, students may notice signal or transition words such as *for instance, for example, such as, in addition*, or *furthermore*. These signal words indicate that the text is describing or explaining important concepts. The following steps may be helpful in having students complete a concept map:

**Step 1: Preview the Passage.** Previewing can help students determine which kind of structure might best display the ideas in the text.

**Step 2: Sketch a Concept Map.** Looking at the boldfaced type, headings, and general structure of the text, students should sketch out a map to display the ideas in the passage.

**Step 3: Read the Passage.**

**Step 4: Construct a Map.** Using boxes, lines, arrows, bubbles, circles, or any other figure, students can display the ideas in the text in a concept map.

## Using the Strategy in Your Classroom

When first introducing the concept map to students, you may wish to create most of the map yourself and have students complete it after they have used a prereading strategy and have read the text. The mapping strategy is most effective, however, if students create their own concept maps. They can embed definitions and examples within the maps to help remind them of the meaning of particular concepts. As students create their own maps, they should consider the content of headings, the signaling power of boldface type, and the organization of the text to help them choose the most important points.

Concept maps work best with text that explains one or more ideas and provides supporting examples. A concept map may be displayed hierarchically, in the example below, or in a more free-form style, in the example on p. 165.

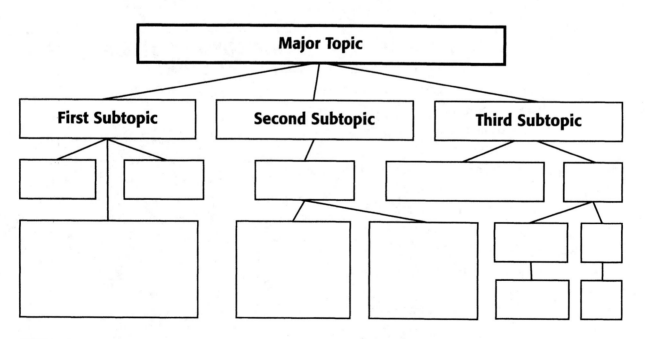

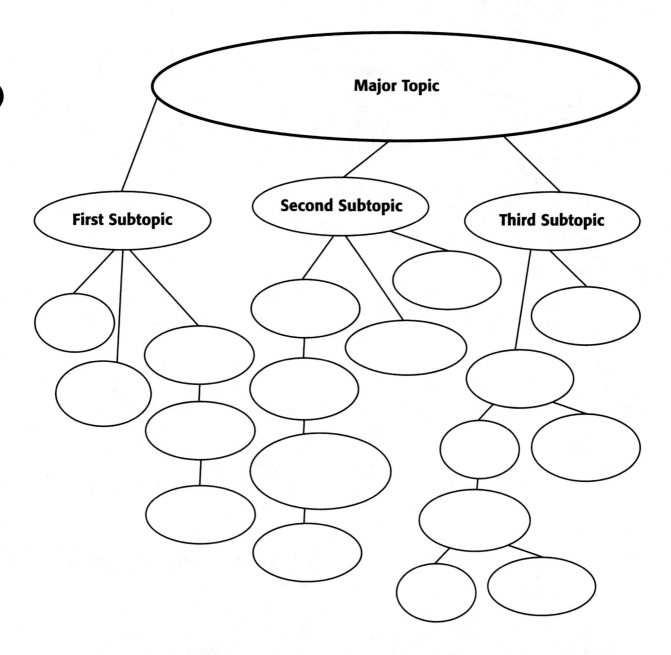

Any combination and organization of circles, bubbles, squares, triangles, lines, or arrows can be used to construct a concept map. Previewing helps students see the overall picture. Sketching gives students an idea of how the key concepts can best be displayed. Constructing the final map helps students understand how the concepts relate to one another. Some teachers suggest sketching the ideas via self-adhesive notes and then constructing the final concept map when students are happy with the display. If some students are more comfortable having a structure to work with, offer them cluster diagrams (**See Graphic Organizer 3**),

and ask them to fill in as many levels as they need and to add boxes if appropriate.

### Extending the Strategy

Struggling readers may need more help to begin a task such as creating a concept map. A Cloze Concept Map may support such readers. After students complete a pre-reading strategy on the topic at hand, you can give them an almost-completed map. Some of the boxes should be left blank and have bold lines around them, as shown in the example on the following page.

If you think students may have difficulty even with this task, you may wish to provide a word

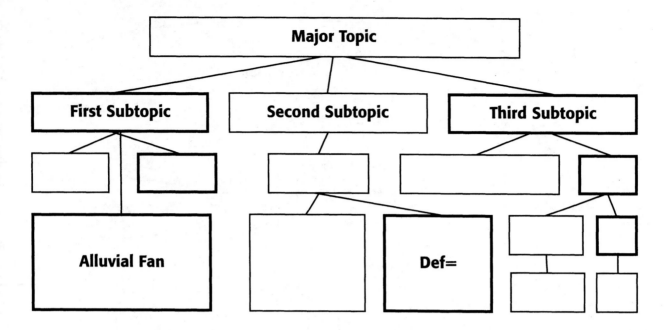

| Major Topic | | |
|---|---|---|
| **First Subtopic** | **Second Subtopic** | **Third Subtopic** |
| **Alluvial Fan** | **Def=** | |

box with the deleted items listed. As students become more proficient at completing this Cloze Concept Map, more boxes can be left blank. As time goes on, once students have finished a pre-reading strategy, you can give them a blank concept map to fill out as they read. Eventually, they should be able to construct their own maps after previewing the text and making a sketch.

## Some Final Thoughts

When first introducing a concept map, use a short and fairly simple text before moving on to a more complex and longer one. Although it is sometimes a challenge, it is best to limit concept maps to one page. That way, when students prepare to study for a test or use the information in writing, the text's most important ideas are displayed in a handy and easy-to-use format.

## Read More About It

Chen, H. S., and Graves, M. F. "Previewing Challenging Reading Selections for ESL Students." *Journal of Adolescent and Adult Literacy* 41 (7) 1998: 570–71.

Cunningham, J. W., and Moore, D. W. "The Confused World of Main Idea." In *Teaching Main Idea Comprehension*, J. Baumann. Newark, DE: International Reading Association. 1986.

Dana, C. "Strategy Families for Disabled Readers." *Journal of Reading* 33 (5): 30–35.

Huffman, L. E. "What's in It for You? A Student-Directed Text Preview." *Journal of Adolescent and Adult Literacy* 40 (1): 56–57.

Salemblier, G. B. "SCAN and RUN: A Reading Comprehension Strategy That Works." *Journal of Adolescent and Adult Literacy* 42 (5): 386–94.

# STRATEGY 5: VISUALIZING INFORMATION

Textbooks are full of charts, diagrams, pictures, illustrations, cartoons, and maps. These visual aids enhance the learning of the content. In their rush to complete an assignment, students often skip over the visual information that may actually improve their comprehension.

The Information Age has certainly bombarded students today with visual images. Some say that the beautiful picture books, the television, the Internet, CD–ROMs, and so forth may have taken away a student's need (and perhaps ability) to visualize. Others may argue that youth today think in visual images. Whatever the case, proficient readers visualize as they read—struggling readers generally do not.

## How Can the Strategy Help My Students?

Visual information displayed in a textbook can be flipped over and ignored or studied and incorporated. What students *do* with the visual information is the important ingredient to comprehending text. Rakes, Rakes, and Smith (1995) suggested that a teacher can help students use information on increasingly interactive levels. The teacher can:

- Provide written or oral directions immediately before students "read" the visual information, such as "On this map, you will notice . . ."
- Direct students' attention through study questions to the important accompanying visuals, such as "This chart displays the most common transportation in America during the Industrial Revolution . . ."
- Encourage students to evaluate the graphics in the text and think about how the graphics and text relate to one another. You might ask, "Given the most important point of this passage, is this graphic representative of . . ."
- Ask students to create their own visuals depicting the information represented in the text. When students draw a sketch or picture of the information in the text, they have made a connection between what they know and what they are reading. Illustrations can be used to summarize text, and graphic organizers and concept maps (Strategies 3 and 4) can assist students in integrating new knowledge with existing knowledge.

The more that students are involved in creating visual images, the more engaged they will be with the ideas in the text. Depending on the purpose of the assigned reading, you may wish to direct students to visuals, have them evaluate the visual information presented, and/or have students create their own graphic representations of the ideas presented in the text.

## Getting Started

Here are the basic steps to the Visualizing Information strategy:

**Step 1: Preview the Text, Noting the Visual Information Presented.** This information may be in the form of charts, diagrams, pictures, or illustrations.

**Step 2: Ask How the Visual Information Relates to the Text or Why the Author(s) Included This Information.** It is important that students create a link between the text and the visual. You may wish to have students use a transparency over the text to draw arrows between the text and the visual.

**Step 3: Generate Questions Raised by the Visual Aid.** Students should list two to three questions that arise from this visual aid.

**Step 4: Read the Text.**

**Step 5: Go Back and Review Visual Aids in the Text.** Students should evaluate whether the visual accurately displays the most important ideas in the text.

## Using the Strategy in Your Classroom

This strategy can, of course, be modified to suit the needs of your students and their purpose for reading. Based on Rakes, Rakes, and Smith's levels of interaction presented above, you could:

- simply direct students to notice the visual element
- provide study questions based on the visual element
- have students evaluate how the visual element helps them better understand the text
- have students sketch their own understanding of the topic of the reading

In addition, questions can direct students' understanding of how the visual element fits with information presented before and after it.

## Extending the Strategy

Some educators suggest that after reading, students be asked to draw the visual from memory. This works particularly well for diagrams explained in the text. The act of creating a graphic helps students process it better and connect to the information presented in the text. In addition, this activity can certainly be used to assess how well students understood the text.

Student-created graphics can be extended through group work by having students explain their graphic to other students. They benefit from hearing and seeing the various perspectives of other students. Without employing competition such as "whose graphic is the best?", students can be guided to give feedback on other students' graphics. Giving and soliciting feedback helps them process the ideas in the text more deeply and become better consumers of displays of visual information.

Some teachers have used a Visual Reading Guide (Stein, 1978) for many years. This study guide is simply constructed to direct students to preview the visual information in the text before they read, answering some preliminary questions before and after reading.

The graphic organizers and concept maps presented in Strategies 3 and 4 are additional ways of encouraging students to visualize and organize the ideas in the text. (**See Graphic Organizer 2, Cause-and-Effect Chart; Graphic Organizer 9, Problem and Solution Chart; Graphic Organizer 11, Venn Diagram; and Graphic Organizer 3, Cluster Diagram.**) Some computer software allows students to flip between graphic representations and an outline of the material.

### Some Final Thoughts

Not all text has strategically placed visual information that is well explained and connected to the text in the caption. If this is the case, then having students evaluate and/or redraw graphics may be useful. Also, because of time constraints, a teacher can not give this type of attention to every visual aid in the text. But when the visual information does help students better understand the ideas in the text, this strategy can be most helpful. Most students—but especially struggling readers—can benefit from learning how to use the visual aids that often accompany texts.

### Read More About It

Hyerle, D. *Visual Tools for Constructing Knowledge.* Alexandria, VA: Association for Supervision and Curriculum Development. 1996.

Rakes, G. C., Rakes, T. A., and Smith, L. J. "Using Visuals to Enhance Secondary Students' Reading Comprehension of Expository Text." *Journal of Adolescent and Adult Literacy* 39 (1) 1995: 46–54.

Scevak, J., and Moore, P. "The Strategies Students in Years 5, 7, and 9 Use for Processing Texts and Visual Aids." *The Australian Journal of Language and Literacy* 20 (4) 1997: 280–88.

Stein, H. "The Visual Reading Guide (VRG)." *Social Education* 42 (6) 1978: 534–35.

## STRATEGY 6: BUILDING BACKGROUND INFORMATION

Have you ever tried to read a computer manual or some other highly technical book when you lacked the background knowledge really to understand it? It is frustrating to read something on a topic you know little about. Students encounter that feeling often when they attempt to read many textbooks. You can help students build the information they need to be successful before beginning a reading assignment.

One strategy for achieving this goal is the Predicting and Confirming Activity (PACA). Teachers find this strategy a good way to teach their content. The strategy helps build background information before students read about something they know little about so they will have a context for understanding the ideas presented. (**Graphic Organizer 8, PACA.**)

### How Can the Strategy Help My Students?

Students often have no personal connection with much of what we hope they learn in classrooms. They have a context for American history and geography, but often struggle with subjects such as world cultures. For students to learn anything new, they must connect it in some way to something they already know. Good teachers help students make the connection between new information and what students already know.

## Getting Started

Here are the steps for the Predicting and Confirming Activity. The Predicting and Confirming Activity uses student predictions to set a purpose for reading. Students make these predictions based on an initial set of information provided by the teacher. Given additional information, students can revise their predictions (or hypotheses) and pose them as questions to be answered during reading.

**Step 1: Provide Some Initial Information and Pose a General Question.** Provide students with a list of words containing the important concepts in the reading as well as 10 to 15 more familiar terms that students will know. Then, ask them questions about the reading. A word list and a question are usually enough to help students make predictions. But if they are not, you can couple the word list with a short overview of the topic.

**Step 2: Write Predictions Based on the Initial Information.** These predictions can be discussed and written on the chalkboard or written by individual students or groups of students.

**Step 3: Provide New Information.** This can be in the form of pictures, charts, diagrams, maps, or other visual information from the textbook, a video, or from reading a story.

**Step 4: Review Predictions.** Students may revise, confirm, or reject their original predictions. Then they turn the predictions into questions for reading. Based on the new information, students discuss—as a class or in small groups—which of their original predictions they want to keep and which they think no longer apply. They may also revise some predictions to be more accurate. They then turn these predictions into questions they want answered during reading.

**Step 5: Read the Text.**

**Step 6: Revisit Predictions and Answer Questions.** Students once again look at their predictions and answer the questions they generated earlier. At this point, students go back to their original predictions and see which ones may be revised or confirmed. They may also check to see if their questions were answered. From here, depending on the purpose of the reading, you may wish to ask students to write about their new learning, formulate study questions and answers, or use some graphic representation of their learning.

## Using the Strategy in Your Classroom

The Predicting and Confirming Activity is simply a method for building background information before reading. When students read after completing this strategy, they will be able to connect what they are reading and what they now know about the topic. The predictions turned into questions help guide their reading as well.

When constructing the initial word list, it is important to include both words students will know and some they will encounter in the reading. While discussing these words in small groups in order to write their predictions, students may guess at the meanings of unknown words, or someone in the group may know the word.

If students do not know enough about the topic even to begin predicting, then you could start off with a reading or an overview of the topic or have students leaf through the textbook to get some ideas. You could also direct students to write a sentence using two or more words in the list to construct the prediction.

## Extending the Strategy

After questions are formulated and predictions are made, you may wish to use a jigsaw design to complete the reading. Groups would be assigned to answer specific questions about the topic— each group forming an expert group. Then one student from each group would share his or her "expert" information with the base group to complete the synthesizing activity.

If students need additional help in processing new information, you could ask them to visualize. They could also organize their newfound knowledge into a graphic organizer or employ a sketch or diagram. Additionally, they could extend and organize their thoughts by writing a summary or report.

## Some Final Thoughts

When using a Predicting and Confirming Activity, students risk forming misconceptions by making predictions based on limited information. Revisiting the predictions is an important part of this strategy, because it is your opportunity to correct these misconceptions and expand students' knowledge about the topic. For this reason, some teachers prefer to display the predictions on an overhead or on the chalkboard. A classroom environment in which students are free to guess and be wrong is an essential component to implementing this strategy.

Some pictures in books are rich with information and some are not. You may need to supplement the text with videos, pictures, or stories. The purpose is to build background information where none or little exists so that students can be more successful when they read their textbook. In the process, students may learn that making and confirming predictions is an essential part of effective reading.

## Read More About It

Beyer, B. K. *Inquiry in the Social Studies Classroom.* Columbus, OH: Charles E. Merrill Publishing Company. 1971.

Harmon, J. M., Katims, D. S., and Whittington, D. "Helping Middle School Students Learn From Social Studies Texts." *Teaching Exceptional Children* 32 (1) 1999: 70–75.

Nessell, D. "Channeling Knowledge for Reading Expository Text." *Journal of Reading* 32 (3) 1988: 231–35.

Weir, C. "Using Embedded Questions to Jump-Start Metacognition in Middle School Remedial Readers." *Journal of Adolescent and Adult Literacy* 41 (6) 1998: 458–68.

# STRATEGY 7: MAKING PREDICTIONS

Making predictions is one of the most important strategies students can use when approaching a new reading assignment. Hilda Taba (1967) was one of the first educators to suggest a method for encouraging even young children to think at higher levels. Her concept-formation model was later adapted as List-Group-Label, a strategy to activate what students know about a topic, build and expand on what they know, and organize that knowledge before they begin reading.

Building on Taba's original work, reading educators later added the "map" step. This strategy can also be used as a diagnostic instrument to find out what students know about a subject before they read and as an organizational tool to facilitate higher level thinking through making predictions. Because the strategy involves the categorization and labeling of words, List-Group-Label-Map also makes an excellent preceding strategy for a vocabulary development lesson.

## How Can the Strategy Help My Students?

When students begin reading without activating what they know first, they often miss the connections that would help them store that information in longer-term memory. In addition, many students lack the ability to categorize and classify information. This process of grouping concepts helps students understand the relationships between ideas. Classifying and categorizing concepts before reading helps students connect to what they already know about a topic and better understand the concepts in the text. Creating a concept map before reading gives students the opportunity to "see" the ideas and their relationships while reading.

## Getting Started

Here are the steps in the List-Group-Label-Map Strategy.

The List-Group-Label-Map strategy works best when students already know something about a topic. During the initial discussion, teachers may ascertain how much students already know about a topic and correct any misconceptions they may have.

**Step 1: Make a Word List.** Direct students to an initial piece of information and ask them to list as many words related to the topic as possible. Pictures are the best and easiest stimulus for this activity, although other visual information in the textbook can be used. These words may be associations they come up with from memory if the topic is very familiar. Many teachers also use videos to elicit words. If you conduct the discussion with the entire class, write the word lists in columns on the chalkboard or on an overhead transparency. If the discussion occurs within a small group, a student can record the words.

**Step 2: Look for Word Associations.** Students group items by indicating which words belong together. Only one student in a group should indicate which words go together. The teacher (or a student in a group) then marks the words with an *X* or *O* or some other symbol. If another student wants to add to the grouping, it is important that the first student be consulted because he or she may be thinking of a different category. Students can use words more than once.

**Step 3: Label Word Groups.** Then the student who came up with the original groupings goes back and labels each group. These labels represent concepts, and the words are then examples of these concepts.

**Step 4: Make a Concept Map.** Individually or in small groups, students use the words listed to create concept maps, following the process described in Strategy 4. (**See Graphic Organizer 3, Cluster Diagram.**)

**Step 5: Read the Text.** During reading, students may note whether the concept map they created was consistent with the ideas presented in the text.

**Step 6: Revisit the Concept Map.** After reading, students take another look at their concept map and add information from the reading. Encourage students to elaborate on their maps using the

ideas in the text. These expanded maps connect what they knew before reading with what they learned while reading.

## Using the Strategy in Your Classroom

Any picture, video, or other information can be used to generate the word list. Pictures that give a lot of information work best and can be used to build the background information necessary to understand the text. Pictures also help students visualize what they read. To get students started, simply ask them what they see in the picture (or remember from the video). Since the next step is to classify and categorize words, encourage students to choose words that describe what they see rather than make interpretations from the picture.

When students group words, it is important that one person state his or her grouping. If more students get involved, the original labels for the groups may be confused or lost. Words can be categorized in endless ways.

Whenever students are engaged in making predictions, they may form misconceptions about the information presented in the text. You can correct these misconceptions while reviewing their concept maps or during the ensuing discussion.

## Extending the Strategy

After you have completed the List-Group-Label-Map process, you may wish to try any or all of the following extension activities:

- *Possible Sentences.* Students connect two or more words from the list and write sentences inferring what the text will be about. These sentences can be formulated into a paragraph, and students can compare their predictions.
- *Writing Summaries.* Using the list and the concept map, students can write a summary of the information after reading. A visual display of the ideas and words in a list can help students who have difficulty writing summaries.

- *Comparing and Contrasting*. One approach is to lead students to compare and contrast one piece of information with another and then lead them, through carefully designed questions, to make a generalization using both sets of information. **(See Graphic Organizer 11, Venn Diagram.)**

List-Group-Label-Map can be combined with other strategies such as Understanding Text (Strategy 2). Depending on the needs of your students, how familiar they are with the topic, your instructional objectives, and the purpose for the reading, many of the strategies presented in this book can be used to support one another.

## Some Final Thoughts

The List-Group-Label-Map strategy can be used by itself to generate information and inferences about a text before reading it, or it can be used with other strategies to extend students' thinking and help them summarize and make predictions. The strategy is a vehicle for using the wonderful visual information generally displayed in textbooks to connect readers with text.

## Read More About It

Blevins, W. "Strategies for Struggling Readers: Making Predictions." *Instructor* 108 (2) 1990: 49.

Caverly, D. C., Mandeville, T. F., and Nicholson, S. A. "PLAN: A Study-Reading Strategy for Informational Text." *Journal of Adolescent and Adult Literacy* 39 (3) 1995: 190–99.

Foley, C. L. "Prediction: A Valuable Reading Strategy." *Reading Improvement* 30 (3) 1993: 166–70.

Nolan, T. E. "Self-Questioning and Prediction: Combining Metacognitive Strategies." *Journal of Reading* 35 (2) 1991: 132–38.

Stahl, S. A., and Kapinus, B. A. "Possible Sentences: Predicting Word Meanings to Teach Content-Area Vocabulary." *Reading Teacher* 5 (1) 1991: 36–43.

Taba, H. *Teacher's Handbook for Elementary Social Studies*. Reading, MA: Addison-Wesley. 1967.

# STRATEGY 8: ACTIVATING AND USING PRIOR KNOWLEDGE

Strong readers know that asking questions and thinking about ideas while reading help them understand and remember text. Students who begin reading a text with no preparation and no thought about the topic often can complete an assignment but do not seem to remember much about what they read. One way to help students clear this hurdle is the KWL strategy, which was developed by Donna Ogle in 1986 and further refined by Carr and Ogle (1987). KWL stands for What I *K*now, What I *W*ant to Know, and What I *L*earned. The purpose of this strategy is to activate students' prior knowledge:

**BEFORE** reading by adding background information and helping students monitor their learning

**DURING** reading by thinking about what they want to know or the questions they want answered about the topic, and

**AFTER** reading by helping them organize what they know through listing the things they learned about the topic.

The KWL chart looks like this:

| ▶ What I *Know* | ▶ What I *Want* to Know | ▶ What I *Learned* |
|---|---|---|
| | | |
| | | |

## How Can the Strategy Help My Students?

Students do not tend to use their prior knowledge about a topic when they read unless it is "activated." The KWL helps students review what they know about a topic, set a purpose for reading based on what they want to know, and organize what they learned after reading.

For struggling students, extra support can be given by the teacher or other students by helping them study the charts, diagrams, maps, and pictures in the book to make some inferences or guesses about the topic. Nonproficient and second-language learners can gain background information by listening to the discussion of others.

## Getting Started

Here are the steps in the KWL strategy.
The KWL activity is most successful when students know something about the material but need to build on what they know to comprehend the text. Students can complete the KWL activity individually, in a group, or as part of a class discussion.

***Step 1: Fill Out the First Two Columns of the KWL Chart.*** Students should write down everything they *know* for sure about the topic. Then they should write down everything they *want* to know about the topic in the middle column. There is no set of correct answers, but misconceptions or wrong information can be flagged for further discussion. What they want to know should be phrased as questions.

***Step 2: Read, View, and/or Listen to Content about the Topic.***

***Step 3: Fill Out the Learned Column.*** Students should work in small groups to elaborate on their answers.

***Step 4: Construct a Concept Map.*** This map represents an integration of what students knew before reading and what they learned.

***Step 5: Write a Summary.*** Using the concept map, students can write a summary of what they learned about the subject. The summary helps students focus on the most important points in the reading.

## Using the Strategy in Your Classroom

The KWL strategy works best with topics about which students have some prior knowledge. If they know very little about a topic, students will have trouble filling in the first two columns of the chart. The purpose of the strategy is to *activate* what students know about a topic and, through discussion and further learning, *build background information.* If students are unsure how to identify what they know, they can scan their reading and make questions from subheadings. If the topic is too broad and students know a lot about it, they may get bogged down making a list. Sometimes you will not know how much prior knowledge students have until the brainstorming begins. To solve this problem, you might have your students create a concept map first so they can organize their thoughts about the topic. Then have them summarize the key points in the What I Know column. (**See Graphic Organizer 6, KWL Chart.**)

Another possibility is that when you ask students what they want to know, they will respond "nothing." That's why I like to refer to the middle column as "what you *think* you know." These statements of what they think they know can then be turned into questions they want answered in the reading. (**See Graphic Organizer 7, KWLS Chart.**)

## Extending the Strategy

Because KWL is such a popular strategy, teachers have devised numerous variations. One variation, known as WIKA, was developed by Richardson and Morgan (2000). WIKA stands for *What I Know Activity*. Some teachers find that the original format for KWL does not fit into the before-during-after framework, which is more clearly identified in the WIKA.

In this variation, the before-during-after instructional framework is clearly identified above the five columns.

### WIKA

| Before Reading | | During Reading | After Reading | |
|---|---|---|---|---|
| What I Already Know | What I'd Like to Know | Interesting or Important Concepts from the Reading | What I Know Now | What I'd Still Like to Know |
| | | | | |

Other teachers have used these variations:

### KWHL

| What I *Know* | What I *Want* to Know | *How* I Will Find Out | What I *Learned* |
|---|---|---|---|
| | | | |

Or:

### KWLS

| What I *Know* | What I *Want* to Know | What I *Learned* | What I *Still* Want to Know |
|---|---|---|---|
| | | | |

## Some Final Thoughts

Feel free to modify the KWL strategy for your topic and the special needs of your students. If your students need more help thinking of what they know about a topic, you can show them a video, bring some pictures to class, have them leaf through their textbook, or read them a story. The first time you use any strategy, pick an easy text and keep the directions clear and simple. As students become more proficient using the strategy, more difficult text and variations may be used.

Some teachers are frustrated using a KWL because it takes longer to get "through" content. Keep in mind, however, that students tend to retain the information longer when they use this strategy. True, it takes some time for students to understand the KWL steps, but the purpose is to get them in the habit of thinking of what they know about a topic before they start reading.

## Read More About It

Bryan, J. "K-W-W-L: Questioning the Known." *The Reading Teacher* 51 (1) 1998: 618–20.

Cantrell, J. "K-W-L Learning Journals: A Way to Encourage Reflection." *Journal of Adolescent and Adolescent Literacy* 40 (5) 1997: 392–93.

Carr, E., and Ogle, D. "K-W-L Plus: A Strategy for Comprehension and Summarization." *Journal of Reading* 30 (7) 1987: 626–31.

Heller, M. "How Do You Know What You Know? Metacognitive Modeling in the Content Areas." *Journal of Reading* 29, 1986: 415–22.

Huffman, L. E. "Spotlighting Specifics by Combining Focus Questions with K-W-L." *Journal of Adolescent and Adolescent Literacy* 41 (6) 1998: 470–72.

Ogle, D. "K-W-L: A Teaching Model that Develops Active Reading of Expository Text." *The Reading Teacher* 39 (6) 1986: 564–70.

Richardson, J. S. and Morgan, R. F. *Reading to Learn in the Content Areas*. Belmont, CA: Wadsworth. 2000.

# STRATEGY 9: ANTICIPATING INFORMATION

Anticipating what a text is going to be about helps readers connect the text with what they already know. Activating and using prior knowledge is an essential component of comprehending text. A strategy known as the Anticipation Guide was developed by Harold Herber in the early 1970s and has been used and modified over the years. The strategy is particularly well suited to teaching informational or expository content and helping students clarify their opinions and ideas about a topic.

## How Can the Strategy Help My Students?

Middle- and high-school students love to debate, discuss, and voice their opinions. The Anticipation Guide uses this natural tendency to connect the ideas in a text with students' experience and knowledge. The Anticipation Guide helps students

- activate knowledge about a topic by voicing an opinion before they read
- focus their attention on the major points during their reading
- provide a structure for discussing the text after they read.

As students state their opinions about a text's topic, they become more engaged and invested in supporting their viewpoint. This discussion alerts them to the important ideas in the text. In addition, students have a structure for discussing these ideas, and teachers can ask additional questions or make comments that expand student thinking.

## Getting Started

Here are the steps to the Anticipation Guide strategy.

Anticipation Guides work best with material that prompts students to form an opinion. For example, one teacher started a unit on comparative governments with this statement: "It is fair that some people make more money than others." The impending discussion on either side helped students understand socialist and democratic philosophies before reading about them. The steps of an Anticipation Guide are as follows:

**Step 1: Identify the Major Concepts.** Before students begin the activity, determine the main ideas of the reading selection, lecture, or film and write several statements that focus on the main points in the text and draw on students' backgrounds. Four to six statements are usually adequate to generate discussion. The statements can be presented in a chart like one below. **(See Graphic Organizer 1, Anticipation Guide.)**

**Step 2: Identify Agree/Disagree Statements.** Students point out statements with which they agree or disagree, then write *agree* or *disagree* in column A. Rather than analyzing too much or second guessing, students should merely respond to the statements. Students respond individually— either negatively or positively—to each statement and can then compare responses in small groups.

**Step 3: Engage in a Prereading Discussion.** You may wish to get a hand count of responses to the statements and ask students to justify their responses with reasons or evidence. Then engage students in full discussion of the pros and cons of each statement. You may wish for students to compare answers within a small group before moving to a large group discussion.

**Step 4: Read the Text.** Students should be directed to look for ideas either that support or contradict the statements they just discussed.

**Step 5: Revisit the Statements.** Students should look at the statements they chose earlier to see if they have changed their opinions and then write *agree* or *disagree* in column B. The purpose of this strategy is not to engage students in competition to see who is right or wrong, but rather to activate their opinions about issues that are related to the text and to expand their thinking.

**Step 6: Engage in a Postreading Discussion.** Looking again at the statements, students should compare their before-reading reactions to their after-reading reactions. Ask them to justify their new or continuing beliefs based on the reading.

## Using the Strategy in Your Classroom

The challenge in designing an Anticipation Guide is creating statements, rather than questions that may signal students that there is a right or wrong answer. The statements also need to connect what students already know with the major ideas in the text. In a sense, the statements represent the "so what" of the reading; that is, how this selection relates to the lives of the students.

Duffelmeyer (1994) maintained that effective statements

- convey a sense of the major ideas that the student will encounter.
- activate and draw upon the students' prior experience.
- are general rather than specific.
- challenge students' beliefs.

After reading, students may wish to add to the statements or modify them in some way. The statements can be the basis for a writing assignment or an essay answer for a test.

## Extending the Strategy

Writing assignments are a natural extension of the Anticipation Guide. Writing a persuasive essay

| A | Statements | B |
|---|---|---|
| **Before Reading** Agree/Disagree | | **After Reading** Agree/Disagree |
| | | |
| | | |
| | | |

is required on many standardized tests. Students could be encouraged to take one or two of the statements, document them with evidence found in the text, and construct a persuasive essay. You may wish to work with an English/language arts teacher on this assignment.

As students get more proficient at using an Anticipation Guide, you can include some distracter statements that have little to do with the content. Critical readers can detect irrelevant comments as not central to the main argument. For students who are not yet ready to read this critically, these statements can be discussed after the reading.

### Some Final Thoughts

While exchanging information with their class-mates, it is easy for students to form misconceptions. It is particularly important that you correct these misconceptions during the prereading and postreading discussion. Creating a classroom environment where students are free to make predictions and venture opinions is the key to stimulating discussions. But monitoring those discussions is also an important role of the teacher.

The Anticipation Guide is an excellent method for promoting active reading, directing students' attention to the major points in the text, and helping them to use evidence to modify erroneous beliefs. Using the natural propensity of adolescents to debate and argue engages them in the content by connecting the topic to their lives.

### Read More About It

Conley, M. "Promoting Cross-Cultural Understanding Through Content-Area Reading Strategies." *Journal of Reading* 28 (7) 1985: 600–05.

Duffelmeyer, F. A. "Effective Anticipation Guide Statements for Learning from Expository Prose." *Journal of Reading* 37 (6) 1994: 452–57.

Erikson, B., Huber, M., Bea, T., Smith, C., and McKenzie, V. "Increasing Critical Reading in Junior High Classes." *Journal of Reading* 30 (5) 1987: 430–39.

Herber, H. L. *Teaching Reading in Content Areas.* Englewood Cliffs, NJ: Prentice-Hall. 1978.

Merkley, D. J. "Modified Anticipation Guide." *Reading Teacher* 50 (4) 1996–97: 365–68.

## STRATEGY 10: TAKING EFFECTIVE NOTES

Identifying the most important ideas in a text and capturing them in the form of notes for study or writing a report can be a formidable task for many students. Any of the prereading strategies suggested in this book can help students focus on the most important points before they read. The INSERT Method (Interactive Notation System for Effective Reading and Thinking) was developed by Vaughn and Estes (1986) to assist students in clarifying their understanding of the text and making decisions while they read. This strategy can help students concentrate on important information and can provide the structure to organize those ideas after reading.

### How Can the Strategy Help My Students?

Most students, especially those who struggle with reading assignments, do not understand that comprehending text involves *responding* to it in some way. In fact, some struggling readers do not realize that *thinking* is necessary while reading. Strong readers integrate the information in the text with what they already know. They constantly make decisions or have a running conversation with themselves such as the following:

- This point is important, but this one is a detail.
- This seems like an example used to help me understand the text.
- I already knew that.
- I didn't know that.
- This is in boldfaced type—must be a major concept.
- I don't understand this explanation.
- This map must be here for a reason— probably to illustrate the important ideas.

The INSERT Method prompts students to have these types of conversations while they read. It also provides a structure for students to organize effective notes after they read.

## Getting Started

Vaughn and Estes suggested that the INSERT Method helps students think more and better while they read. I adapted this method into the steps below to extend this strategy and help students capture the most important ideas into effective notes.

**Step 1: Introduce Students to Symbols in INSERT.** An endless set of symbols can be used to help students focus on the text. Which ones you choose depends on the purpose for reading and type of text. Some examples are listed below.

✔    Knew this already
***    Important information
++    Supporting detail
Ex    Example of important concept
??    Don't understand this

**Step 2: Read the Text and Respond Using Symbols.** Students are not normally allowed to write in textbooks. But the INSERT Method requires that students respond in writing to the ideas in the text. Some teachers fold a sheet of paper lengthwise into three sections, place the INSERT symbols at the top with a line to indicate the page number, and instruct students to place this sheet alongside the book for notetaking. Other teachers have students record their responses with a felt-tip marker on blank transparency sheets. Still others prefer to have students mark passages in the text using self-adhesive notes with colors corresponding to symbols or with preprinted symbols.

**Step 3: Use Symbols to Organize Notes from the Reading.** This is a good time to have students compare notes. Students can meet in small groups to share what they thought were the most important points, the details, and/or the examples presented in the text. The discussion helps

students understand how to find the main idea in passages and organize information. They can then organize these main ideas in the form of notes. Depending on the purpose for reading, the notes could be arranged in different ways. The information could be placed in a concept map or used as part of a larger essay.

## Using the Strategy in Your Classroom

The INSERT Method engages students in the major points of the text and helps them organize their thinking. Feel free to change the symbols depending on your purpose for having students read a selection. For example, if students are reading a position statement of some sort, you may wish to use the following symbols:

A    Agree with this statement
D    Disagree with this statement
I    Interesting statement

Categorizing the ideas in the text engages students in thinking and making decisions about the text. In time, students will make these distinctions on their own as they comprehend text.

## Extending the Strategy

Taking notes from text is an important skill that must be used to write a report or make a presentation. The Cornell, or divided-page, note-taking system is a popular system used in many middle and high schools. In this system the important points are listed on the left side of the paper, and the details are listed on the right. The page might look like the example on the top of page 179. (**See Graphic Organizer 5, Key Points and Details Chart.**)

This information can also be translated into a concept map (see Strategy 4) or a graphic organizer (see Strategy 3) to help students see the relationships between ideas.

## Some Final Thoughts

The INSERT Method is a simple yet powerful strategy for helping students respond to reading informational or expository textbooks. This strategy is most effective when used with a prereading strategy that activates what students

| ▶ Key Points | ▶ Details |
| --- | --- |
| | |
| | |
| | |

know about a topic before reading or a postreading strategy such as creating a concept map or graphic organizer. The purpose of this strategy is to help students think about and respond to text.

## Read More About It

Czarnecki, E., Rosko, D., and Fine, E. "How to Call Up Notetaking Skills." *Teaching Exceptional Children* 30 (6) 1998: 14–19.

Randall, S. N. "Information Charts: A Strategy for Organizing Student Research." *Journal of Adolescent and Adult Literacy* 39 (7) 1996: 536–42.

Rankin, V. "The Thought That Counts: Six Skills That Help Kids Turn Notes into Knowledge." *School Library Journal* 45 (8) 1999: 24–26.

Tomlinson, L. M. "A Coding System for Notemaking in Literature: Preparation for Journal Writing, Class Participation, and Essay Tests." *Journal of Adolescent and Adult Literacy* 40 (6) 1997: 468–76.

Vaughn, J. L., and Estes, T. H. *Reading and Reasoning Beyond the Primary Grades.* Needham Heights, MA: Allyn and Bacon. 1986.

Weisharr, M. K., and Boyle, J. R. "Notetaking Strategies for Students with Disabilities." *The Clearing House* 72 (6) 1999: 392–95.

# STRATEGY 11: DEVELOPING VOCABULARY KNOWLEDGE

All readers encounter words they do not know; strong readers have strategies for determining what to do about those words. Proficient readers use any or all of the following strategies when they encounter an unknown word:

- Skip it and read on.
- Reread.
- Think about what they are reading.
- Sound out the word to see if they have heard it before.
- Look at the headings and subheadings of the text.
- Guess at whether the word is a noun or an adjective.
- Associate the parts of the word (prefixes, root words, suffixes) with more familiar words.

In my opinion, teaching students strategies to use when they encounter an unknown word is more useful than teaching them a host of vocabulary words in isolation. If they don't use these words in writing or see them in reading, students tend to forget them after the weekly vocabulary test.

The Contextual Redefinition strategy helps students learn to use context and structural analysis to determine the meanings of unknown words. An important element in this strategy is teacher modeling of the process of determining the meanings of words. This can be done by sharing the associations that come to mind when using structural analysis.

## How Can the Strategy Help My Students?

Structural analysis (or morphemic analysis) involves determining the meaning of an unknown word by associating the word's prefixes, root words, or suffixes with meaningful parts of other words. When applied to informational or expository texts, structural analysis can be paired with contextual analysis to create a powerful strategy for determining the meanings of unknown words.

Context present at the sentence level is not always helpful. The larger context of the paragraph or the entire passage should be used.

Questions such as "What is this passage about?" or "What type of word would go there?" help students make good predictions about the approximate meaning of a word. Depending on the word or its function, an approximate meaning is often enough to comprehend the text.

Another helpful question is "How important is this word to understanding the passage?" Strong readers make good decisions about when to simply guess at a word's meaning and when to stop and determine the meaning. Consider the following sentence: "Her mauve skirts fluttered as she fell over the precipice." A proficient reader might guess that *mauve* is a color and move on without determining the exact color. However, the same reader might stop to determine the meaning of *precipice* since it explains what the woman fell over.

## Getting Started

Contextual Redefinition is a good strategy for introducing the key vocabulary in an informational or expository selection. The strategy helps students learn and engage deeply with the important concepts of the reading selection, and helps them practice the behaviors and thinking that proficient readers use to figure out unknown words.

**Step 1: Identify Unfamiliar Words.** Before students begin reading, select the word or words likely to be unfamiliar to them. Words that contain meaningful morphemes for analysis work best, so select words with familiar prefixes, suffixes, and root words that students can associate with other words. Having students guess the meanings of particular morphemes is far better than just telling them the meanings. By guessing, students become actively involved in the reading.

**Step 2: Guess Word Meanings.** Present the word in isolation and ask students to make guesses about its meaning. The only clues they have at this point are their associations with the prefixes, root words, and suffixes. Some of these guesses will be wrong or even funny. Remember that the

process of using structural analysis is important, not proving someone's guess right or wrong.

**Step 3: Refine Guesses.** Using the unfamiliar word, write (or borrow from the text) a series of sentences, including more contextual cues in each one. Have students refine their guesses about what the word means as you present each sentence.

**Step 4: Verify Meanings.** Have students verify the word's meaning in a dictionary or glossary. If students have no idea what a word means, a dictionary or glossary may not be helpful because many words have more than one meaning. Therefore, a dictionary or glossary should be the last place they go, not the first. The purpose of these references is to verify an already good guess about the word's meaning. (**See Graphic Organizer 4, Contextual Redefinition Chart.**)

## Using the Strategy in Your Classroom

Most people use a variety of strategies simultaneously to comprehend text. Structural and contextual analysis are two of the most helpful. Another helpful strategy is to examine the syntax of the sentence or the way that the word functions in the sentence. While presenting the sentences with increasingly rich context, make sure to help students see how each sentence gives them the very important clue of syntax.

When using structural analysis to help students associate new words with known words, you should point out that these conventions do not always apply. For example, *-er* at the end of a word usually means "someone who does something," so a painter is one who paints. But is a mother one who moths? Is a father one who faths?

The powerful component of the Contextual Redefinition is the teacher modeling. Struggling readers in particular need to experience successful models of reading behavior and thinking.

## Extending the Strategy

Wordbusting, also known as CSSD, is a parallel strategy to Contextual Redefinition. The steps to Wordbusting are as follows:

- *Context.* Use clues from the surrounding words and sentences.
- *Structure.* Look for familiar roots, prefixes, or suffixes.
- *Sound.* Say the word aloud. It may sound like a word you know.
- *Dictionary.* Look up the word.

## Some Final Thoughts

Educators are desperate to teach vocabulary because students can use these words to write, speak, and think more clearly. Vocabulary is also a common component of standardized tests. Well-meaning teachers often assign lists of words with instructions to use them in sentences or copy their definitions. When presented in relative isolation from any meaningful content, these words are only slightly learned and rapidly forgotten.

Contextual Redefinition enables students to determine the meanings of unknown words during reading. In addition to learning strategies, students need to practice these strategies by reading narrative and expository text that contains unfamiliar words.

## Read More About It

Cunningham, J. W., Cunningham, P. M., and Arthur, S. V. *Middle and Secondary School Reading.* New York: Longman. 1981.

Gifford, A. P. "Broadening Concepts Through Vocabulary Development." *Reading Improvement* 37 (1) 2000: 2 –12.

Ittzes, K. Lexical "Guessing in Isolation and Context." *Journal of Reading* 34 (5) 1991: 360–66.

Simpson, P. L. "Three Step Reading Vocabulary Strategy for Today's Content Area Reading Classroom." *Reading Improvement* 33 (2) 1996: 76–80.

Watts, S., and Truscott, D. M. "Using Contextual Analysis to Help Students Become Independent Word Learners." *The NERA Journal* 32 (3) 1996: 13–20.

# NOTES

# GRAPHIC ORGANIZER *for Content-Area Reading Strategies* ⓵

## ANTICIPATION GUIDE

| A<br>**Before Reading**<br>Agree / Disagree | **Statements** | B<br>**After Reading**<br>Agree / Disagree |
|---|---|---|
| | | |
| | | |
| | | |

GRAPHIC ORGANIZER *for Content-Area Reading Strategies* **2**

# CAUSE-AND-EFFECT CHART

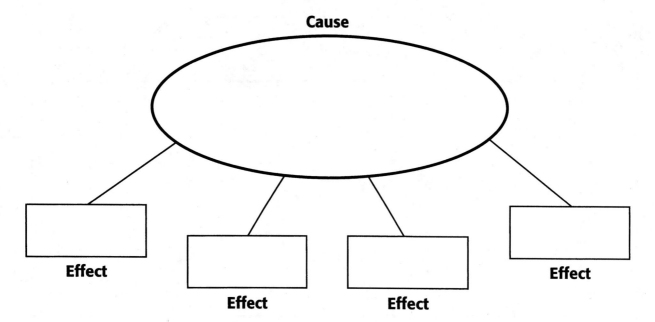

**Cause**

**Effect**

**Effect**

**Effect**

**Effect**

## GRAPHIC ORGANIZER *for Content-Area Reading Strategies*

## CLUSTER DIAGRAM

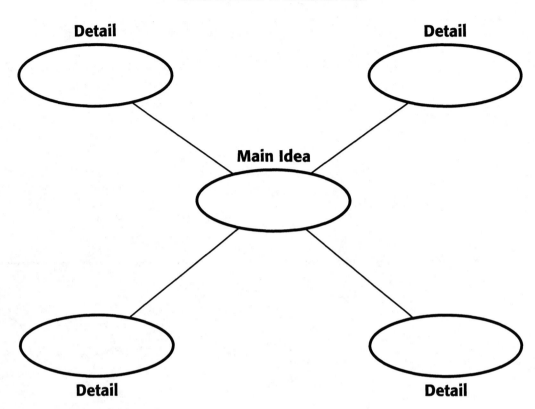

**Detail**

**Detail**

**Main Idea**

**Detail**

**Detail**

## GRAPHIC ORGANIZER *for Content-Area Reading Strategies*

**4**

# CONTEXTUAL REDEFINITION CHART

| ▶ Identify Unfamiliar Words | ▶ Guess Word Meanings | ▶ Refine Guesses | ▶ Verify Meanings |
|---|---|---|---|
| | | | |
| | | | |
| | | | |
| | | | |

Name ______________________ Class ______________ Date ____________

GRAPHIC ORGANIZER *for Content-Area Reading Strategies* 5

## KEY POINTS AND DETAILS CHART

| Key Points | Details |
|---|---|
| | |
| | |
| | |
| | |

Name ______________________ Class ______________ Date ____________

GRAPHIC ORGANIZER *for Content-Area Reading Strategies* 6

# KWL CHART

| What I *Know* | What I *Want* to Know | What I *Learned* |
| --- | --- | --- |
| | | |
| | | |
| | | |
| | | |

## GRAPHIC ORGANIZER *for Content-Area Reading Strategies*

# KWLS CHART

| ▶ What I *Know* | ▶ What I *Want* to Know | ▶ What I *Learned* | ▶ What I *Still* Want to Know |
|---|---|---|---|
| | | | |

## GRAPHIC ORGANIZER *for Content-Area Reading Strategies*

# PREDICTING AND CONFIRMING ACTIVITY (PACA)

| ▶ General Information | ▶ Prediction | ▶ Confirmation |
|---|---|---|
|  |  |  |
|  |  |  |
|  |  |  |
|  |  |  |

GRAPHIC ORGANIZER *for Content-Area Reading Strategies*    **9**

## PROBLEM AND SOLUTION CHART

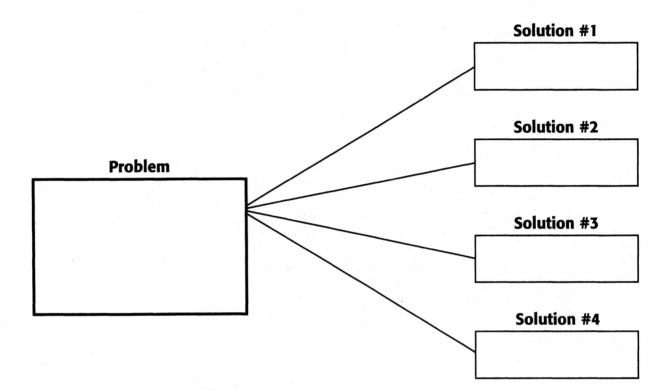

GRAPHIC ORGANIZER *for Content-Area Reading Strategies*  **10**

## SEQUENCE OR CHRONOLOGICAL ORDER CHART

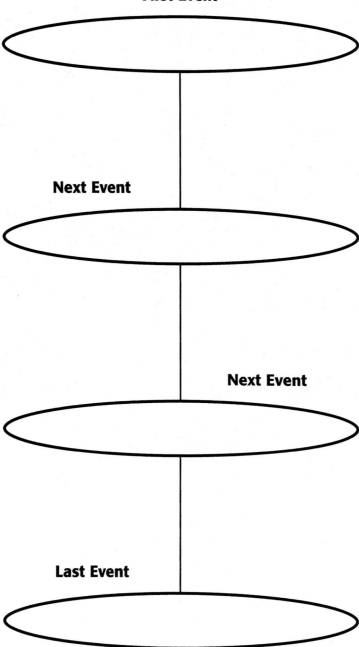

**First Event**

**Next Event**

**Next Event**

**Last Event**

GRAPHIC ORGANIZER *for Content-Area Reading Strategies* **11**

## VENN DIAGRAM

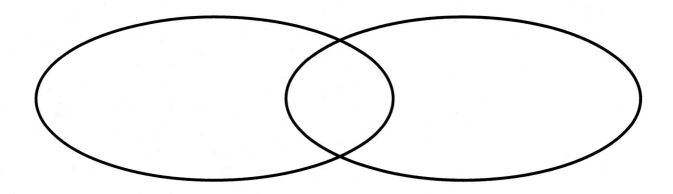